VILLA VICTORIA

Villa Victoria

The TRANSFORMATION of SOCIAL
CAPITAL in a BOSTON BARRIO

Mario Luis Small

THE UNIVERSITY OF CHICAGO PRESS
CHICAGO AND LONDON

The University of Chicago Press, Chicago 60637
The University of Chicago Press, Ltd., London
© 2004 by The University of Chicago
All rights reserved. Published 2004
Printed in the United States of America
13 12 11 10 09 08 07   2 3 4 5

ISBN: 0-226-76291-2 (cloth)
ISBN: 0-226-76292-0 (paper)

Library of Congress Cataloging-in-Publication Data

Small, Mario Luis.
  Villa Victoria : the transformation of social capital in a Boston barrio /
  Mario Luis Small.
     p. cm.
  Includes bibliographical references and index.
  ISBN 0-226-76291-2 (cloth : alk. paper) — ISBN 0-226-76292-0
  (pbk. : alk. paper)
     1. Social capital (Sociology)—Massachusetts—Boston.   2. So-
  cial participation—Massachusetts—Boston.   3. Social ecology—
  Massachusetts—Boston.   4. Poor—Social networks—Massachu-
  setts—Boston.   5. Puerto Ricans—Massachusetts—Boston—Social
  conditions.   6. South End (Boston, Mass.)—Social conditions.
  I. Title.

  HN80 .B7S63 2004
  302'.14'09744'61—dc22

                                                        2003021999

The paper used in this publication meets the minimum
requirements of the American National Standard for Information
Sciences—Permanence of Paper for Printed Library Materials,
ANSI Z39.48-1992.

A mis padres y a mis hermanos

CONTENTS

ILLUSTRATIONS

Villa Victoria

Study area

Streets

Parks

0   0.1 Miles

What first struck me about Villa Victoria, a subsidized housing complex in Boston's South End, was the landscape. Several rows of three-story concrete houses with high front stoops, pitched roofs, and Spanish ironwork abutted a small brick-layered plaza. The plaza was framed all around by *maceteros,* soil-filled banks in which small trees and shrubs had been planted. Permanent tables and benches were installed throughout the plaza. Surrounding it lay a short, almost quaint, cobble-stoned *paseo.* Only one tower in the complex's twenty acres rose over five stories, to about a dozen stories. The complex evoked intimacy. Villa Victoria's landscape had seen better times—paint had peeled off walls, garbage was strewn about, and occasional rodents scurried along the sides of the streets. But the structure's understated dignity, hidden within layers of peeling paint and grime, was evident to anyone willing to pay attention. I had never thought of housing complexes as physically appealing, but if these "projects" underwent some refurbishment, they might be quite beautiful.

Villa Victoria's uniqueness seemed to extend to social relations. It was inhabited almost entirely by Puerto Ricans, in a neighborhood, and city, with few of them. Its construction had resulted not from a policy decision but from a grassroots struggle by migrants from rural Puerto Rico during the 1960s. It was managed not by an impersonal bureaucracy but by a group of current and former residents along with professional staff. It had not been a disengaged inner-city ghetto; it boasted a rich history of community participation, with hundreds of cultural programs and events accumulated over the years. Everyone knew everyone else. There was little violence. Families remained there generation after generation. It even held a yearly festival of Puerto Rican arts and culture attended by thousands of people throughout New England. The Villa, as it is known, bore little resemblance, either physically or socially, to the impersonal high-rises in Chicago and New York with which we usually associate housing projects. *xi*

For years, social scientists had argued that the concentration of poverty in housing projects would produce distrust, alienation, apathy, and social isolation—the disappearance of what sociologists have called social capital. At the community level, the disappearance would reduce community participation and social organization; at the individual level, it would cut off ties to mainstream society, producing social isolation and indifference to community engagement. The effects on the individual had received special attention, for W. J. Wilson's (1987) influential book *The Truly Disadvantaged* had argued that a neighborhood's poverty level would affect people independently of their own poverty or hardship. Many studies confirmed his theory; poor people who were given vouchers to live in middle-class neighborhoods did better than comparably poor people in poor neighborhoods. But few researchers had examined systematically *how* concentrated poverty affected social capital, had examined exactly what reasons simply living in a poor neighborhood contributed to apathy and social isolation and other unwanted outcomes. The question of how was known as the "black box" of neighborhood effects.

Villa Victoria seemed to present an exceptional opportunity to open the black box. If we could understand how residents maintained social capital here despite living in concentrated poverty, perhaps we could learn how to prevent the deterioration of social relations in other poor neighborhoods. This became the objective of the study: to rely on Villa Victoria to open the black box. As I pursued this task, however, two things became clear.

First, I discovered that Villa Victoria was unique only in some senses, quite ordinarily poor in others. Some residents were highly integrated into middle-class networks, but others were profoundly isolated from mainstream society, as Wilson and others would expect. The neighborhood had experienced times of high community participation, but it had also witnessed prolonged periods of apathy and social alienation. The Villa seemed less unique than heterogeneous and dynamic. One might say the concentration of poverty had produced its expected effects but in certain respects more than others, at some times more than others, and on some individuals more than the rest. To open the black box, therefore, I had to investigate what accounted for this variation, over time and across individuals, in how residents responded to the concentration of poverty.

As I pursued this question, I came to another conclusion. The real quagmire was not why the Villa seemed so dynamic and heterogeneous but why the theories would lead me to expect otherwise. Much of what I uncovered in the Villa seemed at first to be counterintuitive, such as the high levels, during some periods, of community participation or the presence of many individuals with ties to the middle class. Yet on reflection, much of it seemed quite logical as well, provided I asked the right questions. For example, despite living in concentrated poverty, several residents did many things outside the Villa, in middle-class neighborhoods, where they had opportunities to meet middle-class people; that these residents were not isolated from the mainstream was not surprising. Most of the time, social scientists think of these as rare examples, statistical outliers in the overall phenomenon. (This occurs even in the reading of ethnographies, which often uncover heterogeneity in neighborhoods.) But taking seriously the incongruity between what I expected in theory and what I witnessed in the field became critical, since the mismatch was so salient and on so many different aspects of social capital. The more seriously I addressed the incongruity, the more the theories seemed simplistic and implausible as commonly understood. In fact, some of them would push me to look for answers repeatedly in the familiar places, resulting in the stereotypical pictures of poor neighborhoods and the people who live in them prevalent in society and represented in the media. If I tried to find that neighborhood poverty produced apathy in the Villa, it was easy for me to do so, since over the two years I conducted the study I met many residents who had no interest in participating in "the community." But when I tried to explain why some residents were not apathetic despite living in concentrated poverty, it became clear that the original theory had relied on a number of unstated and possibly unwarranted assumptions.

Rather than side issues, these became the central concerns of the study. The result was a book different from most ethnographic case studies of housing complexes or poor neighborhoods. Instead of an overall description of life in the Villa, a community study, it became a sustained critique of specific theories about the effects of concentrated poverty, a critique based on my attempts to understand heterogeneity and differences over time in this neighborhood. The resulting product is five analytical essays on different aspects of social capital, all of which use the Villa as the central empirical case. The essays are introduced by a chapter on the general theories to be addressed and another on how Villa Victoria was created. They are concluded by a chapter systematizing the perspective from which I believe the black box should be opened.

In chapter 1, I discuss the social scientific research on neighborhood poverty. I outline the main sociological approaches to be examined, social isolation, and social disorganization theories; I also address the questions of culture and agency, especially thorny issues in a study of this nature.

Readers not interested in an abstract discussion of sociological research may skip to the next chapter without fear of missing substantive findings about the Villa.

In chapter 2, I relate how this poor, predominantly Puerto Rican housing complex came into existence in the 1970s in one of the most affluent sections of Boston, the South End (which, it should be noted, is not South Boston or "Southie"). In the 1960s, the section of the South End that is now the Villa, parcel 19, was designated as an urban renewal area—residents were to be relocated, the buildings bulldozed over, and the area redeveloped as luxury condominiums and commercial space. Something similar had occurred a decade earlier in the predominantly Italian-American West End, as described in Herbert Gans's (1962) classic, *Urban Villagers*. Whereas the West Enders were ultimately displaced from their neighborhood, the mostly Puerto Rican residents of parcel 19 organized and successfully fought their relocation, producing, rather than a luxury condominium, an affordable housing complex, Villa Victoria. I describe, in this chapter, the historical conditions that resulted in the parcel's residents' different fate. The neighborhood's early history would influence, for years to come, the residents' capacity to develop and sustain social capital.

In the next two chapters I address the Villa's transformation in one aspect of social capital—community participation—from a historical and analytic perspective. I explain, in chapter 3, how the neighborhood's level of community participation, which had peaked in the mid-1980s, declined over time in ways one would not theoretically expect. Indeed, based on the tenets of social disorganization theory, the structural conditions of the neighborhood were such that community participation should have risen or, at the very least, remained stable over time. The chapter shows that education levels rose dramatically, residential stability increased markedly, and material hardship appeared to remain stable. The chapter introduces this dilemma: Why, then, did participation in the Villa decline?

I continue examining, in chapter 4, two important issues neglected by existing theory: the role of cohorts and the role of cultural framing. I show that, contrary to common assumptions, shifts in a neighborhood's structural conditions (such as its residential stability level) do not necessarily produce shifts in community participation; the latter result primarily from transformations at the level of the cohort. Indeed, the significance of the cohort has been missed by much of the discussion of community participation. In the Villa, a highly participating cohort was replaced by a relatively nonparticipating one. To address why the cohorts showed different levels of participation, I examine their framing of their neighborhood. The frames through which residents perceived their neighborhood affected how they reacted to their common structural conditions. The most recent cohort saw the peeling paint and grime and perceived an undesirable ghetto; the earlier one saw the same and perceived a "beautiful" community. Though living in an undesirable ghetto was insufficient reason to participate in local activities, preserving a beautiful community was a powerful motivator. The evidence presented in that chapter demonstrates that not everyone sees the same neighborhood through the same eyes— and that how residents see their neighborhood affects how they react to it and whether they are willing to "get involved."

An issue rarely mentioned in the study of community participation is introduced in chapters 3 and 4. Even in the Villa's periods of high participation, only a small minority of residents were "community activists" in any meaningful sense. When many people think of a highly engaged neighborhood they imagine large numbers of residents knocking on doors, leading neighborhood clean-up drives, and passing out leaflets for upcoming events. Yet community participation might well be what business economists have termed an 80/20 phenomenon, where a large portion of the activity (say, 80%) is undertaken by a small proportion of the population (20%). Understanding community participation as an 80/20 phenomenon (or perhaps a 95/5 phenomenon) helps understand why community participation may be high even in the poorest neighborhoods.

In the subsequent three chapters, which are more ethnographic in the traditional sense, I set aside the issue of community participation to examine the residents' social networks. In chapter 5, I distinguish individual from collective social isolation and focus exclusively on the latter. Within any given neighborhood, some residents may be more isolated than others; but a neighborhood as a whole might be, on average, more isolated than another neighborhood or more isolated than one would expect given its circumstances or location. The Villa as a whole is rather (collectively) isolated from the surrounding South End. Despite being surrounded by thousands of liberal, socially minded middle-class residents, Villa residents tend to have almost no contact, intimate or superficial, with the middle-class residents who are nearby. The question is why. The material presented in this chapter demonstrates that the ecological characteristics of the neighborhood itself—the composition of streets and buildings, the configuration of houses and their distribution across blocks—was partly to blame for the fact that residents hardly interact with their middle-class neighbors across the street. This suggests that social isolation should be thought of not as a necessary product of concentrated poverty but as an outcome partly conditional on context-specific characteristics of the neighborhood.

In chapter 6 I examine the relationship between social capital and the number of institutional resources and businesses in the neighborhood. In his famous depiction of Chicago, Wilson (1987) described in convincing detail how the departure of the middle class led to the erosion of institutional resources in Chicago's South Side, the disappearance of grocery stores, banks, churches, and recreational areas. Many social scientists, in turn, came to think of inner-city poor neighborhoods as places that, by definition, are deprived of institutional resources. But Villa Victoria, it is clear, is rich in neighborhood resources and not for accidental reasons. This counterintuitive finding is shown to be a rather logical result of the development of poverty in this neighborhood and city.

I then ask whether this prevalence of resources affects social capital. I show that resource prevalence might, ironically, contribute to social isolation, by reducing residents' opportunities to interact with persons of other neighborhoods. However, this relationship is conditional on, among other things, internal cultural dynamics affecting which groups claim implicit ownership of the available resources.

I investigate the social ties of individuals in chapter 7. While some of the Villa's residents indeed seemed socially isolated, others were strongly connected to middle-class people, society, attitudes, and expectations. (These connections were generally not to residents in the surrounding South End but to those in other, farther neighborhoods.) Relying on an in-depth analysis of the lives of five residents, I examine why some were socially isolated and some were not (casting doubt, along the way, on the utility of overarching categories such as "socially isolated"). I show the significance of generational status, employment status, and neighborhood attachment to the likelihood of developing ties outside the neighborhood. I also uncover the persisting, multilayered conflict some second-generation Puerto Ricans in the neighborhood feel between local and external allegiances and social ties. This "labyrinth of loyalties" reveals much of the dilemma residents have between allying themselves to local causes and pursuing opportunities for moving up and moving out.

In chapter 8, I conclude by systematizing the approach I employed to open the black box. I elaborate on the usefulness of the "conditional" perspective adopted in the book. Social scientists tend to read community studies of single neighborhoods as roughly representative indicators of "the ghetto." Despite years of statistics courses teaching that samples of

Be wary of
Universalism and Particularism
in looks at case studies

PREFACE   *xvii*

one are inappropriate for generalizations, we often want to generalize, to read such studies precisely as depictions of *the* inner-city ghetto, perhaps because there are few such studies but also because of an implicit conception of the inner-city ghetto as a single, overarching institution that manifests itself in roughly the same way from city to city. Conversely, some social scientists explicitly read single case studies as particularistic tales with no legitimate universal applicability, as stories of a single neighborhood in a single place in a single time. Chapter 8 suggests that we should be concerned about generalization but that the common approach to generalization is inappropriate to open the black box. It presents an alternative that is neither universalist nor particularist, that takes the specific context of the neighborhood seriously while not succumbing to the scientific dangers of particularism. It suggests that case studies should be read as conditional accounts, in which the observed patterns of relations, no matter how consonant with standard expectations or stereotypes, are due not to neighborhood poverty in the abstract but to the specific conditions under which poverty manifested itself in the neighborhood—conditions that, nevertheless, may well manifest themselves in other settings.

The foregoing description should give an indication of what this book is and what it is not. It is not a community study. Community studies, such as Gans's aforementioned classic and most ethnographic studies of urban neighborhoods, explicitly provide readers a general or comprehensive snapshot of the community's life or social structure. This book does not. Community studies address issues as varied as teenage pregnancy, school attrition, unemployment, and crime—serious problems in this and many neighborhoods. By contrast, this book is focused exclusively on the relationship between concentrated poverty and social capital. Readers expecting a traditional "ethnography" of Villa Victoria are likely to be disappointed.

In addition, despite its persistent investigation of the historical foundations of present-day phenomena in the Villa, this book is not a history of the neighborhood, an enterprise best suited for a historian, not a sociologist. Moreover, even though the residents' identity or self-conception is examined where it is relevant to understanding social capital, this is not a study of "Puerto Rican identity" or "Latino identity" in the inner city. (I was born and raised in Panama, a small but diverse nation, and I often worry about attempts to subsume ethnic groups under a single comprehensive "identity.") Though the lives of the Villa's residents have much to teach about migration among Puerto Ricans, they are but one case in one city among a rich and complex Puerto Rican culture. The lessons Villa Victoria offered are not predictions about Puerto Ricans in housing complexes or about poor neighborhoods as a whole. They offered, instead, hypotheses about how concentrated poverty affects social capital conditional on residents' framing of their neighborhood, on the influence of cohorts, on the ecological characteristics of the neighborhood, on the prevalence of institutional resources, on generational status, on employment, and on the complexities of residents' loyalties and sentiments toward where they live.

This book examines concretely the diverse ways individuals respond to living in concentrated poverty. I make use of that diversity to critique, to analyze closely and systematically, the standard assumptions about neighborhood poverty, to shed light on the black box—to help develop explanations that neither rely on worn-out preconceptions nor deny the harsh effects of poverty. What follows is an empirically based meditation on the prominent theories of social isolation, social organization, and community participation—a critique from the bottom up.

This project would have been impossible without the help of my friends and respondents in Villa Victoria. I cannot divulge their names in the interest of confidentiality, but I thank them.

For their help, guidance, and constructive criticism on the dissertation on which this study is based, I thank Katherine Newman, William Julius Wilson, and Christopher Winship. Both professionally and scholarly, Kathy Newman has done much more for me than anyone could ask. I feel privileged to have been her student. Bill Wilson has been a significant role model and intellectual mentor, pushing me to my limits and encouraging me to think critically about the literature on neighborhood effects, including his own work. Chris Winship has been supportive and encouraging of my interests in both quantitative and qualitative methods. My work will also bear evidence of the intellectual influence of several of my former teachers, especially Christopher Jencks, Stanley Lieberson, Orlando Patterson, and Nader Saiedi.

The two reviewers for the University of Chicago Press, Howard Becker and Robert Sampson, provided invaluable feedback that has improved the book measurably. Douglas Mitchell, at the press, was encouraging and enthusiastic throughout the process. Yvonne Zipter, also at the press, was a pleasure to work with. Mitchell Duneier provided sharp, constructive criticism on every aspect of the manuscript. Marion Fourcade-Gourinchas, Monica McDermott, Ann Morning, and Bel Willem also read and provided feedback on one or more sections of the book. Judie Miller read the manuscript from cover to cover and caught many errors. Several staff members at Inquilinos Boricuas en Acción and Emergency Tenants' Council helped me throughout the years and I thank them. I especially would like to thank David Cortiella, Mario Devis, Jenny Gray, Kathleen Rivera, Madeline Soto, and Wanda Torres. The following people, a few of whom I have never met in person, were kind enough to provide comments, criticisms, encouragement, advice, or their expertise on a particular issue:

Ricardo Acevedo, Carmen Barrientos, Xavier De Souza Briggs, Blanca Cardona, Silvia Domínguez, Gwen Dordick, Father Dwyer, Thomas Espenshade, Ron Ferguson, Luisa Heredia, Tomás Jiménez, Jennifer Johnson, Gabriella Gonzalez, Judith Gonyea, Michèle Lamont, Mercedes Lebrón, Felix Matos-Rodríguez, Alejandro Portes, John Sharratt, Elisa Soltren, Cynthia Suárez, and Bel Willem. In addition, Fabia Gumbau, Martine Haas, John Jackson, Karyn Lacy, Ezell Lundy, Monica McDermot, Omar McRoberts, Gesemia Nelson, Miguel Salazar, and Celeste Watkins helped sustain my mental energies during my last two years in graduate school, the incubation period of most ideas in this book. Fez Aswat, Jeremy Hauch, and Sally Shiels were supportive and stimulating roommates in our South End apartment, from which I conducted much of this study.

I thank the staff at the South End Historical Society, the South End Public Library, the Government Documents Reference Desk at Harvard University's Lamont Library, the Archives and Special Collections Department at Northeastern University, and graduate students and faculty at the Harvard Sociology Department. The map of Villa Victoria was prepared by Marcia C. Castro. Wangyal Shawa, at Princeton's Geosciences and Map Library provided expert assistance in preparation of the map. The early part of the research on which this book is based was conducted with the Welfare, Children, and Families Study. This book would not have been possible without a Graduate Prize Fellowship from Harvard University, a National Science Foundation Integrative Graduate Education and Research Traineeship Grant (NSF No. 9870661) to Harvard, a research grant from Princeton University, and the support of the Office of Population Research (OPR) at Princeton. A research associateship at OPR provided me the space, time, and stimulation necessary to complete this manuscript. My colleagues at both OPR and the Princeton Department of Sociology have been phenomenal.

A version of chapters 3 and 4, which included some of the observations in the concluding chapter, appeared originally in the *American Journal of Sociology* 108, no. 1 (June 2002): 1–54. Those passages are reproduced here with permission. I thank the editors and reviewers of the journal for their feedback. Earlier versions of some chapters were presented at Princeton University, Wellesley College, the University of Michigan, and the American Sociological Association's annual meeting, in Anaheim, California, 2001. Though I have benefited greatly from the comments of all these persons, I alone bear responsibility for any errors or omissions.

Finally, and most important, I thank my family for their enduring faith and support.

ONE

How Does Neighborhood Poverty
Affect Social Capital?

The problem is straightforward. How does neighborhood poverty affect social capital?[1] In particular, by what mechanisms does living in a poor neighborhood decrease local community participation, reduce ties to the middle class, and weaken social ties among neighbors? Opening this black box of neighborhood poverty has proved both empirically and conceptually elusive.

The intention of this study was to use the case of Villa Victoria to help open the black box. It soon became clear, however, that this would require thinking differently about what a "ghetto" is and about how ethnographic case studies should complement large sample research on this question. To explain why divergent thinking is needed is, in a sense, my objective in this book. The following chapter frames what will follow by reviewing the recent literature on poor neighborhoods and by discussing several problems in identifying how neighborhood poverty affects people.

---

1. The term "social capital" has been subject to multiple definitions in sociology, political science, and economics (Bourdieu 1985, Coleman 1988; Wacquant 1997; Portes 1998; Lin 1999; Sampson 1999; Putnam 2000). It has been used to refer to the gains we obtain from our social ties, to the responsibilities they demand of us, to the norms they enforce, to the ties themselves, and to the presence of a high number of such ties among communities or neighborhoods. I will not, in this book, provide yet another definition, which would only confuse matters further. Instead I use the term merely as shorthand for the specific phenomena that have been studied under the general rubric of social capital, such as the number of middle-class friends and acquaintances poor individuals have, the trust they have toward others in their neighborhood, and the amount of time they devote to local volunteer activities.

The Effects of Neighborhood Poverty

After a relative lull during the 1970s and 1980s, research on the effects of neighborhood poverty increased at a rapid pace, driven in no small measure by Wilson's (1987) work (Small and Newman 2001; Sampson, Morenoff, and Gannon Rowley 2002). Although sociologists for years had believed that neighborhoods had important consequences for life outcomes, Wilson explicitly hypothesized that living in a poor neighborhood negatively affected a person's life chances independently of the person's own poverty level and offered plausible explanations for why this would be the case. The research, aided by influential early reviews such as Jencks and Mayer's (1990), settled on two basic questions. First, does neighborhood poverty affect life chances? If so, how?

Answering the first question, the "neighborhood effect" hypothesis, became a major preoccupation for an interdisciplinary core of demographers, economists, quantitative sociologists, and developmental psychologists, all of whom quickly pointed out the previously underappreciated difficulty in demonstrating such an effect quantitatively. An especially difficult issue, one that economic and demographic studies tended to treat more seriously than sociological ones, was the issue of selection bias (Jencks and Mayer 1990). Since people likely to evince the social problems we worry about are also likely to end up in poor neighborhoods, it is difficult to ascertain statistically that such neighborhoods, independent of people's own characteristics, increase their likelihood of evincing those problems. Over the past fifteen years, researchers have produced better, more rigorous, and more convincing evidence on this question than had previously been the case. An important advance were the Moving to Opportunity experiments, in which residents applying for housing vouchers were randomly assigned either standard vouchers to be used anywhere (the control group) or vouchers to be used exclusively in nonpoor neighborhoods (the experimental group).[2] Careful tests showed that residents in the second group did better on several outcomes, mostly regarding health and teen behavior, suggesting that neighborhood poverty did, indeed, have at least some negative effects on people (Kling 2000). Even these results are not sufficient for strong individualists, who remain unconvinced that neighborhood poverty makes enough of a difference to de-

---

2. The tests were conducted in several cities. In Boston, applicants were assigned to one of three groups: Experimental, Section 8, and Control. Those in the first group received a voucher to be used only in a census tract with a poverty rate less than 10 percent, as well as counseling assistance. Those in the second received a voucher to be used anywhere. Those in the third received nothing (Katz, Kling, and Liebman 2001).

mand serious attention. But most experts on this question seem increasingly convinced that neighborhood poverty does independently affect people in at least some of the ways we worry about (for reviews of this literature and its critical concerns, see Jencks and Mayer 1990; Furstenberg and Hughes 1997; Gephart 1997; Sampson and Morenoff 1997; Small and Newman 2001; and Sampson, Morenoff, and Gannon-Rowley 2002).[3]

The second question—How?—has proved difficult to answer. To be sure, one version of this problem has been the subject of sociological research in the United States since at least the 1960s, when scores of field-based books on life in poor urban neighborhoods were published (Gans 1962; Lewis 1965, 1968; Liebow 1967; Hannerz 1969; Rainwater 1970). But as social scientific research has advanced, the questions have become more subtle and the potential pitfalls more numerous. An important problem is how to interpret what an ethnographer has observed in a particular neighborhood. Did a given outcome result from the neighborhood's poverty level or from another characteristic, such as its ethnic makeup or the cultural characteristics of its inhabitants? Can these variables be disentangled analytically? Was the neighborhood the ethnographer studied representative of ghettos? (The term "ghetto" will refer, broadly, to an urban neighborhood with a high concentration of poor people, regardless of their ethnic makeup.) Earlier field researchers simply did not think in these terms. Many of them saw as their task to depict the ghetto to a middle class largely unaware of the ghetto's inner workings. Even the highly analytical thinkers, such as Hannerz (1969), were more concerned with holistic depictions than with identifying neighborhood mechanisms in the way required to answer these questions.

In recent years, several hypotheses have been advanced to answer the *how* question. Researchers have argued that neighborhood poverty results in the lack of, for example, good role models (Wilson 1987; Cutler and Glaeser 1997), reduced social control and increased disorganization (Sampson and Groves 1989), and greater social isolation (Wilson 1987; Fernandez and Harris 1992), which then contribute to lower educational and occupational attainment, among many other outcomes (see Small and Newman 2001). When compared to research on the first question, research on mechanisms has been relatively scarce, even though a number

3. For a sampling of the hundreds of studies on the issue, see Crane (1991); Jencks and Peterson (1991); Rosenbaum and Popkin (1991); Moore and Pinderhughes (1993); Brooks-Gunn, Denner, and Keblanov (1995); Elliott et al. (1996); Aber et al. (1997); Brooks-Gunn, Duncan, and Aber (1997a, 1997b); Cutler and Glaeser (1997); Duncan and Aber (1997); Duncan, Connell, and Keblanov (1997); Furstenberg and Hughes (1997); Furstenberg et al. (1998); Sucoff and Upchurch (1998); South and Crowder (1999); Tolnay and Crowder (1999); and Katz, Kling, and Liebman (2001). For a recent critique, see Wacquant (1997).

How to understand social processes + mechanisms?

of new ethnographies have addressed one or another aspect of them indirectly (Duneier 1999; Pattillo-McCoy 1999; Venkatesh 2000). Most researchers agree, however, that ethnographic research provides an important, if not the most important, tool in answering this question, for it has great leverage into understanding social processes.

For most of the sociologists, demographers, and economists working in this field, the objective of ethnographic research would be to use a case to uncover daily life in an average ghetto. The idea is that most ghettos share a host of characteristics and that by studying in depth the workings in one (representative) ghetto, one would understand how neighborhood poverty affects social capital in such neighborhoods in general. For example, a researcher might try to uncover the mechanisms by which neighborhood poverty decreases local participation. He or she would study a poor neighborhood and find, for example, that the high poverty levels reduce trust among neighbors. After conducting interviews and making observations, the researcher might find that this lack of trust translates into an unwillingness to participate in local voluntary activities; the ethnographer would depict, in depth, how people conceive of trust and make choices about involving themselves locally. On this basis, one would then hypothesize that neighborhood poverty (cause) decreases local participation (outcome) by decreasing trust (mechanism). This could then be tested on a large sample.

This approach is relatively standard, but it did not work well in Villa Victoria. In fact, my research in the Villa indicated that this approach would fail to identify many of the important mechanisms by which neighborhood poverty affected social capital. It was clear that many of the intermediary mechanisms at work in the Villa would probably not operate across all poor neighborhoods. *These mechanisms evidently resulted from the fact that this was a poor neighborhood, and they could conceivably operate in other poor neighborhoods as well. But these were not mechanisms one would expect to find across all or even most poor neighborhoods.* Furthermore, when compared to other ethnographies of poor neighborhoods—such as those of Gans (1962), Liebow (1967), Suttles (1968), Rainwater (1970), Anderson (1990, 1999), and Venkatesh (2000)—the idea of the Villa or of any neighborhood as a representative sample of the ghetto, as a "typical" ghetto, seemed less and less sensible. By extension, the idea of the ghetto itself as a single institution seemed increasingly less tenable.[4]

ethnography @ research design

weakness

4. The most elaborate conception of the ghetto as an institution is Wacquant's (1997), an extension of Wilson's (1987; also Wacquant and Wilson 1990). The Villa is consistent with some of these observations but inconsistent with several of the conclusions of the top-down approach in Wacquant (1997).

The task that lies before me in the remainder of the book is to explain why this was the case and in what ways, then, one can use ethnographic case studies to inform large-scale cross-sectional research and to open the black box. The Villa posed both empirical and conceptual challenges to the existing work. The discussion below sets the stage for confronting these challenges by describing the main theories to be addressed. It is followed by comments on the issues of culture and agency, particularly difficult and arguably central questions in the study of poor neighborhoods.

Theories

Main Theories

Most of the issues to be covered in this book relate to the theories of social disorganization and social isolation, both of which are part of the distinguished research tradition of the Chicago school of sociology (Park, Burgess, and McKenzie 1925). Social disorganization theory argues that neighborhood poverty (among other factors) produces socially disorganized communities. The theory was originally developed to explain variations across neighborhoods in crime rates. In the 1940s, Shaw and McKay (1942, 1969) studied a cross section of neighborhoods in Chicago and showed that crime rates varied by the strength and organization of local institutions and the ability and willingness of residents to become involved on behalf of the common good and exercise informal social control. Neighborhoods were high in crime, the thought was, because they were "socially disorganized." Social disorganization, in turn, was caused by ethnic heterogeneity, residential instability, and high neighborhood poverty (see also Sampson 1988, 1991, 1999; Sampson and Groves 1989; Sampson and Wilson 1995; Sampson, Raudenbush, and Earls 1997; Pattillo-McCoy 1999; Sampson, Morenoff, and Earls 1999). Neighborhood poverty, therefore, would reduce social control, community participation, and the number of strong local institutions.

Throughout its history, the theory has had its critics, most of whom have argued that poor urban neighborhoods are not disorganized but, rather, are characterized by alternative forms of organization (Whyte 1943; Gans 1962; Suttles 1968; Wacquant 1997). Many critics relied on ethnographic studies, which seemed to paint pictures sharply at odds with the idea of disorganization (see Susser 1982; Gregory 1998). An early example is Whyte's (1943) study of a Boston "slum." Whyte writes, "It is customary for the sociologist to study the slum district in terms of 'social disorganization' and to neglect to see that an area such as Cornerville has a complex and well-established organization of its own. . . . I found that in every group there was a hierarchical structure of social relations binding the individuals to one another and that the groups were also hierarchically related to one another" (1943, viii). The question becomes, then, how to reconcile the theory with ethnographic studies such as Whyte's *Street Corner Society* (1943, 1955), Gans's *Urban Villagers* (1962), and Suttles's *The Social Order of the Slum* (1968)—all important works that take issue with the disorganization thesis. Is the theory out of touch with reality? Or are the field studies unrepresentative of poor neighborhoods?

Thus far, researchers have not produced very clear answers. Part of the difficulty is that social disorganization has been defined in too many different ways to constitute a falsifiable concept. The term has denoted attributes as varied as neighborhoods' inability to supervise and control teens, the lack of mutual trust among neighbors, the low density and limited range of local social networks, the unwillingness to intervene on behalf of the common good, the lack of participation in formal voluntary associations, the lack of voluntary participation in informal activities, the absence of institutional resources in a neighborhood, and even the prevalence of crime, sometimes referred to as "disorder" (Wilson 1987, 1996; Sampson 1988, 1991, 1999; Sampson and Groves 1989; Sampson and Wilson 1995; Sampson, Raudenbush, and Earls 1997; Pattillo-McCoy1999; Sampson, Morenoff, and Earls 1999; Rankin and Quane 2000). Each of the field studies said to question the thesis is consistent with at least one different definition of social disorganization. Moreover, neighborhood poverty could theoretically lead to each of these outcomes through a different mechanism.

This confusion strongly suggests abandoning searches for social disorganization or lack thereof in favor of studying specific phenomena that leave less room for interpretation. In this study, therefore, I will address not social disorganization but, instead, the more specific topics of the presence or absence of voluntary participation in neighborhood activities and the prevalence or scarcity of local institutional resources. The issue is to identify what about the concentration of poverty should lead to these outcomes. Studying these processes will also suggest a way to place ethnographic research within the context of wider theoretical and empirical work.

Social isolation theory argues that neighborhood poverty disconnects people from the mainstream or middle class. The basis of this theory is

---

Handwritten margin notes:
- SOCIAL DISORGANIZATION Theory
- Sociological theory mismatch with ethnographic studies
- Definitional problems
- Causes? effects? outcomes
- Focus of This study
- Questions

Wilson's (1987) study of transformations in inner-city African American neighborhoods. In the past, he argued, such neighborhoods were racially segregated but class integrated, as poor blacks lived in close proximity to working- and middle-class blacks, enjoying the institutional resources and businesses the wealthier groups supported. After the economic shifts and Civil Rights victories of the 1960s and 1970s, the middle class left the inner city, leaving the poor with little or no contact with the American mainstream or middle class. In support of this thesis, several studies have found that living in a poor neighborhood reduces a person's likelihood of having middle-class friends and acquaintances (Fernandez and Harris 1992; Tigges, Browne, and Green 1998; Rankin and Quane 2000; see also Kasarda and Janowitz 1974; Huckfeldt 1983; Cohen and Dawson 1993; Kasinitz and Rosenberg 1996; Wilson 1996; Elliott 1999).[5]

However, a radically different literature disagrees that living in a poor neighborhood would have such effect—in fact, it suggests that the effects of neighborhoods, poor or not, on social networks are negligible. The "community liberated" perspective, as Wellman (1979) has labeled it, argues that social networks are not tied to physical neighborhoods in the ways they once were. Owing to rapid advances in transportation, communication, and technology, networks in contemporary urban societies are "ramified" across neighborhoods and cities (see Wellman and Leighton 1979; Fischer 1982; Wellman 1999; but see also Wirth 1938; Fischer 1976).[6]

This alternative hypothesis suggests that we pay greater attention to the issue of mechanisms. Why, in our contemporary society, would merely living in a poor neighborhood limit our social networks? Unless residents of poor neighborhoods work, play, do all their shopping, and conduct all their business in their neighborhood, it is unclear why neighborhood poverty would have any effect, independent of their individual poverty, on their social networks. The question, therefore, demands further inquiry into the mechanisms behind the generation of social ties.

Understanding the mechanisms behind both social organization and social isolation theories may well require paying closer attention to culture and agency. These timeless sociological concerns become especially salient

5. An important literature touched on but not central to this book examines networks within the poor rather than between the poor and the middle class, focusing largely on the family. See Stack (1974) and Bott (1971).

6. Note that both perspectives would agree that being a poor person will decrease the likelihood of having middle-class ties. But only the social isolation thesis contends that living in a poor neighborhood, independent of one's own poverty, will have such an effect.

in the context of urban poverty, for both sociological and political reasons. In fact, however, how they operate within this context has remained in many ways elusive (Sampson and Wilson 1995; Small and Newman 2001).

Neighborhood Poverty and Culture

Until recently, structuralist sociologists were reluctant to examine the effects of culture. As Wilson (1987) argued, after the outcry that followed the Moynihan report (1965)—which argued that problems plaguing blacks were rooted in the deterioration of the black family—researchers had shied away from studying culture for fear of being accused of "blaming the victim" for their problems (Ryan 1976). Independent of politics, many sociologists in the social disorganization field seemed to be convinced that culture made little explanatory difference. In her devastating critique, *Social Sources of Delinquency,* Kornhauser (1978) chastised cultural deviance models for their logical inconsistency and lack of empirical support. But as the political environment has settled, the sociology of culture grown, and critiques such as Kornhauser's faded from memory, researchers have been increasingly willing to grant that, in some fashion, culture mediates or tempers or complicates the effects of neighborhood poverty on social capital. Still, most of them would agree that we do not know enough about how culture operates (see, esp., Sampson and Wilson 1995; Small and Newman 2001; and see also Nightingale 1993; Patterson 1997; Harrison and Huntington 2000).

The study of culture within urban poverty reached a peak during the late 1960s, with several works tackling the interaction between structure and culture in great detail (Lewis 1965, 1968; Liebow 1967; Banfield 1968; Valentine 1968; Hannerz 1969). The current discourse on culture within urban poverty has only made small advances beyond these works, with some important exceptions (Wacquant 1992; MacLeod 1995; Bourdieu and Patterson 2000). It seems increasingly clear that students of the inner city should revisit culture more seriously. In any such endeavor, two issues are important.

The first is how to define, and think about, culture. Much of the discussion of culture defines it either, following Parsons, as a group's norms and values or, more generally, as a group's worldview. The former definition is probably the most common conception of culture in inner-city research. It is also the staple of conservative explanations about what is wrong with the inner city; it is the conception behind the arguments that urban blacks have low marriage and employment rates because they do not value the family unit, education, or hard work. By this account, a person's actions are caused by his or her values and normative orientation. But even though sociologists of urban poverty have done relatively little to improve on this conception, sociologists of culture have developed dozens of more sophisticated conceptions of culture—such as Bourdieu's (1977) "habitus," Goffman's (1986) "frames," Swidler's (1986) "tool kit" or "repertoires," and Somers's (1992) and others' (Taylor 1989; Hart 1992) "narrative." They have shown that culture, in these varied ways, may affect a person's behavior independent of her or his norms and values. Indeed, the notion that people's actions are directed primarily by their norms and values is rather dated and simplistic. This does not preclude that values may affect certain actions, but it does suggest that reducing cultural analysis to the analysis of values is probably a mistake.

The second common conception of culture—that it encompassed a person's overall worldview—was implicit in sophisticated discussions by writers such as Hannerz (1969), who offered a distinction between "mainstream" and "ghetto-specific" orientations and argued that both of these were present among most ghetto dwellers he studied. The strength of this approach is its ability to capture disparate elements of behavior observed in the inner city and organize them into a coherent whole. The weakness is its simplification. The distinction between mainstream and ghetto-specific behavior seems remarkably like that between behavior the middle class does and does not endorse. If so, then why do we need specialized terms to talk about conduct? Why not simply speak of good and bad behavior? The conception, regardless of terminology, is potentially tautological and difficult to falsify, precisely because it is all encompassing. The idea of worldviews makes generating clear processes tied to specific outcomes troublesome: Why, for example, should the same variable be equally valuable in assessing community participation and social isolation? The worldview concept, in talented hands such as Hannerz's, can give a reader the feel for the community, but by attempting to encompass all aspects of observed behavior, it becomes proportionally weaker at explaining any single one.

A sociologist who has noted the weaknesses of the two preceding approaches to culture might be tempted to propose a third, perhaps based on current research in the sociology of culture. I might have, for instance, relied on that research to present the overall conception of culture to be used throughout the book. However, since it is already clear that most approaches to culture are better at explaining certain phenomena than

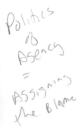

Author's Approach

others, I have adopted a pragmatic approach in this book. When confronted with a particular phenomenon I have observed in the neighborhood, I ask whether a specific conception of culture, such as a narrative of self or a cognitive framing of a situation, helps to understand it.

The second major issue is how to conceive of the relationship between structure and culture. Most structuralist scholars who have agreed that culture matters in the inner city still argue that structural conditions are the ultimate cause of whatever cultural patterns are observed (e.g., Sampson and Wilson 1995). An important example is the oppositional culture thesis, which posits that when certain minorities perceive an inability to overcome structural poverty, they react by developing cultural attitudes and values in opposition to those of the mainstream. If the mainstream values education and hard work, these minorities will denigrate schooling and unglamorous work, rejecting them as paths to upward mobility (Ogbu 1978; Fordham and Ogbu 1986; Massey and Denton 1993).[7] Thus, even though cultural attitudes do affect the academic performance of minorities, these cultural attitudes are ultimately caused by structural conditions. For scholars in this and similar traditions, the causal arrow points in a single direction, from structure to culture to academic underperformance, low social capital, or other unwanted outcomes. Perhaps for political reasons, as in the past, scholars have been reluctant to examine, even in theory, whether other causal relationships are possible, such as whether culture may sometimes act in parallel with, not subordination to, structure. But if we assume, as stated above, that culture may affect behavior through a number of different paths (values, frames, narratives, repertoires, etc.) and that it may affect different outcomes differently, then there is no reason to assume that it should always be caused by structural poverty. Thus, this study allows the possibility of alternative types of interaction between structure and culture.

Neighborhood Poverty and Agency

The question of agency takes on a particular significance in poor urban neighborhoods. Politically, the question has become, essentially, Whose fault is it? Both political conservatives and strong individualists have argued that all persons ultimately dictate their own fates and that by ne-

7. The most recent rigorous tests of this particular hypothesis have found little support for it (Ainsworth-Darnell and Downey 1998; Cook and Ludwig 1998).

glecting the view that the poor are agents in their lives, liberal structuralist social scientists allow the poor to abdicate responsibility for their actions (Mead 1992; Patterson 1997).[8]

Sociologically, the question of agency subsumes two different dilemmas. The first is how to reconcile the theory that structural conditions have such strong impacts on the poor with the fact that poor individuals living within the same conditions manifest such different outcomes; the second is whether choices have any role in sociological explanations. In reference to the first issue, the standard approach to studying poor neighborhoods is to assess whether neighborhood poverty is independently associated with an individual's likelihood of, say, committing a violent crime, becoming pregnant as a teen, or being unemployed. However, as Newman (1999) recently reminded us, most residents of poor neighborhoods have never dealt drugs, never killed or robbed anyone, and are, in fact, employed. What makes them different? If neighborhood poverty causes the aforementioned problems, why does it not affect these individuals? The obvious answer to the latter question is that most research compares people across neighborhoods rather than in a single neighborhood and claims only that neighborhood poverty increases the likelihood of the observed outcome. This is perfectly consistent with the finding that many, or even most, residents of those poor neighborhoods do not exhibit the negative outcomes detailed above. If, after statistically controlling for other factors, say, 40 percent of the residents in poor neighborhoods are socially isolated, as opposed to 10 percent in nonpoor neighborhoods, then neighborhood poverty is clearly associated with social isolation.

The problem is assuming that this information is sufficient. The question of what makes the different cases differ has hardly been addressed. Regarding the above example, for instance, sociologists have spent relatively little time explaining why, in the poor neighborhoods, 40 percent were isolated but 60 percent were not. The scarcity of research on this question probably accounts for much of the waning influence of structural theories in the public imagination for the popularity of arguments that cultural values, laziness, or public assistance policies are to blame for social isolation and its impact. Most research on neighborhood poverty ignores that

8. Note that this position differs from conservatism on culture. Cultural conservatives argue that the poor have alternative cultural valuations, e.g., a disbelief in the work ethic; but agency conservatives argue that the poor have simply not taken agency, e.g., that they have been, essentially, lazy even though they may theoretically believe in the work ethic. Indeed, conservatives have tackled this issue much more forthrightly.

many individuals do not respond to structural conditions as predicted by the literature, relegating these people, in statistical terms, to the error term. To the extent we wish to open the black box, we cannot ignore that many people in poor neighborhoods do the opposite of what they theoretically would be expected to do.

This is especially important because people do, in fact, respond to neighborhood poverty in widely diverse ways. In fact, as Sampson, Morenoff, and Gannon-Rowley (2002, 466) write in a recent review of the literature, "more of the variance in almost any outcome lies within rather than between neighborhoods" (see also Cook, Shagle, and Değirmencioğlu 1997). Since theories have relatively little to say about these differences, they seem removed from reality. How does one conceive of an intermediary mechanism if the outcome varies widely within poor neighborhoods? Such a mechanism can be conceptualized, I will suggest, in part by incorporating that variation into theories about how the mechanisms operate. This study addresses that variation.

The second issue—the role of choice in sociological explanations—is intimately related. Of concern is how to reconcile these structural theories with the fact that individuals make choices about, for instance, whether to participate in neighborhood activities and their networks. Is it that neighborhood poverty only affects those individuals who fail to make choices? Or that it affects people who make choices differently from those who do not? Should choice even be studied sociologically, or is it, essentially, the nonsociological issue of free will?

In addressing these questions, it is helpful to think of choice as an issue of motivation and to ask what affects motivation, as some sociologists studying social movements have done (Snow and Benford 1992; Goodwin, Jasper, and Polletta 2001). For example, some (though not all) of the work on narrative theory has made great strides in conceptualizing the relationship between narrative and action while avoiding relativistic or unverifiable explanations (Taylor 1989; Hart 1992; Somers 1992; Somers and Gibson 1994). Narrative theory suggests that individuals understand their lives in terms of narratives with ongoing and complex plots and that they act not when their actions are rational but when the actions accord with such narratives. Seemingly irrational acts are understandable if we know enough about the narrative a person has of him- or herself. I examine, in the chapters ahead, whether conceiving of choice within the context of motivation improves our sociological understanding of agency among residents of poor neighborhoods.

Basic Approach

My focus in this book are the mechanisms by which neighborhood poverty in Villa Victoria affected local community participation and the residents' social ties to the middle class and to one another, paying special attention to culture, agency, and variation in responses to poverty. I argue that a better way to understand how neighborhood poverty affects social capital in particular and life chances in general is to adopt a "conditional" approach to what is often called the ghetto. The key to this approach is to use not commonality but variation as the foundation for the analysis.

The standard approach, by design, searches for mechanisms to be found in the typical or statistically average poor neighborhood, though this is not always stated explicitly. Reconsider the example at the beginning of the chapter. Cross-sectional research has shown that neighborhood poverty is associated with low local participation. Thus, a researcher would search for a neighborhood that is more or less representative of the ghetto (i.e., one with low local participation). Then, after identifying "trust" as a mechanism linking neighborhood poverty to a lack of local participation, the researcher would hypothesize that the average poor neighborhood evinces a lack of trust, leading to decreased participation. The assumption is that the important mechanism or mechanisms are likely to be found across most poor neighborhoods or, alternatively, in the statistically average poor neighborhood—that is, that these mechanisms operate in a given poor neighborhood regardless of its particular context. I make no attempt here to refute that some mechanisms may, in fact, operate across most poor neighborhoods or within the (statistically) average poor neighborhood. But I show that many of the most important mechanisms will probably not be uncovered by relying exclusively on the standard approach.

I take a different approach. I elect not to choose, as a starting point, that neighborhood poverty is associated with low social capital (in whatever form) but, instead, that neighborhood poverty is sometimes associated with low social capital and sometimes not—and then ask why. The conditions differentiating the two outcomes (low social capital vs. not) are the key to what engenders the association of neighborhood poverty with low social capital. This assumption will guide analyses at the individual and the neighborhood levels. At the individual level, the assumption is that within any given neighborhood some people will have low social capital and some will not and that this variation is not random. At the neighborhood level, I have assumed that two equally poor neighborhoods will evince different levels of social capital and that this variation is also not random. Since this is a single-neighborhood study, systematic study of variation across neighborhoods could not be undertaken, but the case of Villa Victoria can be compared to published field studies to generate hypotheses about the nature of the conditions that cause dissimilarities in social capital. In addition, I assess whether variation over time can be used to the same benefit.

This approach will, I hope, uncover much about how neighborhood poverty affects people, while helping to clarify our current thinking about these processes.

TWO

Villa Victoria and Boston's South End

We shall not be moved from Parcel 19! — EMERGENCY TENANTS' COUNCIL

Tremont Street

In the spring of 2001, having lived in the South End for one year and studied it for two, I tried to imagine what impression the neighborhood might make on a first-time observer. Every observer, I knew, would see the neighborhood through her particular perceptual lenses, but certain aspects of the neighborhood would probably impress anyone.[1] I reminisced about what I had witnessed over the past few years, picturing the red brick walkways and cobblestoned streets, brownstones, townhouses, and ten-story housing projects, children on bicycles, elders with canes, and the yuppies, blacks, *boricuas,* and b-boys whose lives and daily rhythms I had studied and recorded in my notes.[2] Above all, I remembered the South End as a street, as one particular street: Tremont, the main thoroughfare running the length of the neighborhood. There was hardly any aspect of the neighborhood's culture, landscape, and people one could not witness on Tremont; the street epitomized the neighborhood. What first impression, I

---

1. Any ethnographic description is both partial and positional, conditioned by the experiences and characteristics of the observer. Deciding how subjectively, then, to describe one's observations has been the subject of much debate (Clifford and Marcus 1986). This book has little to add to that debate, and the decision here has been more pragmatic than theoretical. Except in some instances where it directly affects the understanding of the phenomenon at hand, I will spend little time discussing how respondents reacted toward me or how a different observer might have witnessed the same events differently. Though not trivial, such a discussion would distract from the objectives of the work. Furthermore, I have attempted to compare much of what I observed and was told by respondents with data from other sources, such as archives, the census, and published oral histories, as discussed in the appendix. Nonetheless, readers should bear in mind the conditional nature of my or anyone else's description of the neighborhood.

2. *Boricuas* is a colloquial term for Puerto Ricans.

wondered, might an observer have of Tremont Street, in particular? No doubt it would seem, to many, like the most integrated mile in America.

I remember my first sight, at the western edge of the neighborhood, just off Massachusetts Avenue, of two tiny barbershops stuffed into the basements of a couple of townhouses. For many African-Americans, the shops were neighborhood staples—their yellowed awnings stubbornly refusing to give in to the elements, mimicking their owners' stubborn resistance to the economic winds of a gentrifying market. Dozens of black men sat waiting for their fades, shaves, and touch-ups. Others stood outside, sporting baggy jeans and sweatshirts or slacks and jackets, one or two of them puffing on a cigarette. They all seemed about the same age, somewhere between eighteen and thirty-two.

A few blocks east, by the large New Hope Baptist Church, several large African-American families congregated outside, exiting mass. Elderly women wearing elaborate, tasteful hats and elegant dresses discussed the minister's sermon with men sporting splendidly matched suits. School-age girls and boys hopped around them in crisp white dresses and miniature ties and jackets. Across the street, by the lobby of a dark brick building, a half dozen elderly black and brown men lounged peacefully, looking out indifferently at the passers-by, and seldom, it seemed, uttering a word.

Further into the South End stood long rows of meticulously preserved nineteenth-century brick townhouses and brownstones. They had high front stoops, charmingly manicured gardens, and finely detailed front doors. The houses ran for blocks in every direction. Few buildings rose more than five stories, creating a squat skyline—an architecturally dense ground that contrasted with the wide-open sky. Young white professionals slipped out of the houses and hurried to the late-model European cars parked alongside the Chevys, Fords, and Toyotas packed into every conceivable space along the street. A young white woman hauled a laundry basket up the high stoop to the door of a townhouse; another, wearing sweats and flip-flops, watered a young tree in front of a brownstone, nurturing her tiny oasis in an aging urban landscape. A woman in her sixties unloaded groceries from the back of her SUV, while her husband, eyes on the streets and sidewalks, carried them to their ground-level apartment. Across the street, a middle-aged white couple read the posters on the window of the small, South End branch of the Boston Public Library.

Sitting on a bench by the park next to the library, two septuagenarians, African-American men, conversed, taking in the summer breeze. Wearing several layers of graying and stained clothing and smelling ever-so-slightly of alcohol, they kept a close eye on a supermarket cart filled with aluminum cans in large plastic bags: their livelihood.

Further east, two Latinos exited a drugstore, one walking, the other riding his bike slowly alongside. Their accents, less melodic than Dominicans' and not as loose as Panamanians', betrayed the men's origins in Puerto Rico. One of the men related what happened when he tested positive for drugs, violating his probation:

> I got dirty urine. . . . Tenia la probación. El probation [officer] told me he would [recommend a] surrender. He said I would get two years [in jail]. Lawyer spoke to my grandmother and told her I would get two years. . . . Said, "I don't care if you talk to *God* [you'll still get two years.]" . . . Because I got dirty urine. But I got in front of that judge and he gave me six months!

Suertudo (lucky one). Across the street, three or four Latino men in their forties gathered by the stoop of a row house under the shade of a tree, laughing and talking loudly in Spanglish, slapping their legs as they did so. A dozen adolescent boys leaned on their bikes outside a bodega, sipping on soft drinks, flirting with the girls who stopped by for groceries. A smaller group of African-American boys strolled up the sidewalks wearing baggy pants, Timberlands, and leather jackets. Near Dartmouth Street, the distinct sound of an old salsa classic floated out into the street from behind a row of houses.

Past Dartmouth there were chic hair salons, boutiques, and restaurants tucked into the basements and the front ground floors of several row houses. Seen together, the establishments resembled less the bottom floors of homes than one long, ground-level, comfortably eccentric mall, whose establishments were alternately chic or utilitarian. At outdoor cafés, attractive white men in their late twenties and thirties ate, drank, smoked cigarettes, and flirted. Gay couples strolled hand-in-hand around the small square before the Boston Center for the Arts' Cyclorama, just past the offices of the *In News Weekly,* a local gay and lesbian paper.

Further along the street, near the Massachusetts Turnpike, sat a small public garden next to a large apartment complex, Castle Square. I remember two Chinese women walking with a half dozen children running around alongside them. Chinese families abounded. Several of these families, returning from a nearby supermarket, carried loads of small grocery bags into the complex. Further up the block, as Tremont rose into an overpass above the turnpike, foot traffic suddenly declined, as the roar of cars and trucks now thundered from below.

The stretch of Tremont Street between "Mass Ave," where the South End begins, and the "Mass Pike," where it ends, is just under a mile. It is not uncommon to witness, within a fifteen-minute walk on a summer weekend afternoon, the full spectrum of American ethnic and class and cultural groups—blacks, Latinos, Chinese, and whites; gay, lesbian, and heterosexual women and men; and the wealthy, middle class, working class, and poor—living peacefully and harmoniously within a few city blocks. It is partly this fact that sustains the South End's reputation for openness and acceptance, a place where anyone might feel at home and where the residential segregation that persists in American cities (Massey and Denton 1993) has failed to materialize.

By extension, a sociologist investigating the social relations of the low-income Puerto Ricans living in this community might expect to find not the "socially isolated" urban dwellers depicted in Wilson's (1987, 1996) works but an uncommonly "exposed" group of poor people. Rather than being cut off from the middle class—and its rich networks and role models—these poor Latinos would be expected to experience more than their share of cross-class contacts. In this respect, they might even outperform the average member of the presumed socially integrated middle class, for their exposure transcends not only class but also race and even sexual orientation.

But like many first impressions, this vision of the South End is misleading, and its concomitant expectations about the Puerto Ricans living there, mistaken. The poor, predominantly Puerto Rican Villa Victoria, while clearly part of a vibrant, diverse South End, remains in many ways isolated from the neighborhood that surrounds it. To many South Enders and even some Victorianos, the housing project is "in, but not of" the South End. The thirty-year relationship between Villa Victoria and the wider South End, rather than harmonious, has often (though not always) been contentious. Certainly the history of the housing complex itself has been contentious. And to understand Villa Victoria's struggle to sustain and develop social capital we must know something about this rich history, how the neighborhood's creation was at once a rare and also a perfectly natural outgrowth of the development of the South End. To present the outlines of that history is the objective of the pages that follow.

The Birth of the South End

As late as the mid-nineteenth century, most of what is known today as the South End was a vast span of salt water marsh between the fat tip of the Boston peninsula and the mainland. At the time, only the thin, long, and winding strip of Washington Street connected downtown Boston and the mainland, through Roxbury. Geographically detached and limited, as a result, in its capacity to grow in numbers, the bustling city of Boston had nonetheless never needed additional space to flourish. Through the eighteenth century, this state of affairs was acceptable to the overwhelmingly WASP city, still reaping the benefits of the high commerce of the early industrial era (see Whitehill 1968; Kennedy 1992).

But by the first quarter of the nineteenth century, rapid demographic and economic transformations had changed the city's outlook. Wave upon wave of Irish and, later, Italian immigrants had begun to undermine the Yankees' numerical majority. The city's traditional and merchant elites, less than enchanted by the increased "ethnic" presence, were inclined to migrate to the outskirts. Indeed, small, attractive suburbs, such as Newton, had sprung up and begun to bloom in the mainland.

It soon became apparent that, as Boston's population of poor immigrants grew and its share of wealthy residents declined, its budgets would be overburdened and underreplenished, threatening the viability of this great city. As a countermeasure, Boston initiated a massive landfill of the swamp on both sides of the Washington Street strip, especially on the Charles River side, setting parcels for the construction of large upper-middle-class townhouses during the 1830s. Thus, Tremont Street was laid parallel to Washington, and then Columbus Avenue was added, narrowing the span of the Charles even further. Between these major throughways, more upper-tier townhouses were built throughout the mid-nineteenth century and sold at auction. To enhance the prestige of the new housing, the city built several neighborhood squares in the English style, such as Chester and Worcester Squares and Union Park (see Whitehill 1968; Goodman 1994a, 1994b).

The new row houses, built around the squares and throughout the new grid of streets, were four or five stories high, of handsome red brick, meticulously finished, and outfitted with basement quarters (with separate entryways) for the servants. In his richly documented topographical history of the city, historian Walter M. Whitehill describes the South End of the mid-nineteenth century as "a region of symmetrical blocks of high-shouldered, comfortable red brick or brownstone houses, bow-fronted and high-stooped, with mansard roofs, ranged along spacious avenues, intersected by cross streets that occasionally widened into tree-shaded squares and parks, whose central gardens were enclosed by neat cast iron fences" (1968, 122). In the charming new neighborhood, several auctions were held for empty parcels of land, where a few wealthy Bostonians built large townhouses and mansions (Whitehill 1968, 125; Moritz Bergmeyer Associates 1979).

For at least a few decades, the experiment in city planning appeared to be working. "By the 1860s, large numbers of middle-class families were moving out of the overcrowded hub of the city to the elegant new bowfront row-houses that lined the freshly surveyed streets between the Tremont Street extension in the Back Bay and Albany Street on South Bay" (Green 1975, 1). The new South End had helped the city keep its affluent residents in town.

But the success was short-lived. It became clear early on that demand for the pricey new real estate had been overestimated: "Although the area was respectable and full of citizens of substantial wealth," writes architect Donald Freeman (1970, 80), "the price of land had been set at an inordinately high rate to insure a uniformly upper-class population; the city found itself with acres of undeveloped land on its hands." Looking to fill the row houses of the South End, the city made a decision that would affect the social, demographic, and political landscape of the budding neighborhood for the next one hundred years: it turned to the working class. As Freeman (1970, 80) writes, "Mayor Smith urged a change in the policy of restricting South End settlement to people of wealth only. 'Mechanics of limited means,' he argued, 'who have not credit on small resources, have a direct claim to indulge beyond all others.' The city then established more favorable loan terms and began to sell the land, preparing the way for a lower-class invasion of the South End. This deflation of prices was a deliberate, positive act of volition on the part of the city; its result was a complete deterioration in the South End's prestige value." Freeman's term "lower-class invasion" is not particularly salutary. One might simply suggest that the city underestimated the desire of wealthy residents to live among their own—and the speed at which the value of real estate can plummet due to demographic changes.

South End real estate eventually collapsed under the weight of two additional forces. The first was the "financial panic" of 1873, which drove many owners to sell their homes and banks to foreclose properties (Whitehill 1968; Kennedy 1992). But perhaps the most important force was the development of the Back Bay. Extending from the railroad tracks at the edge of the South End and into the Charles River, Back Bay was landfilled through the 1860s and outfitted with spacious, beautiful, expensive residential units. It lay at the foot of Beacon Hill, home of the city's wealthy Yankee elite, and within walking distance of downtown Boston. Newer, nearer the traditional elite, facing the river, a few steps from downtown, and unencumbered by democratizing housing policies, the Back Bay swiftly overtook the South End as the hot new neighborhood for the affluent. As historian Lawrence Kennedy (1992, 60) explains, the Back Bay "was a fairly natural and logical choice of residence [for this group] once it came into being." Before long, the affluent class had left the South End.

A Haven for Immigrants

A DIFFERENT SOUTH END

This combination of factors led to a drastic transformation of the South End's population. By the final decade of the nineteenth century, most of the Yankees and wealthy merchants who had hoped the South End would become Boston's newest fashionable neighborhood had fled to the Back Bay and the suburbs. When Aaron Allen, a wealthy furniture dealer, built a large brownstone mansion in 1859 on the corner of Worcester Square and Washington Street, he expected the house to serve as a small landmark in an upcoming, exclusive neighborhood. By 1871, he realized the South End would not live up to expectations and quickly moved back to the Back Bay, never to return (Moritz Bergmeyer Associates 1979; see also Boston Redevelopment Authority [henceforth BRA] 1977). Other homeowners in South End, recognizing the decline in the status of the neighborhood and the value of their properties, followed suit.

By 1900, a new generation of South Enders had settled in the neighborhood. They were immigrants, the working poor, and single men who worked the railroads or in factories. The multiple rooms in the four-story row houses were of little use to this society. They subdivided the houses, converting them into low-rent apartments or rooming houses. On the first floor of the row houses, the new residents erected wood and plasterboard walls to separate the living room from the stairwell, instantly creating new apartments. They turned the second and third floors into two- or even three-bedroom apartments, outfitted with hastily assembled kitchens, small closets, and awkwardly designed hallways. Former servants' quarters, already equipped with separate entries, were rented out as independent units. Other homes were converted into rooming houses, each floor containing even smaller subdivisions and, often, no kitchens. What were once single-family houses for the affluent class now became four- and five-apartment complexes for poor and working-class immigrants and rooming houses for poor, single men.

Housing in the South End was just about the cheapest in the city, and the population of the neighborhood, both of immigrant families and single men, multiplied. A study published by Boston Landmarks Commission (1983, 9) notes that, by 1885, of "the 53 houses on Union Park [on a cross street east of Tremont], half had become lodging houses. Seven years later, only seven still were maintained [as] private residences." Another study notes that by "1900, there were about 37,000 people living in the lodging houses along the cross streets between Tremont and Washington Streets" (Green 1975, 3). As the population grew, so too did the number of restaurants, laundries, tailors, grocery stores, and hundreds of other small businesses. One twenty-four-acre section of the South End had 125 small businesses at one time (BRA 1958). The South End thrived.

Though most of the South End's early immigrants were Irish, they were followed, throughout the first half of the twentieth century, by Greek, Syrian, and Chinese immigrants, Eastern European Jews, African-Americans, West Indians, and, later, Puerto Ricans (see Green 1975; BRA 1978; Moritz Bergmeyer Associates 1979; Boston Landmarks Commission 1983; Lukas 1985). They settled in the South End's roughly three hundred residential acres, in somewhat (though not completely) distinct sections of the neighborhood (see also BRA 1977). The "New York Streets" area, in the northeast, was settled early on by Eastern European Jews. The Chinese lived nearby, further north and west, where the South End, before the construction of the Massachusetts Turnpike, once met Chinatown (see also Keyes 1969, 46). Syrians, Greeks, and Libyans were closer in toward the heart of the South End, mostly near Union Park and along Shawmut Avenue. African-Americans, who had moved in from Beacon Hill and the South, populated many of the cross streets between Tremont and Columbus Avenue, including the area around Massachusetts Avenue and Lower Roxbury. The Mass Ave section of the South End was once a hot nightspot among African-Americans, with several clubs from which to choose (the only current remnant of that period is Wally's Café, a tiny but legendary jazz club). The migrants from rural Puerto Rico who came in the 1950s settled around West Newton Street, between Tremont and Washington Streets.

The neighborhood's ethnic-ecological makeup contained elements of what Suttles (1968) calls "ordered segmentation." In a neighborhood characterized by ordered segmentation, territorial boundaries marking the turfs of different ethnic groups both perpetuate the mutual exclusiveness of the groups and maintain order by minimizing opportunities for conflict. In the South End, however, because of the constant migration of residents, the territorial boundaries among the various ethnic groups were neither fixed nor rigid but fluid membranes expanding or contracting as residents settled in or emigrated from the neighborhood. Moreover, unlike the Addams area in Chicago that Suttles studied, the various immigrant groups in the South End were at least somewhat integrated, living a rather peaceful coexistence. A series of oral histories collected in the mid-seventies by Green (1975) bears evidence to this integration. One Holland native remembers the South End of the late fifties as "one of the most integrated [communities] in the city. There were quite a few Blacks and Portuguese families who were very close. They were all very warm people. I could walk around there any time and be invited to stay at someone's house for dinner" (in Green 1975, 17). A Puerto Rican man who immigrated in the late fifties recalls:

> It wasn't bad being a kid in the South End . . . ; it really wasn't, it was nice. One thing the South End had before that it doesn't have now is that before, everybody was poor; there was poor Syrians, poor Chinese, poor Irish, poor blacks, poor Greeks, and poor Puerto Ricans. . . . Everybody was friends. We all went to school together. I had a lot of Chinese friends. I had a special friend from school who had the same first name as me and I used to go to his house and eat Chinese food and he used to come to my house and have Spanish rice. (quoted in Green 1975, 24)

A former West End resident who was relocated to the South End in 1959 remembers the time: "I met poor white people and black people down here in the South End. We were all in the same boat, and we all got along good. We helped each other out, we loaned each other things, and borrowed from each other" (quoted in Green 1975, 20).

THE PUERTO RICAN ENCLAVE

The Puerto Ricans who migrated to the South End were among the most recent arrivals. Recruited by New England farm companies for seasonal employment (see Matos Rodríguez, unpublished manuscript), Puerto Ricans from the smallest towns in the island had been quietly settling in the northeast for decades. By the 1950s, hundreds of them had moved into the roomy, affordable apartments of the South End. They were, by and large, a rural people (see table 1). As late as 1968, 77 percent of them had migrated from either the countryside or towns with populations of less than 25,000. Once in the city, they quickly found jobs—if often temporary and nonunion jobs—in the many factories in Boston at the time or set up small businesses to join the hundreds of such small businesses already existing in the South End.

Back in the towns of Aguadilla, Comerío, Ponce, and some neighborhoods in San Juan, Puerto Rico, among the kin and social networks of these immigrants, the South End developed a reputation as a place where

TABLE I. Characteristics of Latino Households in the South End, 1968

Characteristic	Number
Migrated from either countryside or city of <25k in Puerto Rico (%)	77
Males with education over 10th grade (%)	11
Females with education over 10th grade (%)	11
Male heads who cannot read and speak English (%)	52
Children per household	3.6
Male heads of household employed (%)	59
Main occupation operative (%)	45.6
In union (%)	14
Working in same job for less than 1 year (%)	60
Having same job for over 3 years (%)	1
Mean weekly earnings ($)	86
Households female headed (%)	38
Female heads who stay at home during the day (%)	88
Female heads receiving some kind of welfare (%)	45
Female heads employed (%)	8
Mean weekly earnings ($)	86

SOURCE. Youngerman (1969).

cheap housing could be found in the center of one of the most vibrant in-dustrial cities in the country (Matos Rodríguez unpublished manuscript). A brother, uncle, or even in-law was enough reason to pull north many is-landers who had been perfectly content with their lives. One such islander was Ernesto, who told me he had lived happily if uneventfully as a con-struction worker and farmer in Ponce; he was married and had several sons and daughters.[3] His older brother, Manuel, had migrated to Boston in the late 1950s and opened a bodega, a little grocery store in the South End. By the turn of the sixties, Manuel realized he desperately needed help to run the establishment. It was not as if Ernesto were a skilled businessman, but in those early years, Manuel simply could not afford the extra help, and if Ernesto moved up they would both, he was sure, be better off. So Ernesto came north at age fifty with his eldest son; the rest of the family would mi-grate within a few years, as soon as it was affordable. The grocery store went out of business anyway, but Ernesto quickly found work at a foundry that paid him enough to afford the $60 monthly rent for a fully furnished,

3. All names, and some identifying details, have been changed to protect the anonymity of respondents. None of the changes bears relevance to the substance of the arguments. Whenever public figures are quoted, real names are used; only in these cases will surnames be included in the narrative.

three-bedroom apartment that had been carved out of the third floor of a brick row house in the neighborhood.

Ernesto was not a high school graduate. In this respect, he resembled most of his roughly 2,000 compatriots living in the South End in the late sixties. A 1968 study of 261 Puerto Rican households in the South End found that only 11 percent of either men or women had more than ten years of education (see table 1). As table 2 shows, the median years of schooling among Latinos in the heavily Latino tract of the South End in 1970 was 6.1 years; 83 percent of persons age twenty-five and older had fewer than twelve years of schooling, and 60 percent had fewer than eight years. Since 77 percent had migrated from the rural or semirural Puerto Rico of the late forties and fifties, the modest years of education are not surprising. Some parents even pulled their children out of school in Puerto Rico to bring them, with the rest of the family, to Boston. Such was the case of Eugenia, who in the midfifties was taken out of school as a twelve-year-old girl. Her parents brought her to the South End, where they settled in a two-bedroom apartment. Her parents did not put her in

TABLE 2. Estimated Characteristics of Latinos in the South End, 1970

Characteristic	Number
Households with female head (%)	19
Median years of school completed among persons 25 and older	6.1
Persons 25 and older with under 12 years of schooling (%)	83
Persons 25 and older with under 8 years of schooling (%)	60
Persons whose residence 5 years earlier was "abroad" (%)	37
Families with incomes less than 150% of poverty level (%)	73
Families below poverty level (%)	26
Families receiving public assistance income (%)	70
Persons below poverty level (%)	31
Median yearly family income ($)	4,721
Male civilian labor force unemployed (%)	20
Males 16 and over in labor force (%)	60
Female civilian labor force unemployed (%)	34
Females 16 and over in labor force (%)	26
Households owner occupied (%)	0
Mean gross monthly rent ($)	93

SOURCE. U.S. Bureau of the Census, 1970. See appendix.

school in Boston, and she never saw another day of formal education, much to her chagrin.

The South End's Puerto Ricans were very poor. A full 70 percent of the families were on public assistance and 73 percent had incomes under 150 percent of the poverty line (see table 2). Only 60 percent of the men age sixteen and over were in the labor force, and 20 percent of these were unemployed. Twenty-six percent of women age sixteen and over were in the labor force, and 34 percent of them were unemployed, as Eugenia was at the time. The 1968 study, which shows slightly higher unemployment rates (table 1), found that roughly 46 percent of the employed men worked, as Ernesto did, in factories as operatives. However, work was unstable: 60 percent had been in their current jobs for less than one year, and only 1 percent had worked in the same job for more than three years. Despite the potential availability of jobs in the manufacturing sector existing as late as the 1970s in Boston, this was not a steadily employed people. Their work was temporary, sporadic, unpredictable, and infrequent.

This fact was reflected in their incomes. The 1968 study and the 1970 census show remarkable similarity in incomes, $86 a week (or $4,472 a year) and $4,721 a year, respectively, enough to cover the average reported 1970 rent of $93 a month. The 1970 census (which, it should be noted, seriously undercounts the number of Latinos in that tract—see the appendix) reports that none of the heads of households owned their homes.

The community was very poor partly because a high proportion of its households were headed by single unmarried women. The 1970 census places the figure at 19 percent; the in-depth 1968 study, at 38 percent. Within that 38 percent, only 8 percent of the women were employed and 88 percent stayed at home during the day, yet only 45 percent were receiving some kind of public assistance. Clearly, women were resorting to alternative sources of income (see Edin and Lein 1997).

Like other South End immigrants, the Puerto Ricans clung passionately to their neighborhood. Many of them remained within the twenty to twenty-five acres bounded by Rutland, Tremont, West Dedham, and Washington Streets for decades. In the 1968 study, among those families who had moved within the past six months, a full 54 percent had moved from another South End dwelling. Consequently, the enclave swelled and quickly became part of the South End mosaic. To insiders and outsiders, this parcel of land became known as the "Spanish" section, flourishing socially and culturally as most ethnic enclaves do. Nevertheless, this attachment to the location also planted the seeds of what Wilson (1987) referred to as social isolation, as we shall see in two later chapters.

The Decline

To their dismay, the honest immigrant families flocking to the South End discovered that less savory characters were also seduced by the neighborhood's modest charms. Dozens of corners of the South End became hubs for drinking, gambling, prostitution, and, as the century progressed, drug trafficking and its concomitant violent crime (see Keyes 1969; Lukas 1985). During the course of the twentieth century, and especially after World War II, two trends combined to cause the deterioration of the South End: the steady increase in the neighborhood's criminal activity and the gradual departure of the stable working families.

As early as the turn of the century, one study reports, there were, "41 saloons, 24 liquor stores, and 11 poolrooms," as well as numerous brothels and gambling operations in the South End (Woods 1898, 3). Over the decades, the neighborhood attracted gangsters, other men and women eluding the law, and the socially alienated. By one estimate, there were as many as 7,000 homeless men in the South End by 1963 (Lukas 1985, 167). Unsurprisingly, the neighborhood developed as a "slum." At the time, the neighborhood was separated from the Back Bay by railroad tracks (now of the Commuter Rail and Orange Line), which cut the South End off from the rest of Boston. Most Bostonians kept to the "good side" of the tracks, except when yearning for drink, drugs, pool, or prostitutes.

After World War II, many of the better-off working families in the South End moved out to their own homes in different parts of the city or the suburbs, following the general pattern of urban flight that affected Boston and most major American cities (see table 3; Keyes 1969). By then hundreds of residents were counting the days until they could make enough to move out. An African-American and lifelong resident of the South End recollects: "A lot of Blacks that lived in the South End, the younger ones, made it their goal to move up to what we called "The Hill," the Humboldt Avenue area right in the middle of Roxbury. The housing

TABLE 3. Population of the South End
and Boston

	South End	City of Boston
1950	57,218	801,444
1960	34,956	697,197
1970	22,775	641,071

SOURCE. BRA (1977, 3).

TABLE 4. Characteristics of the South End and the City of Boston, 1960

	South End	City of Boston
Unemployed (%)	8.70	5.00
Median yearly family income ($)	3,650	5,757
Families with incomes < $3,000 (%)	41	17
Families with incomes > $10,000 (%)	4	14
Units owner occupied (%)	9	28
Dwelling units sound (%)	46	73
Percent population nonwhite	41	10

SOURCE. Adapted from Keyes (1969, 39).

was bad in the South End, cold-water flats and what have you. And so a majority of my friends made it their goal to move out into Roxbury" (quoted in Green 975, 15). The South End's population of roughly 57,000 in 1950 had dropped dramatically to 35,000 in 1960. By then (see table 4), the South End was not just poorer than the rest of Boston; it had two and a half times the percentage of families making under $3,000 a year. It also had four times the percentage of nonwhites (41 percent). But not everyone left. Many South Enders resented outsiders' depiction of the entire neighborhood as a slum. They were quick to point out that, by and large, drug dealing, drinking, and prostitution were limited to certain areas well known to insiders, such as the clubs on Washington Street (see Lukas 1985). These law-abiding residents had never lost their attachment to the South End, avoiding questionable areas or, when that proved impossible, learning to live with them. Eugenia recalls that as a young woman she "wanted to be a teacher and a social worker," so she tried hard to keep out of trouble. Temptation was everywhere, however; the basement of her own apartment building was an illegal casino. This she found neither horrifying nor catastrophic; she made peace with its presence and simply stayed away.

Gambling, it turns out, was a vibrant enterprise in the South End throughout the fifties, sixties, and seventies. Some of the Puerto Rican migrants starting out in Boston accumulated cash quickly by gambling, using their own winnings to buy property or start small businesses throughout the city. These businesses did not always survive, but the financial jump start provided a footing for at least a few families recently arrived. For men who did not break a hundred dollars on a good workweek, poker was an appealing option. Ernesto was a hard, unapologetic gambler. "Sometimes," says Ernesto, who spoke with me in Spanish, "you could make up to a thousand, two thousand dollars in one night." Unfortunately for Ernesto—a competent but not stellar poker player—making a thousand was about as easy as losing a thousand, so gambling did not provide a reliable income source. For others, like Gabriel, gambling made some difference. In an interview, Gabriel explained to me that he had no money to speak of when he came to the South End as a young man, but he clearly had a great deal of business acumen. He worked odd jobs during the fifties, eventually discovering he also had a knack for making relatively vast sums of money in gambling. Gabriel accumulated enough to set up a small grocery store and a make few minor investments in rundown properties. With that money, he brought his family to Boston through the sixties and seventies, settling in the neighborhood until health reasons forced him to move out of state in the 1990s. For most men, however, gambling was not a reliable income source. If anything, playing cards was a way to socialize.

Gambling constituted a small (if persistent) part of a lively nightlife involving music, drinking, and dancing. For many of the Puerto Ricans there, the South End was nothing if not festive. But the nightlife for men like Gabriel and Ernesto sometimes proved dangerous. Ernesto, who spoke to me in Spanish, recalls a tragic experience at a former club on Washington Street where he and his close friend, Roberto, "would stay out until dawn playing poker." He remembers what happened once when he, Roberto, and a few other friends "had spent the whole day drinking beers." He continues:

> Then, in the afternoon, they went out [to run an errand, to later head to the clubs]. They wanted me to go but I said, "No, I'm not going. . . ." Roberto . . . had a brother who loved women. And two women got to the club and [Roberto's brother] headed over to pick them up. . . . He didn't know that the two women had husbands, who were there [at the club]. And—you wouldn't believe it—the son-of-a-guns [*sin vergüenzas*] were upstairs. . . . And they headed down. . . . And one of them came up and stabbed Roberto twice—Holy Mary!—he nearly pulled his heart out. He killed him. . . . That was around ten o'clock at night. . . . The next day in the morning, when I went over there, I saw a large pool of blood right on the road; by then, the blood had frozen over.

The experience pained Ernesto more than it changed him. The potential for violence, he understood, was part of the price he paid for the life he led, a fast life but a relatively honest one. He nevertheless thinks of the South End of that time as a safe place, one where "you could leave your doors open and go to sleep at night without worrying about it. A woman could go out in the streets at 12 o'clock at night alone and nobody would [bother] her."

Regardless of Ernesto's attachment to the South End—a feeling shared by many of his immigrant neighbors (see the testimonies in BRA 1958, 1964; Green 1975)—the South End, by midcentury, was falling apart. Several notable sections of the neighborhood, once beautiful landscapes accented by iron railings, fountains, well-designed public spaces, and numerous parks, had degenerated into dirt and mud pits, garbage dumps, and worse. Dense hedges in certain parks rendered them impenetrable. Back alleys and parks were so piled with garbage as to be indistinguishable from each other. A resident describes the South End during the fifties: "City services were terrible. . . . You could see thirty or forty feet of garbage piled in alleyways, just rotting away there" (quoted in Green 1975, 16–17). The streets, parks, sidewalks, and alleyways became infested with rodents. Ernesto evokes the early sixties: "My friend Nestor and I would get out of work at five and sit by the little park [on West Newton Street, now O'Day Park]—by the 'junky'—to drink beers. That place was full of rats, and roaches, and mice. Five-pound rats would crawl over our feet." He recalls the "huge ditches" running behind the Tremont Street houses, just a short space below the windows of people's homes. The sewer system had been neglected for decades.

As they reached their first century of existence, the townhouses began to deteriorate. One Puerto Rican resident who migrated in 1964 remembers his dwelling on West Newton Street: "The apartment was terrible. There wasn't hardly any hot water and there weren't any storm windows. You could really see through holes in the walls" (quoted in Green 1975, 25). The 1960 Census reported 54 percent of the dwellings as structurally unsound (see table 4), and a 1972 study found that 65 percent of the residential properties in the South End were not up to code (Stainton 1972, 3). Formerly glorious townhouses were abandoned and boarded up. Some were simply rented out at substandard living conditions, with neither heat nor hot water; others were condemned and torn down, leaving behind squalid empty lots, at best, and massive piles of rodent-friendly rubble at worst.

Roberta, an elderly Puerto Rican migrant with a youthful mind and a profound sense of injustice who communicated with me in Spanish, recounts the ubiquitous problem with rodents:

> I'll tell you something. The South End, those were old buildings. And there were so many mice it was scary. One night, my son-in-law and I set up a

mousetrap. And we trapped nine mice . . . the big ones. . . . The big rats. One "shopping bag" full of rats. The next day we called the guy who cleaned the buildings . . . and I told him, "Look, when the garbage truck comes by, take this to get buried out there at the crematory." [The next morning,] the street got full of people to see the bunch of mice I had trapped over night, my niece and I. We [had taken] one of the big mouse-traps. One would fall and after a few minutes another one would. We spent almost the entire night catching mice . . . . Those buildings belonged to—————, one of those rich Bostonians. But he was one of those who would never renovate anything.

Still, Roberta would never leave, not just because of her attachment to the South End but also, as she explains, because "the rents were cheap. My apartment had four rooms. Three bedrooms, living room, and kitchen. And even a little room I turned into a dining room." But the filth of the neighborhood was insufferable.

The squalor of the South End was exacerbated by the construction of the elevated train tracks above Washington Street around the turn of the nineteenth century, which cast a dark, bleak shadow on the surrounding neighborhood. The Allen mansion, once a grand structure dominating Worcester Square, suddenly found its view blocked and its tranquility shattered by the industrial rumble of the elevated train. The distinguished journalist Anthony Lukas (1985, 1666) notes that the el did not even stop in the South End, only at its end points, on Dover and Northampton Streets, as if Bostonians were trying to eliminate all possibility of contact with the neighborhood. The city, for all purposes, had abandoned the South End and left it for dead. A report by the Boston Society of Architects described the city's opinion of the South End as "the no-man's land through which Bostonians pass when traveling between the Roxbury-Dorchester area and downtown. . . . To many, South End and Skid Row are synonymous" (Freeman 1970, 77).

Urban Renewal
A NEW SOUTH END

This state of affairs did not last. The preponderance of deteriorating neighborhoods in the city had contributed to its reputation as an unsafe, undesirable place to live. By the mid-1950s, the city implemented a comprehensive plan for the renewal and redevelopment of several of its neighborhoods, such as the South End, Charlestown, and the West End.

The city's plans for these neighborhoods attracted controversy. In this regard, perhaps the greatest outcry occurred after redevelopment of the West End. As part of Mayor John Hynes's "Boston Redevelopment Tour," a brochure was passed out on January 10, 1957, that articulated the swift, comprehensive, and, for many, obvious plan for renewing the entire, predominantly Italian West End. Unambiguously, the brochure read, "All of the buildings will be cleared except two historical buildings, a junior high school, a health unit, and a Roman Catholic Church" (Hynes and Greater Boston Chamber of Commerce 1957, 9). The plan was executed as promised. By 1960, most of the West End's forty-eight acres of townhouses and small apartment buildings were leveled and virtually all of its Italian and Italian-American families relocated. The drastic clearance of the West End was not the mayor's first urban renewal project, but it was his most politically controversial.

Until the late 1950s, it was a relatively uncontroversial assumption that the best way to "clean up" a "slum" was to tear it down. But the West End was a particularly large neighborhood, and many observers wondered not just whether the disruption of so many families' lives was warranted but also whether this "slum" was really a slum. Perhaps this question was raised in people's minds by the aerial photographs publicized after the leveling, which showed a shockingly vast empty space where the neighborhood once stood, but for whatever the reason, "opposition came quickly," as urban planner John Stainton (1972, 8) writes, "both nationally and locally, to this type of 'bulldozer renewal' with its wholesale destruction of low-income homes and neighborhoods." In his classic ethnographic study of the West End, *Urban Villagers,* Gans (1962) observed that the neighborhood, though poor, was not a slum and that, by clearing block upon block of affordable houses to build luxury condominiums, the city had destroyed a vibrant, working community to please the housing predilections of the affluent. The West End fiasco eventually affected urban renewal in Boston more than any other controversy of the time.

In 1960, a new agency, the Boston Redevelopment Authority, was created to design, plan, and execute all urban renewal projects in the city (Stainton 1972). By then, whatever notions might have floated about of leveling the entire South End had disappeared for good. The South End had already seen the "bulldozer clearance" of one of its subneighborhoods. The "New York Streets" area, twenty-four acres in the northeast region of the South End, had been cleared and replaced with factories and warehouses (BRA 1958). Yet the South End was in desperate need of renewal. Its nearly six hundred acres (roughly three hundred of which were residential) would be rehabilitated through a combination of tactics.

Part of the rehabilitation, such as the improvement of public facilities, tree planting, landscaping, streetlight installation, and sewer renovation, would be relatively uncontroversial (BRA 1965, 5). But the Boston Redevelopment Authority's (BRA) plans concerning housing met a wall of resistance. And it was not a homogenous unified front but a complex and contradictory cacophony of competing parties, ad hoc groups, and special interests.

The early experiments with housing renewal in the South End had disgruntled many lifelong residents. The New York Streets area's 931 families and 125 businesses had been displaced in 1954 (BRA 1958) without residents' input as to what to do with the neighborhood. In 1962, when the Castle Square neighborhood, also in the South End, was cleared, 346 families and 298 single people were displaced (see BRA 1964). Many of the displaced families—about half of New York Streets' and a third of Castle Square's—remained in the South End, registering their unhappiness with anyone who would listen. Often these families complained that renewal had increased their rents. A BRA report of the New York Streets relocation process describes a woman who was shown an apartment where she could be relocated (by then, the BRA had been forced to be particularly sensitive to displaced residents' needs): "After inspecting a five-room apartment in excellent condition, she refused the unit because of the rental, $53.00 per month. She said that she had never paid over $24.00 per month in rent in fourteen years of married life, and despite the urgent and immediate need for housing, refused the apartment" (BRA 1958, 8). Similar reports were made after the relocation of the Castle Square families, where people had been "content with substandard housing at [their] low average rental," since "even a move to public housing required a rent increase for many" (BRA 1964). In this specific sense, redevelopment was bringing increased hardship to the poor and working families who had lived in the South End all their lives.

As reports of these early experiences made their way through the South End's grapevines, residents already disturbed about the massive West End clearance became especially suspicious of any BRA housing renewal efforts in their neighborhood. Political opposition mounted. Dozens of South End community groups—some ad hoc committees, others longstanding neighborhood associations with monthly meetings—fought one or another of the BRA's renewal plans. Among these were the Association Promoting the Constitutional Rights of the Spanish Speaking, the Community Assembly for a Unified South End (CAUSE), the South End Manpower Corporation, the South End Neighborhood Action Program (SNAP), the predominantly Latino Emergency Tenants' Council, the

Committee for a Balanced South End, the Ad-Hoc Committee for a South End for South Enders, and the South End Citizens' Association. The multiple neighborhood groups fought different and often contradictory efforts. For example, the Ad-Hoc Committee and the Emergency Tenants' Council fought for more subsidized housing and less displacement of the South End's poor. But the Committee for a Balanced South, composed mostly of middle-income residents, fought the BRA's efforts to introduce more subsidized housing in the neighborhood. In fact, the Committee for a Balanced South sued (unsuccessfully) the Emergency Tenants' Council's plan to build 181 units of what would later become Villa Victoria (see Urban Field Service 1968; BRA 1978; Lukas 1985).

In the ten years following 1957, attitudes toward redevelopment had shifted so drastically and crystallized so sharply that another swift clearance of the entire neighborhood, as had been effected in the West End, was out of the question. Instead, the South End saw a slow and paced redevelopment, one that involved rehabilitation, the creation of low- and moderate-income housing, and the encouragement of private investment. Though several redevelopment projects had taken place in the neighborhood before then, in 1965 the South End was officially declared a BRA urban renewal area. The process brought about the rehabilitation of streets, sidewalks, and sewer systems, the reconstruction of houses and buildings, and, by 1977, the creation of 4,000 new subsidized units for both low- and moderate-income residents (BRA 1977, 6).

But despite the city's best efforts, the renewal process displaced countless poor families, for no state-enforced renewal process works independently of the private real estate market. Liberal-minded, middle-class artists and others rapidly moved in looking for bargains. In the late fifties, young gay and lesbian men and women, painters, writers, and some professionals, distasteful of the suburbs, had begun looking for cheap housing in the sections of the South End nearest downtown. Lukas describes the newcomers (1985, 168): "Some of them [were] drawn by the bargain prices on Victorian bowfronts, some by the neighborhood's convenience to downtown, still others by the racial and social integration, the opportunity to participate in 'a great urban adventure.' It was the start of a phenomenon later labeled 'gentrification.'" By 1963, several hundred middle-class families had established themselves in the South End, particularly on Union Park and other streets nearest downtown. The neighborhood became a mecca for gays and lesbians throughout Boston, eventually attracting the offices of the *In News Weekly* and other gay- and lesbian-owned businesses.

The city encouraged private investment in the South End for many of the same reasons it had filled in the South End swamps in the first place: to attract and retain wealthy residents. Once the city made clear its commitment to rehabilitating the South End, banks loosened up and the red lines began to disappear. A whole new slew of middle-class professionals, looking for good housing investments, began to move into the neighborhood. Lukas describes this new group perceptively (1985, 427):

> [They were] a different breed of middle-class settlers, more affluent suburbanites with no particular commitment to heterogeneity and little interest in rehabilitating an old rooming house from scratch. Having bought already-restored townhouses for $35,000 to $80,000, this second wave felt a greater stake in their investment, a deeper need for insulation from the poor, the black, and the unorthodox. The most mobile members of a mobile society, often with cultivated tastes, a desire for "gracious living" and pocketbooks to match, they were the quintessential urban consumers, prime targets for every "upmarket" sales-pitch. . . . Gradually, the blocks of restored town houses between Columbus Avenue and Tremont Street became a distinctive enclave, set apart—thanks to the Boston Redevelopment Authority—by brick sidewalks, ornamental streetlights, and ginkgo trees, as well as by its own standards, values, and social proprieties.

At times, the shift was dramatic. Through the early 1960s, the cross streets between Tremont Street and Columbus Avenue, especially those nearest Massachusetts Avenue, were almost exclusively African-American. During the sixties, young white professionals had bought several of the large nineteenth-century houses on the West Newton block between Tremont and Columbus. By 1970, as Lukas (1985, 441) reports, "the block [was] . . . half black"; within another decade and a half it had become almost entirely white.

By the end of the twentieth century, the South End would become one of the most expensive neighborhoods in the city, with several blocks of restored bowfronts occupied primarily by middle-class and affluent white professionals. Many of the former rooming houses were once again reconfigured, this time as condominiums and (sometimes) single-family homes. The poor single roomers, immigrant families, and poor minorities were gone, except for those living in the new low- and moderate-income subsidized housing projects built in lots throughout the neighborhood.

THE EMERGENCY TENANTS' COUNCIL: "NO NOS MUDAREMOS DE LA PARCELA 19!"

In the late sixties, one of the groups most adamantly opposed to redevelopment was the Emergency Tenants' Council (ETC), a small group of mostly Puerto Ricans who lived in Parcel 19, the parcel of land between Tremont and Washington Streets where that small enclave had grown (see Bond 1982; Uriarte-Gastón 1988; Hardy-Fanta 1993). At the time, several of the residents were fed up with the substandard conditions of their housing. In the report of a survey of Latinos in the South End, Youngerman (1969, 9–10) writes that, "one-third of the households said that their greatest problem since they had arrived in Boston concerned housing. In fact, 60% said they would prefer living in public housing to living in their present apartments. . . . Many of them (25%) said [their main housing problem was] that their houses were structurally unsound. Their housing had plumbing which did not work and poor heating. The buildings were in a general state of disrepair. Others (20%) stressed health problems as a result of poor housing." Those living in one section of West Newton Street were particularly disgruntled, since, according to one resident, the "landlord who owned the whole development . . . didn't want to put any heat on" (quoted in Green 1975, 26). Their row-house apartments, after one century of wave upon wave of immigrants, were falling apart. The residents also feared that the BRA, which had plans to demolish the entire area and develop it as a combination of residential and commercial space, would displace them and break up their community. What had happened in the New York Streets area and Castel Square, only a few blocks east, certainly did not allay their fears.

On exactly how ETC was formed, different oral histories among residents and activists of the time tell somewhat different stories. One common account is that, with little outside help, a few residents spontaneously decided to fight their impending relocation against the BRA. A less popular recollection tells that nonresident (and non–Puerto Rican) activists and mobilizers took the initiative and convinced the residents to fight and that the latter only eventually took on leadership roles. The truth seems to lie somewhere in between. Before the demolition plans were known, several ministers of the Saint Stephens Episcopal Church, located in the parcel, noticed that many of the parishioners and their neighbors were living in conditions far worse than even the most sympathetic Bostonians assumed. The ministers, some activists, and several residents of the community began a small effort to reach out to residents in their apartments and seal leaky faucets, patch up walls, refurbish doors, and unclog toilets. It was critical, unglamorous work.

By the spring of 1967, word had spread of the BRA's plan to demolish Parcel 19 over the next few years. Residents held several meetings at a hall in Saint Stephen's Church, where they voiced what they would want upon renovation of the parcel. Minutes for one meeting recorded the residents' relatively uncomplicated wishes for "low rents for low-income families, that we can truly afford to pay, such as $70 for 4 or 5 rooms," "a good supply of housing for large families," and "stores in or close to the area: grocery and meat market, delicatessen, Laundromat, hardware stores" (NU IBA Zo2-20 [henceforth NU], box 3; see the appendix). Some tenants, hearing that demolition would not be complete until 1970, wanted more immediate solutions, such as cleaning up the infamous local junkyard and forcing landlords to fix poor wiring. Hardly political action sessions, the meetings would continue for some time, with resident interest waxing and waning in the coming weeks and months. In a meeting on January 28, 1968, someone finally suggested creating an "Emergency Tenants' Council" (NU, box 3).

In the spring and summer, the campaign gained momentum. As problems worsened and politics intensified, the group grew and its scope expanded. By the fall of 1968, ETC had elected a steering committee composed exclusively of residents. Talented community organizers in the church helped them recruit members, compose newsletters, and develop contacts among activists, church members, and professionals (Meza and Buxbaum 1995; Toro 1998). Funds raised by the ecumenical Cooperative Metropolitan Ministries and the Episcopal City Mission were funneled to the group. By October, the organization and its volunteer architects had composed an alternative preliminary plan for redeveloping the parcel. They called for low- and some moderate-income subsidized housing, a small plaza, and residential space.

In Boston during the 1960s, as in many cities throughout the nation, grassroots housing movements were widely supported by college students, young activists, and radicals. The breadth of cultural support for such activism was probably unprecedented in American history (though there was much polarization as well [Patterson 1996]). The professional and mobilization skills of these groups were critical to the Puerto Ricans of Parcel 19, a population not only formally uneducated but also, until this time, politically apathetic.

Ernesto, who had never, in either Puerto Rico or the South End, so much as attended a Parent-Teacher Association (PTA) meeting, says he quickly became involved, joining the growing task forces that went door to door to register residents' complaints and mobilize them to resist the BRA's plans. Roberta, whose fiery attitude was matched by few, had no formal skills and spoke no English, yet she participated in the task force, passed out leaflets, and encouraged her friends to attend the countless meetings. The documented minutes that survive from these meetings bear evidence to the persistence of individuals such as Ernesto, Roberta, and other residents of Parcel 19, whose participation is recorded again and again. The residents "held a number of community meetings, [which] culminated [in] a gathering of 500 residents who voted to form the Emergency Tenants' Council. . . . [to] '[combat] poverty and the deterioration of the community through the participation of the community in the planning and development of low cost housing . . . with the object of preventing the dispersal of residents, limiting the dislocation caused by Urban Renewal and in general improving the housing conditions of community residents'" (IBA Archives, n.d.; see the appendix). The Emergency Tenants' Council opened a small office in the neighborhood in 1968, thanks to several nonprofit agencies and individuals who donated money and resources. The council needed a motto, and a forceful one was quickly agreed on: "No nos mudaremos de la Parcela 19!" [We shall not be moved from Parcel 19!] (IBA Archives; NU, box 3).

The tenants' council intensified its membership, fundraising, and picketing campaign. Local priests, nuns, and volunteers from Boston's professional and college communities helped the campaign. Roberta helped conduct countless meetings and attended numerous rallies. At times, the group was relentless in its efforts. Ernesto remembers that he and others "used to picket BRA sometimes until 12 o'clock at night," demanding that the Boston Redevelopment Authority hand over the property to ETC. They also mobilized against private landlords who failed to provide adequate heat and insulation in their properties. Residents withheld rent from what many considered a particularly unscrupulous landlord in one of the parcel's blocks. Resistance was well organized, as one resident recaps: "We had many demonstrations against the landlord who owned this block, and he finally gave it up. He gave the whole block to the tenants. There were two tenant councils working then; we [ETC] were working with people from the black community. And soon we got a bill signed so we could rehab these buildings on West Newton Street for poor families. So now Emergency Tenants' Council has rehabbed 106 units of housing for poor families on this street" (quoted in Green 1975, 26). Within a short time, ETC became a prominent activist organization, a major voice in the city's Puerto Rican community.

In 1969, the city and the BRA, after extensive negotiations with professional advisers, contractors, and ETC representatives, and hoping to dispel the BRA's reputation as a tool for the affluent bent on displacing the poor, effected an unprecedented act. They named ETC—now renamed

ETC Developers Corporation—the sponsor-developer for Parcel 19. The decision was contingent on their ability to raise the necessary funds within ninety days. Furthermore BRA, and ultimately the mayor's office, would have veto power on the major aspects of the plans; nonetheless, they no longer ran the show. The tenants council/corporation, after furious and successful fundraising, devoted itself to the complex task of building the housing project.[4]

In this task, they were helped by experienced volunteer planners and architects. Among the most important of these was John Sharatt. In 1966, Sharratt, having recently obtained his architecture degree, decided to volunteer for an advocacy group that advised Roxbury activists working to restore their neighborhood without displacing its people. He explained to me that in 1968, while still working on his professional internship, he decided to offer his services and experiences to ETC, believing there were enough "ingredients" in the situation—the right combination of political, structural, and practical conditions—for the project to succeed. It was in part his and the other architects' work that had given ETC, in its battle with the BRA, the legitimate claim to hold a comprehensive alternative development plan.

With ETC, Sharratt's chief interest was designing a housing project with which the current residents of Parcel 19 would be comfortable. They wanted a community reminiscent of Puerto Rico; they were adamant about this. One of the principal ETC leaders, Leonel, raised funds and personally flew Mr. Sharratt to the small town of Aguadilla, Puerto Rico, to take note of the architecture, the landscape, the colors, the pitched roofs, and, above all, the plaza. Sharratt recalls that Leonel would not even "let me go to San Juan or Ponce because they were too American. . . . So we went around and photographed and measured and tried to find what the typical characteristics were."

Over many neighborhood meetings, residents debated, discussed, and improved on draft after revised draft. The challenge was defining a concept both residents and the city would find amenable. Sharratt remembers that the residents "wanted pictures and they wanted bright colors. Now, . . . the South End [has] got the granite steps and brick faces. So when we

---

4. The oral histories and archival documents are inconsistent on the name of the organization. Most residents, now and in the 1960s, referred to it simply as "ETC"; furthermore, "ETC Developers' Corporation" and "ETC, Inc.," used only after the name change, are often used interchangeably. For simplicity, I will refer to the organization as "ETC"; the reader should understand that this organization changed, at least officially, from a grassroots political orientation to a development and administrative one.

worked on [it, we realized] we needed a combination. [We incorporated] the South End['s] steel rod iron and rails, [and] the brick bases and the steps . . . , but as you go up [the house's facade] you turn to plaster and the brighter colors and the pitched roofs [as in Puerto Rico]." It was on this basis that the new complex was designed.

Construction, which began swiftly, was done in five stages "in order to carry out the development process with a minimum of relocation to places outside the parcel and thus avoid one of the ills of the original Urban Renewal Plan" (IBA Archives, n.d.). The five stages, or projects, were a combination of rehabilitation and new construction, and most of them were finished by the mid-1970s.[5] By then, the residents had given the new neighborhood a name, "Villa Victoria," or Victory Village, a fitting name for a group of poor residents who had fought many battles to remain in their neighborhood and had eventually, indeed, been victorious.

On completion, Villa Victoria became easily one of the most attractive housing projects in the country. The neighborhood was laid on a rectangular plane running lengthwise between Shawmut Avenue and Tremont Street. Against the eastern edge, by West Dedham Street, was Plaza Betances, a small, brick plaza surrounded by permanent benches, chess tables, and trees and shrubs. Next to the plaza was the Unity Tower, a relatively tall yet unobtrusive modern building housing the elderly. On the opposite side of Villa Victoria, by West Newton Street, was O'Day Park, with a small water sprinkler for children, swings, a basketball court, and greenery. Most of the houses—actual houses, not apartment buildings—were located between the plaza and the park.

Rather than either build impersonal high-rise blocks or imitate the nineteenth-century row houses of the rest of the South End, the architects settled for a middle road, inspired by the Spanish and Latin American style Sharratt had witnessed in Puerto Rico. The result was beautiful concrete row houses with sloping roofs, medium-high front stoops, backyards, and iron railings. Painted in bright and earthy colors—soft yellows,

5. The projects were the following: Rehab. I, which rehabilitated several brick townhouses on Tremont Street and Shawmut Avenue to produce seventy-one units; Viviendas La Victoria I, which cleared the area between West Dedham, West Brookline, and Tremont Streets and Shawmut Avenue and built 181 new units, roughly half for moderate-income and half for low-income tenants; Unity Tower and Plaza Betances, which built a nineteen-story structure with two hundred subsidized units for the elderly and disabled and a public plaza off West Dedham Street; Casas Borinquen, which rehabilitated several more brick townhouses; and Viviendas La Victoria II, which built 163 new units and rehabilitated several others between West Dedham and West Newton Streets (IBA Archives, n.d.).

roses, tans, and pastels—the houses gave the once grim area a fresh, clean appearance, appropriate to the community's sense of optimism. Some of the projects in the complex won awards for excellence in design by the Boston Society of Architects.

Plaza Betances was designed to emulate the plaza in Aguadilla. Since the families, like those of many Latin American migrants, were large, ETC commissioned not just two- and three- bedroom units but also four- to six-bedroom dwellings. The residents requested a communal space where children could play outdoors peacefully and safely. The architects drafted a plan to cut three of the cross streets running through the neighborhood and convert them to U-shaped streets that entered and exited the neighborhood on the same side. Residents called one of them Aguadilla Street, in memory of a common hometown. They set a mirror image of Aguadilla on the opposite side of the neighborhood and called it San Juan Street. Most of the townhouses had modest but attractive backyards, and several spaces throughout the neighborhood were reserved for greenery. These elements, in addition to O'Day Park and Blackstone Square Park on the opposite side of Shawmut, made for an inviting residential community in the middle of the city, an urban oasis devoid of the squalor once typical of that section of the South End.

Inside, the houses were stunning. In contrast to the former cold-water flats of the area, the new houses boasted roomy, modern kitchens and dining areas, state-of-the-art heating systems, upstairs bedrooms and bathrooms, double-locked doors, large living room windows facing sidewalks, trees, or parks, and rear doors leading to individual yards and small gardens. Children could play out in front while parents kept an eye on them through the living room windows or out back, where a mother could keep the door open to check on them while cooking. In most houses, the top two levels constituted one apartment, accessed via medium-high outdoor stoops, and the ground floor was another, a welcome feature for some of the elderly Puerto Ricans immigrants who were getting weary of climbing stairs. Nearly all the poor activists moved into Villa Victoria, marveling at the astonishing beauty of their community, incredulous that so much had changed for the better in so little time.

Villa Victoria was an overwhelming success. Most of the families that had been moved out for the rehabilitation and construction of the neighborhood returned to live in "the Villa" (as the residents call it) after each phase of the neighborhood was finished. In their new apartments, most families paid 25 percent of their income (most families now pay 30 percent of their income).[6] As a result of the efforts of ETC, the Puerto Rican residents of Parcel 19 were among the few groups of residents of the South End who were able to remain in the South End after urban renewal.

Villa Victoria and the New South End

I began this chapter by suggesting that the South End's integration is more perceived than real, for social relations in the neighborhood are steeped in a politically charged history whose effects are still being felt. Though the full implications of this past will be discussed later in the book, it is already possible to see how the past has shaped the present. The various groups inhabiting the South End are not integrated in at least one particular sense: they do not live side by side, with each house—or even cluster of houses—in every street representing a different demographic group. On the contrary, different ethnic and class groups live, now more than ever, in separate and relatively discrete (though still somewhat fluid) sections of the neighborhood.

Though much of the South End appears statistically integrated on a census map, it remains highly segregated in real life. The small Chinese community, for example, lives in and on the few streets around the Castle Square subsidized housing complex, near Chinatown and its grocery stores and specialty shops. A few of the Syrian immigrants still linger but not many; one or two grocery stores and an abandoned building reading "Sahara Syrian Restaurant" bear evidence of the fading existence of that once-thriving community. And African-Americans are concentrated in a few subsidized apartments and on several side streets near Massachusetts Avenue. Only a minority of the African-Americans attending churches such as Tremont Street's New Hope Baptist Church are middle-class black South Enders; most are part of a long-gone community whose lingering link to the neighborhood is found largely (though not entirely) in the few still-viable congregations. By and large, parishioners in these congregations commute to church. Indeed, to witness a concentration of middle-class blacks in the area, one must wait for Sunday afternoon, when congregations are exiting mass. As for the South End's Puerto Ricans, most reside in Villa Victoria and in another housing project a few blocks

6. The income limit is now about $36,000 for a family of four. New residents must be earning some income to be eligible. Current residents who lose all sources of income pay a flat fee of $25 in some cases and nothing in others.

east. And by no means are all the affluent whites who stroll around Tremont Street neighborhood residents. Some are gay men and lesbians from other neighborhoods patronizing the city's hub of gay-owned and gay-catering shops and restaurants; others are recent arrivals to the neighborhood heading for their homes on the side streets, where few people stroll about as they do on Tremont.

In fact, it is on Tremont Street, on Sundays, and in the summer that the South End will strike one most as a haven of integration. A different street, on a different day, at a different time of the year might well yield a different impression of the ethnic and class composition of the neighborhood. Place and time matter, a recurring theme throughout this book.

At nearly every stage in the South End's one hundred and fifty–year history, waves of migrants into and out of the neighborhood have altered its social and economic composition. The Puerto Rican residents of Parcel 19 represent but one of these groups, and Villa Victoria itself can be thought of as a neighborhood within a changing neighborhood, subject, as others have been, to the pressures of the South End's demographic shifts, and agent, through its own waves of migration, in the larger shifts that end up shaping its course. It is within this context we must investigate the development and sustenance of social capital, internal and external, in Villa Victoria.

THREE

The Rise and Decline of Local Participation, Part 1

Social Organization Theory

During that time, everyone thought they were community organizers.
— FELIPE, SPEAKING (IN SPANISH) ABOUT THE 1970S

By 1976, the construction of Villa Victoria was virtually complete, and the new community would enter what, by all accounts, were its golden years. The former Parcel 19 could not have seemed more different from the new Villa Victoria, with its clean, safe streets, colorful parks with swings and slides, plush greenery, and houses with backyards. For the first time since they had migrated to Boston, many of the residents lived in structurally sound apartments with fresh coats of paint, adequate heating, electricity, and hot water. To have lived in the former Parcel 19 and move into the new Villa Victoria was to experience a once-in-a-lifetime transformation in quality of life. For many of the women and men who had been involved in the struggle against displacement, the life-altering experience provided a lesson they would never forget.

Roberta, Gabriel, and others of that generation savored this sweet fruit. Theirs was a story of near-overnight improvement in the standard of living, an accelerated version of the American dream. It was not a rags-to-riches story, for they were still poor and unskilled, vulnerable to shifts in the economic cycle. And neither did their story imply the virtues of autonomy of that standard American tale—of a rugged individualist who pulls himself by the bootstraps, starts a business, and attains success. This was a story not of individuals but of groups, of success attained not by following one's own path but by participating in a collective struggle that, in fact, one did not always lead. To witness such radical and tangible change after such difficult and concerted work is truly a rare experience, among poor and nonpoor alike. Not surprisingly, the residents—young women and men at the time of the resistance—came to see voluntary participation in their new community as an inherent good, one that could create palpable results and measurable improvements in the quality of their lives. The lesson was clear: getting involved in your community pays off. The most entrepreneurial among them initiated activities to help sustain the community and get people involved; others volunteered their time to help the activities started by what had become local community leaders. This newfound participation took several forms.

Probably the most formal was the institutionalization of the Emergency Tenants' Council (ETC) and the creation of a new community service agency. After the construction of the property, ETC became the manager of most of the units of the new development. A separate organization was founded that would provide all-around community services: Inquilinos Boricuas en Acción (IBA), or Puerto Rican Tenants in Action, the mission of which became "(a) fostering the human, social, and economic well-being of Villa Victoria residents, (b) promoting and advocating for Latinos citywide, and (c) perpetuating the rich Latino cultural and artistic heritage" (IBA 2000a). It became a full-functioning nonprofit organization, with office space in the neighborhood, professional directors, and staff and volunteers.[1] As with ETC, the mobilization for the creation of IBA was grassroots—not a top-down policy outcome. Its budget would rely both on government grants and, especially, on donations from wealthy individuals and corporations hoping to associate themselves with the neighborhood's success. Both organizations would be overseen by a board—thirteen people for ETC, seventeen for IBA—selected exclusively by the residents of the neighborhood and composed mainly of residents but also of outsiders who had demonstrated their ability and willingness to serve.[2] The neighborhood was divided into eight small dis-

1. At the turn of the millennium, IBA was a complex service-provision organization with three basic departments: residential, finance, and arts and culture. The residential department, the largest, encompasses five separate human-service divisions: the youth department, the Escuelita Borikén day-care center, the family support department, the Batey Technology Center, and the Unity Tower residential center for the elderly.

2. The organizational relationship between IBA and ETC has changed several times over the years. There have been times when a single director managed both IBA and ETC, times when the two organizations were governed by two separate boards, and times when they were governed by one board. The sizes of the boards have also changed. In the early 1990s, the two boards were consolidated into one. Presently, IBA has a managing director and a board of directors (composed primarily of elected residents), while ETC is run as an independent company.

The creation of two separate centers—one for management, one for services and advocating—was part of a general strategy followed by community groups in Boston and other cities

tricts; one board member represented each district, while an additional twelve or so members were selected at large (IBA Archives; NU, boxes 2, 3, 27).

But participation was by no means limited to the formal organizations, as residents quickly involved themselves in their community in forms both elaborate and mundane. Consider a sample: in the early 1970s, the first of several newsletters was published. *El Luchador* (in this context, "The Struggler") was a ten-page item photocopied at the IBA office and distributed through the late 1970s. The newsletter often evoked optimism as it described new associations or recorded the progress of existing ones, such as this item from 1976, translated here from the original Spanish: "A few weeks ago the dance classes of the Areyto program for children began. . . . We are very happy with the reception of this workshop, given that the first day of classes numerous girls showed up with great interest in learning" (IBA Archives). In the mid-1970s, the residents initiated the yearly Betances Festival, a four-day celebration of Puerto Rican music, arts, and culture held in the neighborhood's main plaza. The festival attracted thousands of people every year, celebrating with a small parade and the traditional election of a "reina del festival," a young woman selected to represent the neighborhood during the festivities (IBA Archives). In the late 1970s, a small group of women calling themselves La Cooperativa de Cocina (roughly, "the cooking cooperative") began meeting a few times a month to exchange and discuss Puerto Rican recipes. Occasionally, these recipes—including the popular "*sancocho* with pigs' feet," a stew—were disseminated throughout the neighborhood in local newsletters (IBA Archives). Shortly before 1980, one of the more extroverted residents, Fredo, a man who had migrated to the South End in the early fifties, started informal English courses for adults and for children. The long-running courses were held in one of IBA's rooms and were very popular, earning him the nickname *El Profesor,* for which he is still remembered.

In 1980 a group of young men and women built a small solar greenhouse, which, a reporter marveled, was a "plastic-covered geodesic dome [that] resembles a jungle gym topped with a bubble. Ten and one-half feet tall at the highest point, the sides slope to the ground. Inside, warm humid

during the time. Professionals who were activists often counseled community groups to engage in this strategy, to allow for the separation of activities that could be considered political (and therefore subject to greater scrutiny before obtaining government grants) from those directed at the stabilization and institutionalization of an organized neighborhood. (I thank Ronald Ferguson for alerting me to this set of issues.)

air bathes the vegetables and flowers tucked into the 21-foot circle of soil" (Pollard 1980). When the greenhouse was completed, the residents who organized it expected longevity: "We want kids to run this project, to have a garden growing all year round" (quoted in Pollard 1980). In the early 1980s, Villa Victoria's own television station, Channel 6, was launched (see Rivas 1981). Since its construction, the neighborhood had been wired for cable with a local channel in mind. Staffed by one full-time worker and up to twenty volunteers from the community, the closed-circuit system broadcast the evening news in Spanish and taped and broadcast the happenings at local events, often with interviews from participants. Channel 6 left an archive of thousands of hours of tapes (IBA Archives). In the mid-1980s, a particularly popular cultural program, Areyto, sponsored by IBA, got both adults and children involved in the visual arts, including print making and photography. Once, with the help of outside funding, the youth of the neighborhood assembled a colorful tile mural on a large wall facing Plaza Betances, the plaza built in the center of the Villa in emulation of the central plazas in Aguadilla, Puerto Rico. The mural depicts the history of the Puerto Ricans in the neighborhood and their struggle to create Villa Victoria (see Hoyt and Rivera, n.d.).

In that decade, between 1976 and the mid-1980s, community participation flourished, with activities such as big brother/big sister mentorships, math and literacy workshops, English courses, community gardening, cultural education on the music and rhythms of Puerto Rico (such as the *son* and the *trova*), workshops on the dance styles of Puerto Rico and Latin America (especially salsa and *bomba*), baton twirling for girls, after-school tutoring programs, summer field trips, and celebrations of every major holiday of both the U.S. mainland and Puerto Rico. Scores of boxes of IBA's archives contain fliers, posters, photographs, announcements, meeting minutes, editions of neighborhood newsletters, draft "certificates of appreciation" for volunteers, local newspaper clippings, and auditors' reports bearing evidence to the hundreds of events, group meetings, and ad hoc associations that took place at the time in the neighborhood. The level of participation is striking (see e.g., NU, boxes 1, 2, 3, 22, 44, 49, 102, 132).

This phenomenon, which we can call community participation, differed radically from the earlier political mobilization that had led to the creation of Villa Victoria. The mobilization of the late 1960s was precisely that—a movement aimed at the clear, if complex, goals of resisting displacement and creating an affordable housing community. The participation of the late 1970s and early 1980s was not a movement; it had no particular goals or missions and was hardly of a political nature.[3] Though math and English-as-a-second-language (ESL) courses may possibly be thought of in that light, cooking groups, gardening associations, mural painting, and cultural festivals represent participation in the more general sense of voluntary community involvement for its own sake (e.g., Sampson 1999; Rankin and Quane 2000). Unlike the political mobilization of the 1960s, community participation would not lead to policy changes; but it would, according to urban theorists, improve the quality of life, decrease crime, and lessen the hardships that accompany poverty by increasing social support systems (Wilson 1987, 1996; Sampson 1999). Indeed, Villa Victoria became evidence that poor neighborhoods need not be disorganized, anomic, or alienating (see also Whyte 1943; Gans 1962). As Carla, a lifelong Villa resident in her sixties who spoke with me in Spanish, recalls, "This community used to be a model for other communities."

The Decline

The golden years were short-lived. Community involvement in the Villa declined sometime around the latter half of the 1980s after reaching what appeared to be a peak then. Several transformations took place in Villa Victoria, changes that may or may not have affected one another. One change was in the scope and mission of IBA, as new directors adopted different management styles and implemented different objectives; another was in the level of trust for IBA-ETC, as minor scandals and accusations of favoritism in the allocation of apartment units hurt its reputation among residents in the mid-1990s. The kind of change I am concerned with in this chapter, however, is not institutional but, rather, social: the gradual but precipitous decline in residents' participation in voluntary activities, whether associated with IBA or not.

By the time I began fieldwork in the neighborhood in the late 1990s, most of the associations and activities of the seventies and eighties had vanished. There were no cooking groups; no plays for the elderly; no volunteer-run English or math courses; no print making; no newsletters. There was only haphazard support for new ideas; low attendance at com-

---

3. The Partido Socialista Puertorriqueño (PSP), Puerto Rican Socialist Party, did have some members in Villa Victoria and attempted organizing during the late 1970s around employment issues, education, health, and housing. It distributed an occasional newsletter titled *Voz de Lucha*. The effort, however, was short-lived.

munity meetings; and almost no big brother or sister mentoring taking place. Channel 6 had ceased operation, and its cameras, thousands of tapes, and editing equipment were collecting dust in a storage room closet. Even the board of IBA-ETC suffered a loss of participation, with fewer residents running for election to it, and it had dropped in size from twenty in 1977 to twelve in 1999. In fact, the district' system had to be disbanded, for it was too difficult to find at least one candidate for each of the eight districts.

Some activities, such as the Betances Festival and an after-school program, survived, but Villa Victoria was a different neighborhood. As Tania, a resident in her fifties who talked with me in Spanish, laments, "It's been about ten years now since all of this has disappeared." Although many of IBA's community-service programs were still in operation, most of the neighborhood's volunteer-dependent activities had declined drastically. For instance, several meetings that had been organized to allow neighborhood residents to discuss how to improve their community—for example, by organizing a cleaning day—had few people show up beside the organizers and me. A newly instituted computer center, to give another example, had trouble attracting volunteers to teach courses or even people willing to learn. Since organizers had been unable to find volunteers, I offered to teach a free, fully bilingual, introductory computer course for adults scheduled for the early evenings. The course would cover the basics, such as how to use a mouse, what Windows and the Internet were, and how to create and e-mail simple text documents—skills that, I knew, many of the adult residents lacked. After hours of canvassing along with local organizers, announcements, and word-of-mouth advertising, fewer than ten students attended the first day. Programs in the arts suffered from the same apathy as more practically oriented programs. Melissa, a young, lifelong resident of the neighborhood with a passionate interest in the arts, once arranged a meeting to organize an after-school dance class. Almost no one showed up. "I try to organize things and people don't come," she explained. "It's frustrating!" This was a far cry from the optimism of the 1970s, when organizers for a similar course were "happy" to report that "the first day of classes numerous girls showed up with great interest in learning."

Melissa's sentiment was repeated over and over from the few organizers still invested in community participation—frustration. Gloria, another young woman poised to become a community leader, simply quit the board of directors. She explained why: "Feeling a lack of involvement from the community. Feeling that there was so much work and there wasn't enough help. . . . [So I said] I do not want to do this anymore. So I stopped. . . . I just was not involved."

How did it come to this? Both the archival record and the oral histories suggest that participation declined gradually, if dramatically, beginning the second half of the 1980s and continuing through the late 1990s. An instructive if imperfect indicator of this trend is the number of residents who volunteered for the board of directors of IBA. The board in 1970 had twenty-one active members; in 1977 it had twenty; in 1982, it had twenty; in 1987 it had sixteen; and by 1994 it had twelve. In the latter year, only fourteen people even so much as ran for election (IBA Archives), and in the ensuing years, the board held elections sporadically, rather than annually.[4]

Around 1990, hope for renewed interest blossomed. As IBA's management changed over the years, its mission had shifted, sometimes emphasizing human services, other times financial independence and stability. But by 1990, it was so clear that the ethos of participation had changed for the worse that IBA decided to attempt suppressing the trend. It hired professional community organizers and directed them, in the words of two of them, "to . . . increase resident participation . . . and create a community vision of Villa Victoria" (Meza and Buxbaum 1995, 7). Their campaign, the "Villa Victoria 2000 Initiative," was called a "'back to the future' grassroots effort to get Villa residents re-engaged" in the neighborhood, through community forums and local mobilization (see the newsletter *El Correo de la Villa*, NU, box 30). Yellowing scraps of drafts for handouts and newsletters bear evidence to the organizers' indefatigable efforts to transform the residents' attitudes about participation. A 1994 flier optimistically wrote about IBA's restructuring as a solution to this problem: "IBA/ETC is uniquely equipped to maintain and strengthen the community it helped create 26 years ago. . . . To hear the board and staff at IBA speak is to know why. Just listen to their words: *community participation, resident leadership, responsible representation, the importance of coordination*" (NU, box 132). The same flier also called for the "renewal of the community spirit which marked the early years of the [ETC] movement," emphasizing the campaign's recurring theme—a "renewal" of the former "spirit" of involvement. As part of their effort, the campaigners attempted to revive Channel 6 with support from the neighborhood's youth, calling

4. These figures, I emphasize, are imperfect proxies. Until 1993, there were two separate boards, one for ETC, one for IBA; that year, the two boards were consolidated into one. I have tried to include those years for which I was able to obtain figures on the number of actual persons sitting on the board(s).

for residents to show "evidence for our teens . . . that the community has made a commitment and supports them."

In 1991, the campaign published the first issue of its monthly newsletter, *El Correo de la Villa*, using its editorials to provoke residents to act. The editorials provide rich testimony about the status of the campaign and the ethos of the neighborhood at the time. A 1993 editorial commented optimistically that "we have taken important steps towards achieving unity in Villa Victoria. There have been several community forums, all well attended by residents" (NU, box 31), suggesting the campaign might, indeed, be successful.

By early 1995, the outlook was again more pessimistic. The monthly newsletter had turned into a quarterly, and in the fall issue, the editorial struck a grim note: "Editorial: Fight Negativism. . . . Too often our minds get stuck on the negativity and adversity that surrounds us, and we don't even notice the small victories that are the best evidence of our daily efforts. . . . As small as the victories of our neighbors, co-workers, members of our community, committee or Board of Directors may be, we need to recognize them. If we do not, we perpetuate a culture of negativism that can bury for years to come our dreams of progress in our communities" (NU, box 30). Fifteen years earlier, *El Luchador* celebrated ever-increasing opportunities for engagement; now, organizers discussed "renewal of spirit" strategies and newsletters complained of "negativism" and apathy. The invocations spoke for themselves.

In late 1995, the organizers finally admitted defeat and did so with a good deal of distress, acrimony, and distrust (Meza and Buxbaum 1995). The campaign was indefinitely suspended. The "grassroots effort to get Villa residents re-engaged" had failed.

If one were to produce a line graph indicating the change in community participation from the mid-1980s through the late 1990s, it would not be a smooth, downward line. It would be a bumpy one with sharp highs and lows—momentary bursts of activity and brief collective disengagement—whose messy pattern would only reveal itself from a distance. Historical events over a few months affected the momentary direction of change, yet over time, the direction of the trend was unmistakable: downward.[5]

5. In light of the current controversy spurred by Putnam's (2000) *Bowling Alone* over the nation-wide decline in social capital, it is worth being clear that a decline in local community participation, one form of social capital, by no means implies that all other forms of social capital declined as well (as Putnam 2000 argues). On the contrary, I later show how a different type of social capital—the level of contact some residents had with people from other neighborhoods—might have increased in Villa Victoria.

Change in Neighborhood Participation: The Social Organization Perspective

What happened to Villa Victoria's sense of lively engagement? To explain transformations such as these, sociologists of urban poverty have traditionally relied on one or another variant of social disorganization theory, which ties a neighborhood's level of social organization to structural conditions, primarily poverty, ethnic homogeneity, and residential stability. When poverty is high, homogeneity low, and residents constantly moving, neighborhoods are expected to be "socially disorganized." That phrase has meant different things to different researchers, but two common conceptions are the unwillingness of residents to intervene in a neighborhood situation on behalf of the common good and the lack of participation in neighborhood voluntary associations (Sampson and Groves 1989; Sampson 1999; Rankin and Quane 2000). In fact, these traits, in many ways characteristic of the Villa Victoria in the late 1990s, are part of how sociologists depict and most people imagine standard ghettos. The remainder of this chapter examines this question closely, asking whether social organization theory accounts for what happened in the neighborhood—and, if not, how we can improve on the theory's weaknesses.

Before beginning, we must examine an important problem in the theory itself, which will help place the case of the Villa against the wider question of how neighborhoods transform themselves over time. Consider figure 1A. The theory posits that differences in structural conditions across neighborhoods will result in differences in neighborhood participation. The problem is demonstrating that this relationship is causal. Most tests of the theory have relied on large samples of neighborhoods or census tracts, finding positive associations among these factors. But since most of these samples are cross-sectional, they cannot establish which variable caused or preceded which, a particularly important concern where so many variables at different levels of analysis are involved.[6] Another way to

6. In their tests of this relationship—and of that between social organization and crime—most recent studies employ multilevel or hierarchical linear models (Bryk and Raudenbush 1992), which help adjudicate how much of a resident's involvement is associated with neighborhood characteristics and how much is related to individual characteristics (e.g., Sampson, Raudenbush, and Earls 1997). Even though social organization theory focuses largely on collective, not individual, factors, it cannot disregard the latter; in fact, it must establish that the relationships it observes are rooted in collective not individual processes (see, e.g., Sampson 1991). But hierarchical linear models by themselves cannot account for the most important individual-level problem, which is that individuals are not randomly distributed across neighborhoods (see Jencks and Mayer 1990; Duncan and Aber 1997; Furstenberg and Hughes 1997; Small and New-

look at this problem is to note that although the existing evidence speaks to figure 1*A,* the theoretical relationship is, or ought to be, the one in figure 1*B:* after structural conditions change, participation will change. In this light, Robert Sampson, one of the prominent new thinkers in social disorganization theory, writes that "designs are needed where sequential order can be established" (1999, 269). One such design, which is, as are all others, not without its limitations, involves examining a single case from a historical perspective. Was the Villa's decline in participation preceded, as expected, by a decline in structural conditions?[7]

In the remainder of this chapter, I carefully assess whether the changes in local participation can be accounted for by changes in the structural conditions posited by social organization theory—that is, by a decline in socioeconomic status (SES), homogeneity, and residential stability. As we will see, the theory falls short, but the reasons for which it does so suggest that it should not be abandoned but, instead, improved on—by clarifying how structure affects participation and addressing how culture may play a role as well. We begin by considering the principal structural shifts in the neighborhood.

The Villa's socioeconomic transformations over the past thirty years were positive in some ways, difficult to ascertain in others. Table 5 shows the median family income, percentage of high school graduates, and percentage of persons below poverty level in Parcel 19 in 1970, 1980, and 1990.[8] The 1970 figures correspond roughly to the time of the pre–Villa

---

man 2001). People live in neighborhoods as a consequence of many (measured and unmeasured) factors that affect both neighborhoods' social organization and their heterogeneity, poverty or SES level, and residential instability. If any of these characteristics is highly correlated with both social organization and any of its three hypothesized causes, failing to account for it would inflate the perceived effect of any of the factors on social organization. For example, some people are raised in households that foster volunteer work; if these people, as adults, tend to move into high SES, homogenous neighborhoods, those neighborhoods will likely have high levels of social organization, and the causal factor will not be either the neighborhoods' SES or homogeneity but the familial culture and early socialization of their residents.

7. Historically grounded, case study research has two obvious limitations: the difficulty in establishing generalizability and its post-factum nature (see appendix). Other solutions, with their own problems, are to create randomized experiments (such as the Moving to Opportunity Program [Kling 2000]) and to make use of longitudinal data at the individual and neighborhood levels.

8. The figures must be read very cautiously for several reasons. The most serious is probably the undercount problem. The 1990 census, for instance, only counts about 1,300 who identified as Puerto Ricans in tract 705, which encompasses the Villa entirely; yet we know there are more than 3,000 residents, the overwhelming majority of whom are Puerto Rican or of Puerto Rican descent, in the Villa. The 1970 census counts about 650, even though the historical record points to at least 2,000. Undercounted populations tend to be the poorest and least steadily employed,

FIGURE 1. The relationship between structure and social organization in social organization theory

Cause	Effect
A	
Different structural conditions across neighborhoods ⟶	Different levels of social organization (and local participation) across neighborhoods
B	
Changes in structural conditions within a neighborhood ⟶	Changes in level of social organization (and local participation) within neighborhood

Victoria, antidislocation movement, the period when ETC mobilization against dislocation was in full force. The 1980 figures correspond to the period of high participation in Villa Victoria itself, and the 1990 figures, to the early period of low participation, which lasted through the end of the nineties. Social organization theory would argue that a decline in neighborhood participation between 1980 and 1990 would be caused by a decline in median family income and the percentage of high school graduates and a rise in the percentage of persons below poverty level over the course of that decade. On the contrary, the median family income increased slightly, while the education level increased dramatically, as it had for the previous decade as well. Whereas only 29 percent of residents twenty-five and older in 1980 were high school graduates, 41 percent were in 1990. Residents were wealthier and much better educated.[9]

However, the poverty level also increased, presenting a discrepancy with the income figures. The percentage of poor persons increased by

---

so the figures can be thought of as conservative estimates of the seriousness of the poverty situation.

9. An important issue not shown in the table is the unemployment rate. Consistent with the theory, the unemployment rate increased between 1980 and 1990. However, in 1970, during the tail end of the antidislocation movement, the rate had been high as well. Thus, while the participation trend was downward, the unemployment trend was U-shaped. This is not so much contradictory to as inconsistent with the theory. Regardless of the theory itself, it is unclear what relationship we would most reasonably expect between unemployment and participation. People who are unemployed are likely have more time to be involved, provided they have alternative sources of income, such as subsidized housing and AFDC or TANF checks, as in the case of Villa Victoria. But people who are employed are also more likely to be self-efficacious, as prolonged unemployment can lead to apathy, self-doubt, depression, and low self-efficacy (Wilson 1996). The actions of the Villa's residents are consistent with both hypotheses, for, we shall see in later chapters, highly involved residents have ranged from the chronically unemployed, to the unstably unemployed, to the employed.

TABLE 5. Socioeconomic Characteristics of Latinos in Villa Victoria

	1970	1980	1990
Median family income per year (1990 dollars)	15,991	13,635	14,231
Percent over 25 with 4 years of high school	17	29	41
Percent of persons below poverty level	31	34	44

SOURCE. U.S. Bureau of the Census, 1970, 1980, 1990. See appendix.

about 10 percentage points over the 1980s, but the median income also increased, by about $596 in 1990 dollars. Thus, did material hardship increase or did it not? The available census data will never provide a completely satisfactory answer, but, unfortunately, the census data are the best data we have.

Nevertheless, we may still gain some insight into the question by examining the economic status of adults. Since it is adults who can reasonably be thought of as potential participants in the community, the ideal (and unavailable) figures might be the percentage of poor adults and the median income for adults after controlling for the number of children. The question would be whether the average adult had greater material difficulty over time. If families grew bigger over this period, then hardship would increase, contrary to the implication of the income figures; if families grew smaller, hardship would decrease contrary to the implication of the poverty figures. The censuses do provide the percentage of people who are children, which can be used as a proxy for family size, given that we are only interested in the relative hardship of the collective of adults in the entire neighborhood. The greater the number of children that adults have to support, the greater their hardship. In 1980, 61 percent of the Latino residents in Parcel 19 were age nineteen and under (eighteen and under figures are unavailable for 1990), suggesting that the median annual income of $13,635 per family was spread thin. In 1990, the percentage of children nineteen and under dropped to 38 percent. Thus, the number of children per adult declined dramatically, which suggests—but cannot demonstrate—that hardship may have decreased among adults over this period. If material hardship decreased, then social disorganization theory would expect participation to increase, not decrease.[10]

10. When reading a different version of this chapter published in a scholarly journal, a perceptive reviewer suggested that children often motivate parents to get involved, so that a greater proportion of children might lead to higher, not lower, rates of participation. I do not know of tests that adjudicate between this and the alternative hypothesis presented here. Assuming that

The second issue is ethnic homogeneity. In this respect, the neighborhood remained relatively stable over that period. It is not possible to obtain precise racial data over time for the ethnic composition of the Villa (see the appendix). Furthermore, defining "ethnic homogeneity" is difficult among Puerto Ricans, who do not ordinarily conceive of themselves in racial terms. Generally, there are two ways of identifying the ethnic makeup of the neighborhood or, in fact, any group: through self-identification and through a measure defined by an external social scientist. In the Villa, both measures suggest that the ethnic composition did not change radically over time. An ETC-commissioned study in 1985 showed that 76 percent of the heads of household self-identified as "Latino," 10 percent as "black," and 8 percent as "white." In 2001, the figures I obtained from ETC indicated that roughly 77 percent of heads of households self-identified as "Hispanic," which, in that particular survey, could be of any race (of this 77 percent, the overwhelming majority selected "white" as their race). This indicates that there was no change in ethnic heterogeneity (NU, box 24).[11]

The staff member who provided the data, however, was skeptical of these figures, as was I. From both our experiences, the neighborhood seemed closer to 90 percent of Latino origin, at least by sociological definitions of the term. She explained, "We have lots of underreporting, and

---

children do, indeed, drive parents to participate, one would have to determine whether the conducive effects of having more children outweigh the deterrent effects of greater material hardship. More children may mean greater motivation, but it also means more expenditure, more work, and less time to get involved.

Regardless, I later show that the relationship between poverty and participation is probably not so straightforward, independent of the number of children. We will see that participation tends to be limited to a minority of the population, even in "highly involved" neighborhoods, so that positing one-to-one relationships between poverty and local participation is unlikely to tell us much. In addition, the next chapter argues that the relationship between poverty and participation is affected by the residents' cultural conceptions of the neighborhoods, which, I hope, adds subtlety to this issue.

11. A note on the figures. The 2001 figures are for the 395 households ETC managed at the time. In the late 1990s, ETC had lost the right to manage most of the housing project after several irregularities; it regained the right to manage several of the properties in 2000. The figures are for four of the developments, Viviendas Associates, Casas Borinquen, Victoria Associates, and South End Apartments. The 1985 figures are for these four developments plus a fifth named ETC and Associates, which housed 125 individuals at the time. Thus, the figures are closely, if not strictly, comparable. All of these developments are within what is known as Villa Victoria. Villa Victoria's additional developments are West Newton Street, about 140 units on that street, and Unity Tower, both always owned and now managed by the Boston Housing Authority, not ETC. Unity Tower is explicitly designated as housing for the elderly and disabled; the housing authority has always selected its tenants, and it has always been conceived somewhat separately from the rest of the project.

people living [in units] who are not on the lease" (a problem they have addressed aggressively in 2001). "I know [the 77 percent figure] is not true. I would say it's about 95 percent Latino. More conservatively, 90 percent." Each year, IBA runs a "membership drive" to get residents to become "corporate members," which means they will obtain a card (for $1) stating that they are members of IBA and allowing them to vote in the yearly (or near-yearly) elections for the IBA board of directors. I volunteered with IBA one year on several door-to-door membership drives. For the drives, volunteers were given lists with the head of household (or whoever paid rent) for every house in every street in the neighborhood, and the streets were divided among the volunteers in pairs. In our list, for every fifty or so names, roughly three derived from a language other than Spanish, which would indicate a Latino population of about 94 percent of households (also note that many Latinos have first and last names that derive from the English language).[12] Thus, many individuals with surnames in the Spanish language were identifying themselves as either black or white, which is what brought the self-reported figure down to 77 percent. In any case, the homogeneity of the neighborhood did not decrease and may, in fact, have increased.

It is still possible, however, that within the Latino population, ethnic heterogeneity or diversity increased, driving down the level of neighborhood participation. According to the 1980 census, of the Latinos living in Parcel 19 at the time, 11 percent were non–Puerto Rican (the 1970 figure was the same). In 1990, however, the figure was 2 percent, suggesting a more, not less, homogeneously Puerto Rican population.

Finally, what about the changes in residential stability? There are two separate issues in residential stability: home ownership and retention. The home ownership rate is obviously zero, given that Villa Victoria is a subsidized housing complex, so it is not a relevant explanation in this particular case.[13] With respect to the retention rate (100 minus the turnover rate),

12. This figure excludes the Unity Tower, a tall building in Villa Victoria that does not have a random sample of residents. The Tower, with roughly two hundred wheelchair-accessible units, has been, since its construction in the 1970s, reserved for the elderly and the disabled. Throughout its history, residents have been low-income people of all ethnic backgrounds, and it has always had a much higher proportion of non-Latinos than the rest of the Villa.

13. A few residents, in fact, as of the mid-1990s, have owned their property, with the help of a grant from Housing and Urban Development (HUD). By contract with one of the companies helping to finance the housing project, a small row of houses (fewer than fifty households) facing Tremont Street were up for purchase by the residents. With the help of the HUD grant, the residents purchased their homes. Including these would bring the ownership rate to about 5 percent. This would constitute an increase in home ownership, which should have led to more participation, not less of it.

TABLE 6. Retention Rate among Latinos in Villa Victoria

	Lived in Same House 5 Years Ago (%)
1970	47
1980	34
1990	57

SOURCE. U.S. Bureau of the Census, 1970, 1980, 1990. See appendix.

consider table 6. The table shows the percentage of heads of households who, when asked where they lived five years prior to the census, answered that they lived in the same house. In 1980, the figure is 34 percent. According to social organization theory that figure should be lower in 1990, to account for the decline taking place in and after that period. The 1990 figure, however, is 57 percent, which, of course, represents a dramatic increase in the retention rate.[14] By the standard structural measures of social organization theory, and, in fact, by most common expectations, participation in the Villa should have flourished, or at least remained stable, but certainly not declined. Most measures did not change as the theory would predict, and many changed in the opposite direction. This failure results not from the irrelevance of these factors but from the way they are expected to function. I begin the discussion of why these factors functioned as they did by expanding the theory itself in ways contemporary researchers have done (Sampson and Wilson 1995).

14. These are conservative estimates of the neighborhood retention rate in each of the years, since it only asks people whether they lived in the same house. A common practice in the neighborhood is for residents to move from one house in the neighborhood to another, perhaps larger for its growing family, or closer to the park, or with elevator service, or with a vacancy downstairs where in-laws can live. Melissa, for example, a resident in her midtwenties, has lived in three different houses within the neighborhood. Ernesto has lived in two different apartments. Oscar, a man in his midtwenties, says, "We've only lived in two houses. And it's on the same street. I live on————Street. We moved from one house to around the corner to another house." Tania moved from one apartment to another on the ground floor, so she and her family would not have to climb stairs. Thus, the percentage of people in each year who remain in the same neighborhood in each of the years is, in fact, higher. Indeed, the bulk of the changes in families occupying apartments do not come from new residents (the waiting list was closed during much of the study) but, according to a staff member at ETC, from "transfers. Lots of transfers."

Beyond Social Organization Theory:
The Political Economy

An important standard critique of social organization theory stems from the political economy tradition. Social organization theory and the Chicago school of sociology are ultimately rooted in a free market paradigm of the urban landscape, whereby the natural competition among groups for space and resources in the ecology of cities results in more or less orderly rings, from the inner cities toward the peripheries, of increasingly wealthier groups. As poor immigrants increase their social and economic standing, which they eventually will, they move further out from the inner cities in which they started (Burgess 1925; Park, Burgess, and McKenzie 1925; Park 1952). Critics have countered that the distribution of groups across the urban landscape results not merely from free competition but also from willful, political acts by the state and powerful urban interests—with redlining, block busting, urban renewal, forced relocation, and housing discrimination being but a few of the tactics and practices employed by multiple parties in what is ultimately as much a political and racial contest as an economic one (Logan and Molotch 1987; Massey and Denton 1993; Sampson and Wilson 1995; Sampson and Morenoff 1997). The importance of this critique is borne out by creation of the Villa itself, resulting less from the natural outgrowth of the city than from an ethnically charged political contest. The politico-economic forces affecting neighborhoods will surely also affect neighborhood participation, and if we hope to understand the latter we must find some way of accounting for the former.

How do we think about this situation in the Villa? Throughout the seventies, eighties, and nineties, Boston experienced a transformation from an industrial into a technology-based economy, the widespread departure (during the sixties, seventies, and eighties) and subsequent return (during the nineties) of white middle-class professionals, an influx of immigrants to the greater metropolitan area, and a relatively robust economy that kept unemployment low, even among low-skilled workers (Bluestone and Stevenson 2000). In most local neighborhoods, this resulted in rapid demographic transformations over the past thirty years, most recently evidenced in the heavy gentrification of formerly minority and poor or working-class neighborhoods, such as the South End and Somerville and, in the last few years, parts of Dorchester and Roxbury (see Gamm 1999). The lifting of rent control in the early nineties and the sustained robust economy placed heavy burdens on low-income families, many of whom saw their rents double in less than ten years. For many poor, working poor, and lower middle-class Bostonians, the housing crunch was the single biggest economic burden of the 1990s. The residents of Villa Victoria, which is self-managed and subsidized, were relatively insulated from this situation. This was especially true because residents were able to keep their units even if they became unemployed.

The difficulty with assessing the influence of these larger politico-economic factors is that they can include anything and everything—from the drug economy, to the political makeup of city hall, to rent control, to the national attitude toward welfare. My objective, here and throughout this book, is not merely to account for what happened in the Villa but to use the neighborhood as a case to push for clearer thinking on these issues. A comprehensive historical explanation accounting for each of those factors will make for interesting reading but will hardly serve this objective. And yet these issues cannot be ignored. Thus, to apply them systematically to our question, I make a heuristic distinction between environmental effects and institutional effects. The former term refers to the effects of political or economic transformations on the general neighborhood environment under which residents would be inclined to participate; the latter, to the effects on the local institutions that sustain participation. Politico-economic effects on environmental conditions are addressed in chapter 4, where I elaborate on their relationship to residents' perception of their neighborhood. With respect to factors affecting institutional conditions, I now address how they affected IBA—the most important institution with respect to local participation—and whether and how these changes contributed to the decline.

The tenants' organization, IBA, relies on government funding and both donations and loans from private organizations such as United Way; state, local, and federal sources currently account for roughly a third of its funding (see Rivas 1982; Teltsch 1982; IBA 2000b). The group's funding is very much at the mercy of changing politico-economic winds. The political makeup of Congress, Housing and Urban Development, the governor's office, and the mayor's office each could have an effect on the economic viability of the organization. Consider one straightforward example: during the summer of 2000 the state's governor, a Republican, threatened to cut nearly 4 million dollars in funding for summer youth employment programs, despite pleas by the city's mayor, a Democrat, to keep the funds intact, since 1,950 teenagers in the city would lose their jobs (Jonas 2000; Marantz 2000). This cut would have direct implications for the thirty or so adolescents working in IBA's summer youth program that year, most of whom were paid with city funds. The situation seemed particularly precarious on the Thursday before the decision would be made, and one community organizer worried that the youth might be out of work by Monday. The governor did cut the funds, but the mayor "found" emergency funds for the program, amid much political fanfare. A minor shift in the state's attitude toward its urban poor, fueled by a political feud, could have had great consequences for the ability of IBA to fulfill its functions. As this example illustrates, the political and economic landscape directly affect IBA.

But how does IBA affect voluntary community participation? Although IBA is, above all, a human services–provision organization, it can also help sustain community participation, whether by providing rooms for brainstorming ideas (e.g., clean-up day), running programs (e.g., computer courses), helping publicize events in newsletters (e.g., *El Correo de la Villa*), or providing the institutional backing to formalize a budding activity (e.g., a community garden). Thus, if an external factor, such as the politico-economic environment of the state, has a direct effect on IBA's financial stability it will affect its power to sustain these activities. And, indeed, between 1996 and 1997 IBA suffered the single biggest institutional crisis in its history, as internal and external politics led to conflicts between the board and the head of IBA, the resignation of the head, the firing of board members by the community, and the election of an entirely new board (see Chacon 1997 for an account; also, With 1996a, 1996b).

This crisis, however, arose long after participation had declined. This was the only time in its history when IBA-ETC's institutional viability was in question. Ironically, however, IBA's crisis acted as a spur, not a blow, to participation, though a targeted and momentary spur. It is easy to overestimate what a service-provision organization can do, for such organizations represent, in the minds of many, the key to solving much of what ails poor neighborhoods. They resonate with conservative visions of self-help and liberal beliefs in self-empowerment; they are known to accomplish many tasks well, and they are (often) run by people connected to the neighborhood. But community participation by unpaid volunteers—not for a few programs but for many programs over the course of two or three decades—may well be a different matter. By definition, voluntary community participation requires volunteers, which IBA ultimately cannot produce but can merely sustain. Recall that IBA's early 1990s "campaign to get residents reengaged" failed. Indeed, participation declined in spite of

IBA's sustained fiscal and institutional stability over two and a half decades, suggesting the decline lay in deeper transformations occurring at the social level, among the residents themselves.

Something was happening among the residents of the neighborhood that institutional efforts may have affected but did not fundamentally change. Villa Victoria, I suggest in the chapter that follows, was experiencing changes that could be labeled as cultural. [15]

15. It may be suggested that the very institutionalization of IBA played some role in the decline. Here, two hypotheses are possible. One, a descendant of Weberian theories of rationalization and bureaucratization, is that when voluntary-based organizations become institutionalized, certain roles formerly occupied by volunteers are subsumed by paid staff, as organizations become more concerned about accountability and regulation (Smith and Lipsky 1993, 111 ff.). The other is that when community-based organizations become more institutionalized, they become an infrastructure that facilitates local participation by providing meeting space, telephones, copy machines, computers, etc., previously unavailable to neighborhood activists. This can be thought of as the benefit of resource accrual (e.g., McCarthy and Zald 1977; McCarthy and Wolfson 1996). The two hypotheses are not incompatible, for the former refers to volunteers working for the organization, while the other refers to participants who may or may not wish a formal relationship to the organization. My general concern in this book is with local participation by residents, regardless of whether it was related to IBA. A great deal of useful research could disentangle these issues.

FOUR

The Rise and Decline of Local Participation, Part 2

Cohorts and Collective Narratives

This was a fight! And hard work! . . . And for us to be letting it go to waste. We haven't valued everything they [the pioneers] have done. — EUGENIA

In this chapter I examine why local participation in Villa Victoria declined even as the neighborhood's structural conditions would lead us to expect it to rise or, at the very least, to remain stable. I suggest that structural conditions may not bear the one-to-one cause-and-effect relationship to participation in poor neighborhoods that researchers have implicitly assumed. The case of the Villa forces us to think of structural conditions differently and, I suggest, more clearly and consistently with the lived experience of residents.

In Villa Victoria, culture mattered. Cultural conditions affected participation in ways separate from and irreducible to the neighborhood's structural conditions, even as the latter set constraints on the effects of the former. In the context of urban poverty, "culture" has been defined as something akin to Parsons's "norms and values"; in the context of urban policy, it has been interpreted as the conservative counterpart to liberals' "structure," as the prescription that if we could change ghetto dwellers' basic value system we would change their basic behavioral patterns as well. This conception of culture, nonetheless, explains little about what happened in Villa Victoria. As we shall see, to the extent that "cultural" factors mattered, it was not in their capacity as value systems but in their role as framers of the lenses through which residents viewed their neighborhood. The role of culture, that is, was not normative but cognitive.

Thinking about Neighborhood Change

Before the importance of cultural factors is discussed, a short but critical digression is in order. Any discussion about local participation should clarify two assumptions, one about neighborhoods, the other about individuals. The first regards what we expect to happen over time in a neighborhood; it is strictly hypothetical: If all causal factors were held constant, what would happen to a neighborhood's level of participation over time—would it rise, fall, or remain the same? Selecting the first option (rising) assumes that neighborhood participation is inherently self-regenerating, a type of contagion or epidemic phenomenon; the second (falling), that it is inherently difficult to sustain, a type of degenerative phenomenon; and the third (remaining the same), that it is an inertia-driven entity—like physical objects in nature, it will remain in its current state unless affected by an external force.

Inherently self-regenerating phenomena reproduce themselves without external intervention; examples are a group's teenage pregnancy rate (Crane 1991) or the rate of middle-class white flight (Schelling 1978). In this category would fall most peer effects among adolescents and most social epidemics; these phenomena often have tipping points, after which the rate of self-perpetuation accelerates rapidly (see Gladwell [2000] for an accessible discussion). Degenerative phenomena are inherently difficult to sustain; over time, they will tend to exhaust themselves regardless of any external intervention. Examples are the influence of charismatic authority among a population (Max Weber in Parsons 1947) and the membership rate in a given commune (Kanter 1972); these factors naturally tend toward zero. Static phenomena are those unlikely to change in the absence of external intervention; an example is the voting rate in presidential elections, which hardly changes from year to year unless the nation is faced with a major crisis.

Being explicit regarding one's assumptions makes it clear what causal factors to look for and not look for. For example, if we believe neighborhood participation would tend to decline over time by itself, then looking for factors that cause it to decline is not the best route. Such a research approach is also potentially misleading, for it might tempt us to conclude that had the causal factors not been in place the change would not have occurred. Not knowing what our assumption is has contributed to the confusion about the mechanisms linking neighborhood poverty to local participation. Of the three assumptions, the last one—that neighborhood participation would remain stable—appears to be more intuitively correct, since, as sociologists, we typically attempt to explain change, not the lack thereof. And indeed, when we ask why neighborhood participation declined, we are implicitly assuming that it should have either remained the same or risen. However, I suggest the assumption truest to reality is that the Villa's decline in participation might well have taken place even if no other factors were in play. To explain why, I return to the traditional work on social organization.

Traditional social organization theory does not answer explicitly which assumption about neighborhoods is fundamentally sounder; it does, however, provide an instructive starting point. The Chicago school assumed that neighborhoods were fundamentally in flux (Park 1952; see also Schwirian 1983; Wilson 1987, 1996). Burgess's (1925) theory of concentric circles relied on the idea that populations in each circle of neighborhoods were in constant succession, as old immigrants became upwardly mobile and moved out and new immigrants supplanted the old ones in less desirable neighborhood circles. This assumption would carry over to the theory of neighborhood participation, suggesting that our assumption should be that participation would inherently change over time, either rising or falling. However, this conclusion is unwarranted. Part of the problem with the original theory of concentric circles (and the Chicago perspective in general) is the assumption that the processes the scientists observed in Chicago were universal across cities and, by extension, that the processes they observed in Chicago neighborhoods could be applied to all neighborhoods (Sampson and Morenoff 1997; Wacquant 1997). That is, the school often failed to distinguish between traits inherent to neighborhoods and those simply common across the neighborhoods in Chicago. Assuming that common or frequent social traits are also inherent or endemic is a common tendency.

To determine whether change (in either direction) in local participation is endemic to neighborhoods we should ask whether any inherent attribute of neighborhoods will tend to force local participation to change over time. Consider the case of a neighborhood's socioeconomic status (SES). It is certainly the case that SES levels in neighborhoods change a great deal—either through gentrification or middle-class flight; but these changes are not inherent to neighborhoods. Neighborhoods may and do remain poor for extended time periods. Parcel 19, for example, has remained poor for at least a half century. The same is true with respect to ethnic heterogeneity, as well as residential stability, if the term refers to the rate at which residents are moving in and out within a given time period (e.g., five years).

In fact, one may posit that the only trait guaranteed to change in a neighborhood over time is the population itself, since life is finite. In this particular sense, neighborhoods are inherently unstable over time, by mere virtue of the life course. That is, neighborhoods are inherently unstable not because their turnover rates will always change (these may well remain constant for years) but because they will always have turnover.[1]

Related to this issue is the question of human nature rather than neighborhoods. Are individuals inclined to engage in neighborhood participation or are they inclined not to? Here we must distinguish between voluntary participation in neighborhoods and voluntary participation in general. The question of voluntary participation in general figures large in the debate over altruism. A version of this question has tormented thinkers as diverse as Tocqueville, Durkheim, and philosopher Charles Taylor. It is unclear if we will ever arrive at an answer, and I do not pretend to provide one. But even among analysts who believe that altruism, the need to give, and the need to participate are intrinsic human needs, few would be prepared to argue that participation in one's neighborhood (or proximate physical surroundings) is an inherent human need or inclination. Many analysts suggest that such an inclination was in place under certain social conditions—it was the gemeinschaft of small towns in preindustrial Europe that seduced thinkers as early as Ferdinand Toennies. Yet these patterns were, by definition, not inherent to human nature, for they were only present under certain social circumstances. Though general altruism may or may not be an inherent human inclination, participating in neighborhood activities, it is safe to say, is not.

At this juncture, we may turn to the question of neighborhood changes over time. Among a population, any trait that is not innate will tend toward zero in the absence of intervening factors. In a neighborhood with a given rate of participation, each succeeding cohort would be expected to have rates closer and closer to zero if no other factors intervened. Thus, the more reasonable basic assumption about neighborhoods is not that local participation will remain stable over time unless affected by external forces but that it will tend to decline over time unless counteracting forces intervene.[2] In this light, we should think of stability, homogeneity, and high

1. Either this or the elimination of their populations which would, in effect, constitute the end of the neighborhood as such.

2. One well-researched counteracting force is the institutionalization of participation (Piven and Cloward 1977). The creation of IBA itself is an example of this process. Yet institutional organization is not neighborhood participation; the latter is an act of individuals in a community who are willing to act on behalf of the common good and is ultimately dependent on the wills of individuals. The factors should be factors that affect individual willingness to intervene.

SES as sustaining or intervening factors rather than think of their opposites—instability, heterogeneity, and poverty—as factors that produce declining rates.

(I emphasize the difference between positing a logical relationship and advancing an empirical statement. The above discussion suggests that if all exogenous factors *could* be held constant, participation would tend to decline. It does not argue that participation is always declining in all neighborhoods in our cities.)

These assumptions will make a difference in how we interpret the relationships in figures such as 1B in the previous chapter. None of this discussion precludes that social conditions, structural or otherwise, contribute to a neighborhood's decline in participation. But it does force us to be explicit about the way in which those relationships manifest themselves. We are now poised to address the changes in Villa Victoria (and the role of cultural factors in this process) directly.

Change and Cohorts: A Highly Engaged Cohort

One of my most surprising discoveries about participation in the Villa came as I investigated who, among the neighborhood's current residents, was still involved. The current level of participation in Villa Victoria is not zero; it is simply much lower than it had been during the late seventies and early eighties. The neighborhood still boasts a board of directors (though it holds elections at irregular intervals), a summer beautification campaign (though it is sporadic and weakly supported), and a Betances Festival (though it sometimes has difficulty attracting local volunteers). However, many of the people who volunteer their time now are the same older cohort that has been doing so since the early 1980s.

An imperfect but useful indicator of the makeup of current participants is the composition of the board. A list of the board of directors of the mid-1990s contains many of the names from a similar list dating to the 1980s. Over the last few years of the 1990s, most members were in their late forties and older, with three people in their thirties and one younger, even though there were no age requirements (other than being an adult) to run. During the membership drives in which I participated, part of our goal was to get residents to consider running for the board by informing them what board members and IBA itself did. In all of my rounds of the neighborhood, only three persons considered running: an energetic African-American lifelong resident in her fifties, a Latina lifelong resident of roughly the same age, and another Latina in her early sixties, who had been involved for thirty years in the neighborhood.

The few occupied seats at community service meetings are generally filled by middle-aged and older people and rarely by young adults, the likes of whom had energized ETC meetings in the 1960s. At a recent, symbolically important public ceremony in the plaza to designate Villa Victoria a historic place fewer than a dozen young adults were present. At meetings for membership drives, most volunteers are over forty, except for a few young men and women who attend over and over. As part of a cultural festival one summer, one of the organizers, Melissa, asked for volunteers for a simple activity in which young children would be provided paints to decorate a set of cement tree and plant holders in an area of the neighborhood that needed the upkeep. On the date of the event only two adult volunteers under the age of thirty-five (and one of them was me) showed up. In recent years, several residents under forty have been approached by the elders to run for the board, nearly to no avail. Overwhelmingly, participation in the Villa is the practice of an older generation. Much to the chagrin of the remaining community leaders, the second cohort of residents refuses to be engaged. In the words of one of them, "We need new people. I mean, I hate to say it like that but we have an older generation in there."

By and large, it was not quite the case that those individuals who were once involved gradually lost their interest in their neighborhood. Instead, as the first cohort of adults grew older and died, their activities were not carried on by the second cohort of residents. Participation has not stopped completely thanks to the efforts of the same residents, for the most part, who were leading the way during the early 1980s and contributing to the maintenance of community in the Villa. Not all of them can do so. Many of them, especially those who were part of the ETC campaign, are now elderly or have died. Again, though, this is not a matter of a cohort's resignation but, rather, of its successor's failure to continue its work. In the Villa's past, young adults were involved locally; now, young adults are doing other things.[3]

Why have the two cohorts participated locally at different rates? The issue of cohort differences is echoed in the recent book *Bowling Alone* (2000), in which political scientist Robert Putnam argues that "social cap-

---

3. Of course, lest we romanticize the 1970s and early 1980s, many young adults of that time did nothing in the community as well. The issue here is one of proportion.

ital" has declined throughout American society as a consequence of recent cohorts' failure to live up to the civic potential of their parents and grandparents, the "civic generation" that fought World War II. In light of this book, two observations are important. First, many of the highly involved residents of Villa Victoria were, in fact, baby boomers, the population who, in Putnam's work, were civically disengaged relative to their parents. Second, Putnam's book serves as an occasion to clarify one issue. Putnam argues that, from one cohort to the next, social capital declined in just about all forms, including local and national participation, civic and political engagement, networking and friendships—even bowling, card playing, and praying became less social, more personal activities. We certainly cannot make such claims about the Villa. Here, although local participation in neighborhood activities declined, other forms of social capital actually rose, such as friendship networks among residents across race and culture and residents' relations with non–Puerto Ricans and non-Spanish speakers. Villa Victoria is not a "bowling alone" story.

In any case, it is not enough simply to note the differences between the cohorts: they must be accounted for. In the Villa, different cohorts participate locally at different rates because they "frame" the neighborhood—its history, its structural characteristics, its landscape, and its people—differently.[4]

Local Participation and Neighborhood Framing Processes: The Cohorts' Framing of Their Neighborhood

Relying on recent work in social movements and culture (Morris and Mueller 1992; Snow and Benford 1992; Johnston and Klandermans 1995) and in narrative theory (Taylor 1989; Hart 1992; Somers 1992; Somers and Gibson 1994), I suggest that the cohort differences reflect, above all, a

---

4. The question of cohort participation highlights an interesting but little-discussed fact about the peculiar macro-micro nature of neighborhood participation (see Huber 1991; Sampson 1991). The level of participation is presumably a macro- (i.e., neighborhood-) level problem; yet the mechanisms I suggest operate at both the macro- and the microlevel. Furthermore, much of the evidence discussed below about collective narratives is, by definition, microlevel evidence. Microdata can help understand macrochange in participation because neighborhoods' participation levels are so small that even small changes—of, say thirty persons—can mean large differences in a neighborhood's participation rate. This issue is addressed in greater detail in the final chapter.

difference in the narrative-related frames through which the cohorts perceived and made sense of their neighborhood. Neighborhood narrative frames (NNFs) are the continuously shifting but nonetheless concrete sets of categories through which the neighborhood's houses, streets, parks, population, location, families, murals, history, heritage, and institutions are made sense of and understood. Contrary to common assumptions about poor neighborhoods, residents do not merely see and experience the characteristics of their neighborhood "as it is"; their perceptions are filtered through cultural categories that highlight some aspects of the neighborhood and ignore others. These perceptions become part of an often explicit narrative about the neighborhood's role and significance in residents' lives. Residents' framing of the neighborhood will, in turn, affect how they act in or toward it.

The concept of NNFs borrows from work on "collective action frames" in the social movements literature. Much of that literature, building but expanding on the resource mobilization perspective, has focused on how "frames" affect the effectiveness of mobilization (see Goffman 1986; Morris and Mueller 1992; Snow and Benford 1992; Steinberg 1999). Snow and Benford (1992, 137) define a frame as "an interpretive [schema] that simplifies and condenses the 'world out there' by selectively punctuating and encoding objects, situations, events, experiences, and sequences of actions within one's present or past environment" (also Goffman 1986). The framing perspective's critique of resource mobilization theory is that cultural or symbolic elements are critical for the possibility of action; regardless of resources, activists will be unable to mobilize potential participants without transforming their perception of their situation (see also Thomas 1936) by "framing" the issues in such a way that mobilization appears necessary (Gamson 1992; Morris and Mueller 1992; Snow and Benford 1992). Though few would argue that framing processes are the only critical processes at work, most would suggest that frames are necessary, even if not sufficient, conditions for action. This approach to the framing process illuminates much of what has happened in the Villa.[5]

Any discussion of framing theory should be sensitive to three criti-

5. It is important to be clear about how the social movements literature is and is not applicable to our question. The creation of the Villa, as a result of the collective activities of the Puerto Rican residents of the neighborhood during the late 1960s, is certainly a social movement question. Yet if the issue of framing is relevant to us, it is not because the community participation of the 1970s and 1980s is a type of mobilization (it is not), but because both problems concern how meaning-making—in their case, of social injustices (Benford 1997, 415), in this case, of neighborhoods—can be said to result in action.

cisms: that the term "frames" implies cultural perceptions are static; that the theory may assume people are passively subject to reframing but hardly involved in the framing process itself; and that framing theory may be tautological (see Benford 1997; Steinberg 1998, 1999). Recent research on narrative theory can help both conceptualize neighborhood framing as a process and interpret how residents can have a role in the development of their neighborhood frames while being affected by them. The term "narrative" has been attached to a diverse and uneven body of research, some of it dealing with topics more appropriate to literary criticism, and some dealing with political change, historical sociology, and the critique of rational-choice theory. Here, I make use of the latter work (Taylor 1989; Hart 1992; Somers 1992; Somers and Gibson 1994). The theory suggests that individuals understand their lives as narratives with ongoing and complex plots and that they tend to act not necessarily when acts are rational but when the actions accord with such narratives. I suggest the same is true with respect to neighborhoods. Residents act and become involved in their neighborhoods when such actions conform to their narrative of the neighborhood's role in their lives. These narratives, in turn, are shaped by the frames through which the neighborhood is perceived. Frames are assumed to be dynamic entities partly dependent on the experiences of individuals. Specific aspects of the tautology problem are addressed in a subsequent section. Below, relying on observations and on interviews and conversations with most of the highly engaged residents in both cohorts as well as with many unengaged ones, I examine the cohorts' differences in their cultural framing of the Villa.

A "Beautiful" Place to Live

For the Villa's first cohort of residents, the neighborhood is a wonderful place to live. Ernesto, for example, is an elderly man who has lived in Parcel 19 since the 1950s. He now relies on a wheelchair, but as a young man he was one of the first members of the IBA board and, in the sixties, was part of the ETC campaign, picketing the BRA "sometimes until 12 o'clock at night." To explain what he thinks of Villa Victoria, he describes the former Parcel 19:

> They used to call this around here "The Trap" [or "The Catch-All"]. Look—behind [my apartment] here there used to be a huge ditch. The little houses used to lean over into the water. When it rained hard, a spurt of water ran along [behind here] and the houses—and their balconies—were

almost falling over. And people lived in these places! Holy Mary! The houses were falling apart. And I find myself dumbfounded [*me quedo bobo*] at how beautiful this got afterward! It was torn down and refilled with machines, until the houses were all built anew.

Ernesto believes he is fortunate to live in Villa Victoria. That the neighborhood deteriorated markedly over the years (until 2001, when a massive renovation was begun) has had little effect on his belief in its fundamental beauty.

That perception constitutes part of a broader vision of the neighborhood as a place of historic significance. This cohort considers the neighborhood a sort of treasure, the legacy of the group of activists who fought for its creation. These activists are known as "the pioneers," a title considered a badge of honor. The pioneers' struggles and accomplishments imply, in this cohort's mind, the responsibility of the existing residents to sustain the community.

Doña Cotto, known locally, like Ernesto, as a "pioneer," is an elderly woman who has lived in the South End most of her life. She recalls that, in the 1960s, "the living conditions were very bad. The apartments were really rats' nests." With her husband, Leonso Cotto, and often with her daughter, she attended many of the meetings with housing officials before the neighborhood was built. She lacked professional skills, but she believed her presence helped bear evidence of the residents' determination to put up a fight against dislocation. She saw the construction of Villa Victoria as something much larger than herself: "I thought that this would be [a] strong and up-to-date construction that would last for many years, for future generations." Thus, she complains that, "some tenants have moved in without orientation about how this community was forged. And many of the younger generation don't care about [the buildings], and have damaged and vandalized the apartments, as if the housing had just fallen as a gift from heaven. Many people sacrificed [themselves] to build this housing. . . . I believe that the residents must get together and preserve this housing that so many of us fought for" (in *El Correo de la Villa* 4, no. 3 [1995], NU box 30). Just about all of the highly involved residents of this cohort appealed to this narrative when explaining their motivations: there was a difficult struggle that produced a beautiful community that should be preserved any way possible.

Consider the case of Tania, a confrontational, yet optimistic woman in her late fifties who has been a passionate member of the board of directors and has organized after-school arts projects for years. She explains her motivations: "This was a struggle. . . . These people [the pioneers] went to war. They had to go to city hall, at dawn, and picket, fight. That's why I want to join the board. . . . I want to see more programs that provide services for the community. This was a fight of the Puerto Ricans who lived here, and I want to see that [our lives] are even better." Another woman with four teenage sons recently told a reporter: "Puerto Ricans and other Latinos struggled to get this. That's why I moved here. That's why I have stayed and that's why I will fight to keep it" (Manly 1992).

Eugenia, a sixty-year old who migrated to the South End in the 1950s, has the energy of someone fifteen years younger. An on-and-off board member for ten years, she has volunteered for everything from the Betances Festival to an ad hoc coalition to improve the landscape of the houses' tiny backyards. She is known as a bottomless well of ideas for neighborhood improvement. During a recent conversation, she said, referring to younger residents, "they don't know what we have here . . . something *beautiful*." Explaining in Spanish why she is involved, in words nearly replicating Tania's, Eugenia, with her characteristic tinge of indignation said: "This was a fight! And hard work! . . . And for us to be letting it go to waste. . . . We haven't valued everything they [the pioneers] have done." These residents perceive the Villa as a success, something "beautiful" to cherish and preserve.

THE PROJECTS

The second-wave cohort frames the neighborhood as an entirely different place. The term "cohort" rather than "generation" is not accidental; it refers to the second wave of neighborhood residents, who are not necessarily the children of the first wave. The second wave consists of two primary groups: the children, grandchildren, nieces, and nephews of the first wave of residents and residents completely new to the neighborhood, often recent migrants from Puerto Rico who moved into the neighborhood after the 1980s. (The two groups are rough categorizations.) Both groups share certain conceptions of the Villa.

During a meeting for young people in 1999, the attendees discussed what they thought about Villa Victoria, brainstorming on what they believed the neighborhood needed. It is instructive to catalog their opinions of what the Villa needed:

trash cans to get rid of the public litter;
speed bumps to prevent accidents;
elimination of the iron fences surrounding parks and public areas;
roofs over the basketball court;

removal of "the bums" found in the plaza ("they should get [i.e., be offered] jobs");

a bank closer to the neighborhood (the nearest Bank Boston, a few blocks away, was too far for them);

more programs for seventeen- to twenty-two-year-olds;

more programs aimed at cracking down on drugs (too many people were doing heroin and cocaine);

a summer program that would, rather than being "camp-oriented," give people work skills;

more training in good parenting skills (for both men and women);

more police officers (but others in the group disagreed);

a cleanup of local parks;

a better security squad (again, disagreement);

a new laundromat;

a bigger day-care center;

a youth center with foosball, ping pong, and pool that would be open late and have air conditioning;

more street lamps in the neighborhood;

a program for parents with children doing drugs; and

more probation officers, since at the time, one probation officer had "lots of kids."

In addition, they complained that the apartments needed repairs: "The closets come off the racks," "the walls are thin," the "rugs are cheap," the refrigerators often have no handles and too few shelves, the windows often lack screens, and a closet once fell over in one resident's apartment. This meeting was organized to discuss what they thought about the Villa, so one should not conclude from this that the young are always complaining about their neighborhood. What is noteworthy is the category of things they chose to talk about—structural decay and the general manifestations of urban poverty, drug use, police involvement in their lives, and material deterioration. Indeed, for them, their neighborhood is little more than a ghetto. Equally noteworthy is what they did not talk about. The notion of preserving a treasure was absent; the word "beauty" never came up. And, contrary to similar meetings attended by the middle-aged and elders, nobody complained that too few people were involved in the community.

Later, I will address why the two cohorts frame the neighborhood so differently. For now, I note that the second-wave cohort's running narrative of the Villa is not of an attractive neighborhood, much less "something beautiful." The Villa for them is either passable or undesirable. A suggestive detail is the vocabulary that residents use to describe their neighborhood. While the first cohort repeatedly used the words "community" or simply "Villa Victoria," many of the young residents refer to it as "the projects." Papi is a young man nearing thirty with an extended family in the Villa. Once, while boasting about his young nephew's athletic abilities in basketball, he proudly stated, "This kid's gonna get us out of the projects," a phrase indicative not only of his perception of the neighborhood but also of his feeling it is something to leave as quickly as possible. Melissa, a young resident who has been ambivalent about both her involvement with and her feelings about the neighborhood, reminisces about her walks home from school when she was in high school; she explains the clear contrast she felt between the affluent Back Bay/South End and the Villa: "I'd walk in from Back Bay, and I'd get here and right away I'd now—yep, there's the graffiti, and the men going 'Oye, mami' and I'd hate it." If she had a child, Melissa repeatedly states, the child would not be raised in Villa Victoria. Laura, a woman in her midtwenties who has lived her whole life in the neighborhood, frequently laments that many of the younger and newer residents of the Villa do not understand its history; she says, "They basically see this as the projects with a little flavor, the projects with a [Puerto Rican] twist."

WHAT HISTORY?

Laura alluded to an important element of this cohort's perception: its lack of concrete knowledge about the neighborhood's political history. Many of the young women and men raised in the neighborhood know superficially that, during the sixties, a political struggle ensued around the construction of the Villa. Yet, surprising as it may seem, most of them have little understanding of the role that mobilizing, canvassing, picketing, and political negotiation by the earlier generation had in the creation of the neighborhood. This is all the more notable given the several murals throughout the neighborhood that depict, in different ways, the history of the Villa and of the Puerto Ricans who came to live there.

Members of this cohort, furthermore, do not provide a particularly coherent set of reasons for not being involved. For the most part, they do not see the point of it. Don, a man in his late twenties who has a wife and two young children, brushed aside any notion of his being involved saying, "I got a family to take care of." Tommy, a responsible, witty man in his early thirties, is more blunt about why he is not involved: "What for?" He complains about IBA's organizational troubles circa 1996, but he is unsure what he would expect IBA to do to foster participation. In any case, he says, "I do my own thing," serving as a mentor of sorts to one of his younger peers. Most of the second-cohort men and women do not give much of an explanation at all, which is not surprising: most people, regardless of where they live, would be hard-pressed to provide a rationale for why they are not involved in their neighborhoods. But some residents are quite thoughtful. One resident, Daniela, now regularly volunteers at the yearly Betances Festival. But for much of her life she was indifferent. She recalls in Spanish her thoughts during that time: "I never wanted to get involved. I was a very private person. . . . I didn't see the point in getting involved. . . . I didn't see the reason for it. And in truth I didn't know much about the history [of the neighborhood]."

Indeed, people are often able to articulate eloquently social processes larger than themselves. Tania describes the new cohort of residents: "Many people have moved in [to the neighborhood], and they don't know the history, they don't know what happened here. Nobody has told them. They have come in as if they owned the place [*como Juan por su casa*]. I understand that this is an important factor [in why they don't get involved]. I want to make it so that any time a new person moves into the neighborhood, they should be taught this history and about IBA and about why it is possible for you to live here today." This is a common complaint of first-cohort residents about newer residents: "They don't know the history."

If neighborhood frames are those categories that filter our perception of the neighborhood in which we live, and if narrative-related frames are those categories that bear a relationship to an ongoing story we have about ourselves and the neighborhood, then the two cohorts' narrative frames can be articulated both through what their categories highlight and through the generalized story about the Villa to which these categories belong. For the first cohort, such a narrative can be described as follows: the neighborhood has a politically important history; it constitutes a marked improvement in the quality of life of a generation of Puerto Ricans; it is a symbol of their capacity to resist their displacement by forces more powerful than themselves; it would not have existed without the "struggles" of the "pioneers" of ETC in the late 1960s; it is a desirable, even "beautiful," place to live; and its park and plaza are special places where community can be built. For the second cohort, the narrative is starkly different, in many ways more consonant with those of an outside, first-time observer: the neighborhood is physically dirty and deteriorating; it constitutes the poorest section of the South End; it is, above all, a ghetto, "the projects"; its drug use is rampant; the central plaza is full of "bums" and alcoholics; the Villa is no more beautiful or historically important than any other place.

Neither narrative represents a more accurate description of the neighborhood; they simply accentuate different aspects of the complex agglomeration of people, historical events, landscape, and institutions that represent Villa Victoria. Neither cohort has delusions about the neighborhood's current problems; both can see the grime, the rodents, the drug traffic. But how they react to this situation depends on how they frame the neighborhood as a whole, which is why positing automatic reactions to changes in structural conditions (such as low SES → anomie) is a mischaracterization of how people respond to concentrated poverty. In addition, it is not merely that the first cohort "knows" the history while the second does not; the first cohort's perception of history is itself biased and incomplete. The important role of white priests and seminarians, outside professionals and architects, and the church is not denied but is generally neglected. History matters, but this history is fragmented and selective. Participating in neighborhood activities does not occur outside of a personal justification found in a collection of meaning symbols of some type. Here, such a collection of symbols is historically constituted.

Elaboration on the Importance of Cultural Perceptions
DISTINGUISHING NNFS FROM OTHER CULTURAL CONCEPTS

To incorporate culture into social organization theory, we must move beyond stating that "culture matters," by showing how it operates in this situation and how it does not. To this end, I contrast neighborhood frames to other cultural concepts employed recently in related work (Anderson 1994, 1999; MacLeod 1995; Wacquant 1997; see also Valentine 1968; Hannerz 1969). The three most relevant concepts are "master frames" in the social movements literature, generalized belief or value systems in the urban poverty literature, and the "habitus" or cultural dispositions in the sociology of culture and inequality.

The cultural frames through which residents perceive Villa Victoria differ from "master frames" in Snow and Benford's (1992) use of the term because they do not categorize "the world out there" or their general lives, only their conception of the neighborhood. For example, their cultural frames are not frames about what it means to be Puerto Rican or poor, nor are they particularly nationalist frames, even though a nationalist "collective identity" (Melucci 1989) may have been part of the political mobilization of the 1960s (Uriarte-Gastón 1988). That is, the statements quoted above reflect the conception that participation is critical not to Puerto Ricans everywhere or to the poor in general but to Villa Victoria. Those residents most highly involved evince, at best, a weak Puerto Rican nationalism; indeed, most of them have no intention of ever moving back to Puerto Rico. In any case, as we have seen, they do not invoke their origins as Puerto Rican when explaining their motivation to participate; instead, they invoke the specific history of activism in their own neighborhood.

Neither can one equate neighborhood narratives with generalized value systems. That is, the former are independent of the generalized culture-as-values concepts employed by Kornhauser (1978), Shaw and McKay (1969), and, recently, in somewhat different fashion, by Anderson (1994, 1999) in the "street" versus "decent" distinction. Many of the Villa's residents would be characterized in that typology as "decent"—for valuing work, family, and responsibility—who not only do not participate in voluntary activities but also feel no moral dissonance as a result of not doing so. Tommy, the young man who responded "What for?" when asked why he is not involved in neighborhood activities, quickly pointed out that he is still involved, if not in the neighborhood, by mentoring his younger friend. Don, also cited above, expressed no interest in participating as well, but his justification was a sense of responsibility for his family. These individuals lack not "the right values" but, instead, a neighborhood-specific framing process that highlights specific aspects of the neighborhood that render it symbolically important.

Significantly, most of the highly involved residents in the Villa are not and were not "general" participants. Here, again, we must distinguish the Villa's case from Putnam's (2000) "highly civic" generation. Unlike the latter, who, according to Putnam, participated in multiple and diverse types of local and national voluntary activities, the Villa's highly engaged cohort volunteered for nothing, or almost nothing, unrelated to the Villa before, during, or after the neighborhood's construction. Ernesto, the elderly man well known as a pioneer for his extensive local involvement, never attended school PTAs, joined external residents' associations in the wider South End, participated in city-wide political movements, or volunteered his time to civic engagement activities unrelated to Villa Victoria. Outside of her church, neither has Eugenia, though she is a nearly indefatigable local participant. In other words, their community participation is not rooted in the perception that participation is good for humanity at large (though they may well believe this); rather, it is rooted in the perception that it is good for Villa Victoria.

The framing perspective connotes cognitive, as opposed to strictly normative, perceptions and attitudes. In this respect, it resembles, Bourdieu's notion of habitus (1977; Bourdieu and Wacquant 1992), which denotes a cognitive perception that predisposes individuals to act in a particular fashion. Such dispositions are, indeed, site specific (or, in Bourdieu's framework, "field specific") and, in addition, not value dependent. However, Bourdieu's habitus works precisely because it is unconscious; it operates at a cognitive level that individuals do not typically articulate and may even be unable to. The cultural narratives at play here, on the contrary, are conscious perceptions of an entity—the neighborhood—that individuals not only articulate (often in rich detail, as described above) but also consciously act on.

EXCEPTIONS THAT "TEST THE RULE"

That the cohorts differ in both their rates of participation and their NNFs does not guarantee that participation cannot be understood without understanding NNFs, for the cohorts differ in a host of other traits. A more compelling case can be made by examining a group of residents who are members of one cohort but who act like the other. A small group of second-cohort residents participate at the rates of the first: they run for the board of directors, volunteer at fundraising campaigns, and do door-to-door canvassing. These "exceptions"—and there are, indeed, but a handful of them—corroborate the significance of narrative framing processes.

Most young adults are either resentful or indifferent about living in the Villa—unaware and uninterested in its history—just as most of us know little and care less about what happened thirty years ago in our own neighborhoods. But others, such as Laura, a young woman who has volunteered formally and informally with just about every teen-centered activity available over the past five or six years (such as fundraising for ski trips and crisis counseling) can explain in rich detail the birth of the neighborhood, the political tendencies of the city administration of the sixties, the politics of urban renewal, the significance and source of the architectural design of the Villa, the names and familial relations of the activists of the time, and the symbolic significance of the three murals painted throughout the neighborhood. (This was not because of formal education; Laura, like many second-generation Latinas, did not graduate from high school.) Laura repeatedly explains that the "struggles" earlier generations went through to create Villa Victoria drive her to remain involved in her "community."

Oscar, a young man who has served as a "big brother" to many of the neighborhood's children, also frames the neighborhood as a historically constituted community that plays an important role in his life. His answer to a question of why he is involved: "I know what people had to go through to get my community to where it is today. And that means a lot to me. The history of my community means a lot to me. People struggling, and the fight . . . to get affordable housing, to get a piece of land in the city . . . that represents my culture." Gloria, a young woman who volunteered on the board of directors, concurs, punctuating the issues of struggle, history, and the maintenance of community, if perhaps in less articulate fashion: "[In the past,] people were so involved in this neighborhood. Because they knew what it entailed. They knew it was not an easy fight against the city to be able to control this. It was not simple. It was a clash of the minds. . . . And they got together. They started figuring out ways to battle [the city], and they did. They did it. And they were able to be part of the . . . urban renewal project. . . . They took control of this area." And later, "[I hope] people will start realizing the importance of working for this and trying to nurture it and keeping it afloat."

These exceptions among the second cohort share with the first cohort (*a*) a narrative of the neighborhood as something good and sometimes even a privilege (Laura recalls thinking of her new house as a "dream house" in a "dream neighborhood"), and (*b*) a historically constituted conception of the neighborhood. The symbolic element, that is, transcends the cohort and is found in those residents of either group who are locally involved.[6]

NOTE ON THE ETIOLOGY OF FRAMING PROCESSES

The framing perspective has been rightly criticized on an issue bearing direct relevance to our argument: for its failure to deal adequately with the etiology of framing processes (Benford 1997; Steinberg 1998, 1999). How do we know that residents' framing of the neighborhood was not a post facto justification for their acts of participation, acts that would have happened anyway for other reasons? To be clear, the presence of a loop-back effect is not a problem (Stinchcombe 1968). Once residents became involved, their existing perception may have become increasingly historicized and highlighting of the neighborhood's perceived political importance. At issue is that the initial impetus run from framing to action or, stated differ-

6. As we will see below, their narratives of the neighborhood are similar but not identical to those of the first cohort. Though very much aligned on the historical significance of the neighborhood, their perception of the landscape is tempered by their own, different experiences while growing up in the neighborhood.

ently, that the initial action might not have occurred without the "right" framing of the situation.

Among most residents I observed in the neighborhood, participation had been a part of their lives ever since they had developed a concrete idea of where they lived, making it difficult to identify the initial impetus. But one case strongly suggests that the arrow does, indeed, run from perception to participation, even if participation later reinforces perception. Daniela, one of the most active young residents of the neighborhood, was born and raised in Aguadilla, Puerto Rico, where she lived with her family until graduating from high school. An independent, if shy young woman, she did not consider herself a political person, nor was she active in neighborhood or town organizations of any kind. Since economic prospects in her small town were grim in the mid-1980s, she migrated in her late teens to Boston, where one of her uncles had opened a bodega in the South End. Daniela worked for her uncle and lived in his apartment directly above the store. She soon married, bore two children, and applied for a unit in Villa Victoria. In the early 1990s, they moved in.

I met Daniela in the late 1990s, while we were both volunteers for the Betances Festival, and eventually became very close to her and her family. One day, I asked her to sit down with me for a taped interview (see the appendix). I asked if she started getting involved shortly after moving to the Villa. "No, no," she said. I asked why. Her discussion with me, in Spanish, offers some signals about her conception of the neighborhood at the time:

> I never wanted to get involved. I was a very private person. . . . I didn't see the point in getting involved. . . . I didn't see the reason for it. And in truth I didn't know much about the history [of the neighborhood]. I didn't know how this neighborhood was created. . . . I didn't even know—and pardon my ignorance, I didn't have a lot of schooling—what a board of directors was, what its function was, what they did here. . . . Because if I had known [*voice trails off*]. Maybe ignorance. Above all, I would say ignorance. I got involved about three years after being here. If I had known from the beginning how this community worked maybe I would have gotten involved. . . . I was too young, too ignorant. I didn't know what Villa Victoria was about, the community, IBA.

Indeed, she had never been involved in neighborhood activities of any type. When she first moved in, she saw Villa Victoria in the ahistorical fashion any first-time observer would—and saw her neighborhood in the same way most people arguably see theirs, as nothing more important than a place to live. For her, it was "ignorance"; for the sociologist, it is a way of framing the neighborhood.

Daniela came to know the history of the neighborhood and IBA very gradually. She recalls, for example, getting "fliers . . . about workshops to learn [how to use] computers." As she asked about taking the workshops she came to know about IBA and, in turn, the neighborhood, its pioneers, and what had been transpiring during the late sixties in the South End and Parcel 19. In particular, getting to know the pioneers was critical for her. One of them, an elderly ETC activist who, being a father or grandfather to residents in more than a dozen households in the neighborhood, was known to nearly everyone in the community, lived directly across the street. Daniela had heard both fact and gossip about his past and eventually came to know him well, for he enjoyed retelling the oral history of the Villa's creation. Thus, she slowly began to develop a different conception of the neighborhood, coming to understand why others found its history important, why it carried a symbolic appeal, and, not insignificantly, coming to believe it could even be lost to another wave of urban renewal. Indeed, she began to conceive of living in the Villa as a privilege. She recalls a conversation she had recently with this pioneer:

> I was telling Mr.————that he is a person I admire a lot . . . because he is a leader who has been working in the community for so many years. . . . I told him: "You are a person who must sit back and feel proud of what you did because it's thanks to you that I and my children are here, enjoying the privileges of having a low-income apartment, paying a [low] rent, because we cannot pay for more." And I was telling him . . . "I thank you so much. Because all of this we have. . . . We owe this to all of you, people like you, because you worked for so many years." People like him motivate me to do something more for my community.

To be sure, the changes in how she saw the Villa were much more gradual than her words imply, taking place over a three-year period. Yet Daniela has become one of the most active residents of the neighborhood, having done everything from sitting on the board of IBA to contributing to several clean-up campaigns to helping me recruit students for the computer courses I taught. She attributes her earlier lack of participation to her ignorance or what she calls later her "lack of education" about her neighborhood's history. Her distinction between ignorance and knowledge is our distinction between an ahistorical and a historicized way of framing the neighborhood.

Daniela's activism did not precede her narrative framing of the neighborhood, for she was not an activist during the first few years of her residence or, in fact, before she lived in the Villa. But to be clear, it is neither the case that no other factors contributed to her participation (in her case, the fears wrought by the mid-1990s crises in ETC and IBA probably had an impact) nor that her participation did not later reinforce her perceptions about Villa Victoria (it may or may not have). The issue is that coming to conceive of living in the Villa as a privilege—or, more generally, reframing her conception of the neighborhood—was a necessary condition, and principal motivator, for her involvement. Before, there was no point in getting involved; after realizing her position of "privilege," there was. Furthermore, her shift did not make her more likely to participate in general—only to participate in the Villa. Daniela's testament to the motivating effect of her newfound knowledge (her new set of framing categories) bears evidence to an initial impetus from framing to participation.

An issue about the study of framing processes is worth noting. I happen to trust Daniela because we know each other well. This was helpful but not altogether necessary for me to obtain reliable information about how she frames her neighborhood. Although residents may pretend to an interviewer that they care about a neighborhood, they cannot pretend to know a history they do not know. Furthermore, when residents are asked simply to describe their neighborhood, their answers will betray their framing of the neighborhood because they will either discuss its history or they will not, allude to its political significance or not, depict it as beautiful or not. In this sense, it is possible to obtain relatively bias-free descriptions of residents' conception of the neighborhood, addressing an important issue in the study of culture (see also Weiss 1994, 147–50).

Factors Affecting How Residents Frame Their Neighborhood

As important as knowing how framing processes affect participation is knowing why different cohorts frame the same neighborhood differently. The cohorts framed the neighborhood differently, without a doubt, because of the historical experiences through which they came to live in Villa Victoria. These experiences are affected by the poltico-economic environmental conditions each cohort faced as it developed its view of the neighborhood.

The first cohort's perception of the neighborhood is not difficult to understand. With simplification, their collective history can be described as follows: Born in the small rural towns such as Aguadilla in Puerto Rico, they had lived poor and (by their account) uneventful lives. The boys who had grown to be men there had worked in construction, agriculture, or other temporary and low-skilled jobs; the girls who had grown to be women were by and large home workers. Attracted by opportunities in manufacturing and agriculture in New England, they migrated to Boston, and settled in the cheap if overcrowded South End. Many of the women never held stable employment. Their new houses were a century old, cold, dirty, and falling apart (see, e.g., Green 1975, 16–17). Recall, for instance, Roberta's memory of collecting a shopping bag full of rats, described in chapter 2. As young adults in their twenties, thirties, and forties, they had experienced the fear of displacement; picketed, rallied, and negotiated; and succeeded in producing a new complex. The many of them who had done nothing or very little—perhaps signed a petition or two and attended the meeting of five hundred in 1969—enjoyed the success as much as the community leaders, for they had experienced the same deprivation. Moving to the new, attractive Villa Victoria represented the single most significant improvement in standard of living since their migration, one that, for most of them, would never be surpassed. At this juncture they began to construe the Villa as a beautiful and important neighborhood, which it was, given their experience. For many, this process took place at a critical age in their lives—the period of early adulthood—in which significant events have lasting impacts on one's memories and perceptions of history (Schuman and Scott 1989; see also Mannaheim [1928] 1952).

The second cohort's perception of the Villa stems from its quite different historical experience. Some of them, now adults in their twenties and early thirties, were born and raised in the Villa. They never saw the former Parcel 19. Though they might or might not remember the attractiveness of the Villa in the late 1970s, they certainly witnessed the opening of cracks along the cobblestoned paths of the plaza, the resurgence of rats along the sidewalks, and the rise in drug traffic. But this cohort has experienced something beyond simply not living through the history of ETC. Its basic socialization, and associated networks, took place not in Puerto Rico but in Boston's schools, where they met, played with, and dated students from other neighborhoods and were taught by U.S.-born teachers. For all of them, English is the dominant language, and although most of them understand Spanish, the majority only speak what they call "broken Spanish." Gloria, as we shall see later, only spoke Spanish during her first few years. After starting school, her mind "switched," as she explains, and she now prefers English. These residents are invested in the music, style, and symbolism of urban hip-hop culture; many of their friends are African-Americans, and some of them even call themselves "black." Unlike their parents, but in common with their peers in school, this cohort's favorite types of music are rhythm and blues (R&B), hip-hop, reggae, and Spanish reggae. Their story, in many ways, is a tale of modern second-generation assimilation (see Portes and Rumbaut 2001; Rumbaut and Portes 2001).

This cohort, both the second generation and the new residents, assesses its neighborhood from a radically different vantage point than did the earlier generation. Their only conception of the South End is of the new surrounding upper-middle-class area with its accompanying signifiers of affluence in Victorian urban New England: brick sidewalks and cobblestoned roads, elaborate street lamps, meticulously restored brick townhouses, European cars, sophisticated cafés, exotic ethnic restaurants, and cigar and martini bars. When compared to its surroundings, the Villa they witness is a deteriorating ghetto with garbage on the streets and manifestly poorer people in its households. Recall Melissa's comments about walking from work through the South End and hating the graffiti and the "Oye, mami" catcalls when she entered the Villa. Theirs is a peculiar variant of relative deprivation, manifested not merely as one's poverty in light of another's wealth but also as an impoverished ghetto in light of an affluent neighborhood, a perceived deprivation both collective and physical, visible in the community directly across the street.

Both cohorts are rather sedentary, spending much of their time in Villa Victoria. But the first compares it to the former Parcel 19 and sees its pride and glory, while the second compares it to the affluent South End and sees a shameful ghetto. In their respective collective histories lies the source of their framing of the Villa.

The Exceptions: The Importance of the Family

Not all second-cohort residents perceive the neighborhood so unequivocally. Strikingly, the "exceptions that tested the rule," having no direct experience with the political struggles of the 1960s, still framed the neighborhood in terms similar, or at least consistent, with the neighborhood's first residents. One factor links nearly all these "exceptions," a point made succinctly by one of the Spanish-speaking residents themselves: "All of them had parents who were involved." Indeed, with but a single exception, all of the persistent second-cohort participants had a mother, father, aunt, uncle, or near relative who was either a neighborhood pioneer or a community leader during the 1970s and 1980s.

Although many of the current second-cohort residents had parents in Villa Victoria—parents who, therefore, tended to frame the neighborhood as described above—not all of these parents were equally involved in their own time. In the 1970s and early 1980s, many residents were willing to get involved in activities started by others; but, as in even the most active neighborhood, the proportion of persistent leaders willing to initiate activities was much smaller. Most of the second-cohort residents who participate in the community had a near relative in this latter category. Laura, for instance, the woman depicted above who was on the board of directors of IBA, described how her aunt, a neighborhood activist during her own youth, not only educated Laura as to why they were able to live where they lived but also encouraged her to work for a local service agency. Oscar remembers that when he was "a child, my mother was a board member. My mother would *drag* me to the meetings," making it clear why they lived where they did and how the neighborhood had come to be. Gloria, who also once served on the board, relates that her "mother had been on the board . . . and [both my father and my mother] were very involved in the community. My father used to teach" ESL courses in the neighborhood. Melissa is a young woman who, despite her uncertainties about becoming involved in her neighborhood, had tried to start an after-school dance group. She repeatedly explains that one of the few reasons she perseveres is her mother, who, as one of the "pioneers of the Villa," emphasized the importance of helping others in the neighborhood. Consider, finally, the words of Tania, somewhat older than most residents of the second-cohort: "I know about the history [of the neighborhood] because my mother was one of the people who got together and worked [to fight their displacement]. They held activities to raise funds. My mother would bring her musicians, and they would put together shows [to raise money]."

Family socialization shaped their conception of the neighborhood. By relating and repeating (their version of) the story of the birth of the Villa, these relatives shaped the categories through which the children viewed what was now a more deteriorated neighborhood, acting in effect, as mobilizers of their own children. This finding is consistent with much of the literature, which finds that family effects are at least as strong and often stronger than neighborhood effects (Furstenberg et al. 1998). But what the parents witnessed, the children had to imagine and construct, which had implications we unpack in chapter 7.

Understanding the Villa's Change in Participation

In this and the previous chapter, I detailed how the changes in local participation in Villa Victoria were driven by changes not in structural condition but in cohorts and that the most important of these changes was in the cultural categories through which the cohorts perceived their neighborhood. Stated differently, the mechanisms by which participation declined in Villa Victoria were (*a*) not the decline in participation by residents who were formerly involved but the replacement of a participating cohort with a nonparticipating one, and (*b*) the concomitant shift in the perception of the neighborhood by residents. In addition, although framing the neighborhood as a symbolically meaningful entity is not a sufficient condition for neighborhood participation, it is a necessary one and although framing processes involve the participation of the actor, they can be shown to be rooted, at least in part, in external factors—specifically, historical experiences larger than the individual. At this point, it is necessary to expand on what this suggests about change in neighborhoods' participation level over time.

First, we must ask what to make of the apparent inability of changes in structural factors to explain the decline. I suggest that, contrary to the relationship implied in figure 1*B*, in the previous chapter, structural factors by themselves do not cause participation to fall (or rise) in a neighborhood. This by no means suggests, however, that structural factors are irrelevant. Consider figures 2 and 3. Figure 2 presents a revised approach to the mechanisms by which neighborhood participation changes in a neighborhood. The replacement of an existing cohort by a new one will bring about a new set of residents and experiences with their own histories, residents who may or may not have the same levels of participation (but would be expected to have lower levels if all possible factors could be controlled, as discussed above). Whether these residents volunteer their time to their neighborhood will depend on the narrative categories through which they frame it, much as it would among potential participants in social movements. These categories will, themselves, be affected by a host of factors, including, as suggested by the Villa case, personal experience, parental inculcation, social networks outside the neighborhood, perceptions of relative deprivation, and others. (And, indeed, whether framing will translate into action will itself depend on a host of factors, not the least of which is the agency of the actor.)

But this relationship occurs within the constraints imposed by structural factors. Assume in neighborhood *A* the conditions are high SES, high homogeneity, and high stability (*solid line*), while in neighborhood *B*, they are low on all three factors (*dotted line*). As shown in figure 2, any changes in participation would take place regardless of whether the line is dotted or solid (i.e., whether the constraints are weak or strong), yet only within the boundaries (i.e., structural constraints) imposed by the line.

FIGURE 2. The relationship among structural conditions, cohort replacement, and participation.

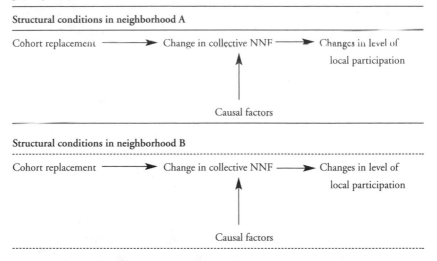

Structural conditions set the constraints under which participation changes, but they do not necessarily predict change. In addition, please note that, for the sake of clarity, the top diagrams do not show the effects of factors affecting participation other than changes in the collective NNF (neighborhood narrative frame). See also figure 3.

Thus, at any given time participation will be expected to be lower in neighborhood *B* than in neighborhood A, as much of the cross-sectional research has shown. And whatever changes are brought about in each neighborhood will be constrained by such conditions, so that *B*'s highest potential level of participation will never be as high as *A*'s, which is also consistent with much of the existing research. But whether structural conditions change or remain the same may not affect whether participation changes or remains the same.[7]

Therefore, although structural changes would not produce changes in local participation, structural conditions certainly set constraints on how high participation is likely to be. In Villa Victoria, the most important structural constraints were its relative homogeneity and its residential sta-

7. Moreover, consider the following: If one could artificially control, e.g., SES and the stability rate and cause a neighborhood to increase only in homogeneity, what would happen to participation? Figure 1*B* suggests that it would rise. I conjecture that a third of the time it would rise, a third of the time it would fall, and a third of the time it would remain the same. However, over time, as participation rose and fell, its highest possible level of participation would be higher than it was before since there is now greater homogeneity. A related but different point about the qualitative difference between how structural factors operate across space and over time was made recently by Quillian (1999).

FIGURE 3. The relationship between structural constraints and fluctuations in participation.

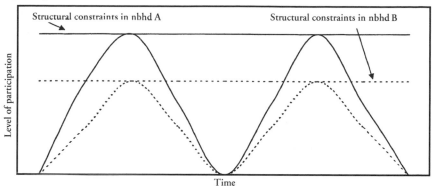

The fluctuations in neighborhood *A* are denoted by a *solid line;* those in neighborhood *B,* by a *dotted line.* As shown in the diagram, participation will wax and wane over time regardless of the structural conditions but only within the limits imposed by those conditions. That is, participation in each neighborhood is unlikely to rise above the constraints imposed by its set of conditions.

bility. The collective narrative of the neighborhood as a historically important place has persisted as long as it has only because the neighborhood is residentially stable, since many residents who lived there in the 1960s, 1970s, and 1980s still live there and have kept the oral history alive, and because it is highly ethnically homogeneous, since the story of the neighborhood's birth, centered as it is on the role of Puerto Rican activists, would have resonated weakly in a heterogeneous neighborhood, complicating the task of sustaining that narrative. It is in this sense, I suggest, that structural factors operate: as constraining or enabling conditions that do not precipitate changes but make them easier or more difficult. The high associations between the independent variables and at least this particular form of social organization demonstrate a relationship not of cause and effect but of constraint and possibility. That we have hardly articulated this distinction has impaired our ability to open the black box linking structural conditions to local participation.[8]

The Villa also helps us better comprehend how cultural processes work, independently of structural ones. Much like contemporary conservatives,

8. The notion that cohorts are important to understand neighborhood change is reminiscent of Ryder's (1965) work. Ryder has argued that the cohort should be as central to the understanding of social phenomena as the social class has become. By understanding cohort-related process, we can learn a great deal about both stability and change in social processes over time.

traditional social organization theorists such as Shaw and McKay (1942, 1969) and Kornhauser (1978) have conceived of culture as the general norms and values of a group of people; they have argued that a group of residents' culture is the natural result of structural urban poverty, a collective response shared more or less equally by all residents. In three specific ways, this approach does not work in Villa Victoria. First, we have seen that culture in this case worked not via norms and values but via the cognitive categories through which the neighborhood was perceived. As we have seen, while norms and values may explain some other particular element of the relationship between structure and behavior, it certainly does not, in the case of local participation in the Villa, account for very much. Culture here operated to frame the lens through which the neighborhood was observed. Thus, we can think about cultural effects on local participation not just more accurately but also more dispassionately, independent of the analysts' preferences and prejudices about whether local participation is a good in itself, or a substitute for government intervention, or a form of self-empowerment, or any prescription from the political left or the right. Second, we have seen that local participation was affected not by a generalized cultural worldview, or even a cultural view about volunteering and altruism, but by neighborhood-specific cultural conception, such that "culture" does not become a catchall category alleged to explain everything from local participation to drug use to teen pregnancy to joblessness. Finally, we have seen clearly the frequently neglected fact that residents respond very differently to the structural conditions they share at any given time—and that at least some of this difference can be understood by asking which cultural categories are shaping their perception of their situation. Thus, positing automatic relationships between structural conditions and, say, an "anomic" local culture, or a "culture of poverty," masks as much as it uncovers, adding unwarranted generalizations to relationships that could be understood more concretely.

The Villa's changes in local participation were at once simpler and more complicated than the previous two chapters suggest. They were simpler in theory because a decline in participation is precisely, I suggested, what one would expect if all possible causal factors could be held constant. But they were more complicated in practice because the Villa changed in a host of other ways over time, especially with respect to landscape and what urban sociologists have termed the ecology of the neighborhood. The effect of these factors on social capital is addressed in the chapters that follow.

FIVE

The Ecology of Group Differentiation

We're a lot like Southie. We don't like outsiders coming in. — LAURA

It's like two different worlds in one section of the city. There is the South End and there is Villa Victoria. . . . They do their thing, we do our thing. — OSCAR

It's completely isolated. It's a community by itself, really. . . . It's very isolated.
— IAN (WHITE SOUTH END RESIDENT)

Betances

One afternoon in the summer of 1999, when I was still finding my way around the South End, I took a walk on Dartmouth Street. A Sunday, the streets were empty and quiet; many stores were closed. I headed toward the Villa, hoping to learn more than I knew then about life in the housing complex on weekends, when people might be out and about the park, streets, plaza, and sidewalk. By the time I reached Tremont Street, I could detect a faint, distant rumble of some sort, though there were few cars on the streets. After crossing the Tremont, I suddenly heard loud beats—the beats of a spiky, contagious *plena,* the rural Puerto Rican rhythm—from behind the row houses before me. I looked up, imagining the music was coming from one of the top-floor apartments, but the sound was too loud, and it echoed. Along Tremont, on either side of where I stood, nothing looked out of the ordinary. I walked around the row houses into the neighborhood and discovered a large stage assembled on a scaffold at the far end of the plaza, facing it. On the stage, a highly professional band played animatedly before an audience of several hundred people.

The spectators, many of them young, wore shorts and cutoffs, flowing skirts, backless tops, and long t-shirts in red, white, and blue, the colors not of Old Glory but of the single-starred Puerto Rican flag. The air was humid, the temperature in the nineties, and the sky devoid of clouds, so most spectators gathered around the several trees in the plaza or by a nearby covered terrace, waiting for the punishing sun to relent. To the left of the stage, about seven or eight food vendors had arranged stands to sell rice and beans (*arroz con gandules*), roasted pork, chicken, beef on a stick, patties, and drinks. A plate of rice and beans and pork went for $8; a lemonade went for $2; bottled water for $1. One woman sold piña coladas in a small plastic cup for $3. To the right of the stage, along the terrace, about three or four vendors had arranged display tables with shirts and caps for sale. Just about all the clothing had a Puerto Rican flag or the words "Puerto Rico" stitched, pressed, or painted on. Further down, from a table with three or four people, hung a banner reading, "It's Time We Made Smoking History," which seemed highly out of place.

Though I did not know it at the time, this was the early part of the final day of the yearly Betances Festival (El Festival Betances), a four-day event that has been celebrated in Villa Victoria every July for nearly thirty years. Organized by IBA, it is among the neighborhood's most anticipated and well-known events, attracting thousands of spectators. The festival is named after Ramón Emeterio Betances, a mid-nineteenth-century "surgeon, ophthalmologist, scientist, politician and writer" (IBA 2000a) who was also an abolitionist and active Puerto Rican nationalist. With the financial backing of corporate sponsors, the festival celebrates Puerto Rican dance, art, food, music, and culture and is held entirely in Villa Victoria. Though most of the attendants are residents of the Villa, the festival attracts an estimated crowd of 15,000 between the Thursday evening it begins and the Sunday night it closes (*Boston Globe,* May 25, 2000).[1]

The festival demonstrates that the Villa's sense of community has not disappeared altogether. For the student of social capital, it is fertile ground, and in more ways than one. Using the festival as a starting point, I address, in this chapter, the social isolation of the residents, their inability to generate ties to the middle class and to further their external social capital.

The Following Year

By the time I attended the festival the following year I knew what to expect and when. On Thursday afternoon, vendors and organizations had assembled stands on the sidewalks and parking lot surrounding Plaza Betances. A few of them were nonprofit organizations offering information on an array of services targeted at the poor or Latino community, such as

---

1. The attendance figure includes people who attend on more than one day.

family planning, the Women, Infants, and Children (WIC) Program, or health care. But most of them were food vendors offering Puerto Rican fare, both full meals and baked or fried pastries (such as *pastelitos* and *alcapurias*).

THE PARADE

The Friday festivities began with a parade led by the neighborhood's children and youth, wearing typical Puerto Rican masks and costumes, and accompanied by a small band playing traditional *bombas* and *plenas*. One large mask at the head of the line was a replica of Betances's face; another, a gorgeous traditional folk mask in bright yellow and green. The resident who made the masks had worked at them for weeks, employing a combination of papier-mâché, heavy-duty glue, and oil-based paints and cluttering her kitchen and living room with materials.

For an hour before the parade began, a troupe of young baton twirlers (*batuteras*) practiced their dance routine and twirling before a steadily increasing crowd of onlookers. The girls, about forty in all between the ages of nine and twelve, paced to the beat of a merengue tune blasting from a van. A few men and older boys, themselves part of the act, tightened the skins on their conga drums; an older man instructed a boy of about twelve-years-old in the proper way to hold a cowbell. Both of them were sitting, with the rest of the percussion crew, on the back of a small pick-up truck near the head of the line.

Other young men just people-watched. I ran into Tommy and Oz, men in their twenties and thirties, who were watching the young women in the crowd and cracking jokes, most of them relating to sex or the women's bodies. Oz was crass: "She's so fat she's got two asses, one in the front and one in the back!" Tommy, in turn, laughed, then matched Oz' quip with a comment of his own. A few minutes later, they commented on the scores of attractive Latinas who seemed to them to have come out of nowhere.

The parade was lively and exciting, yet short. It began at the plaza and headed toward Tremont, where it turned left and continued until West Newton Street; there, it turned left again and ended at O'Day Park, lasting, in all, about twenty-five minutes. In the park, paraders encountered dozens of aluminum pans stuffed with food on several tables lined up against the inside fence of the park. The park, by now, unlike most of the time, was overflowing with people of all ages, not just young men, but women, children, the elderly, and the middle-aged. For the first time in months, the park gave the impression of being a family space.

Tommy, Oz, a few other men, and I sat on one of the benches in the park. Children were running around us playing tag. Most of the men were drinking from beer cans barely covered in brown paper bags. At different times Villa Victoria security members or Boston police officers walked by us, staring at but not approaching us. The men had begun cracking jokes, mostly homoerotic in nature, each man asserting his masculinity by describing in what position and under what circumstances he would force another to succumb. One of the men was openly gay, which seemed to bother no one. Nor did he seem bothered by the homophobic humor, in which he partook with apparent glee. After half an hour of this, they noticed being overheard by a few older women on a nearby bench, so the men lowered their voices, slightly embarrassed. One of the men, just out of jail, suddenly stood up, laughing, and started looking over the crowd of baton twirlers, who were finding their way around the food tables. "OK, let me look around," he said. "I think one of these girls is my daughter!" He laughed. But then he looked again. I do not think he recognized her.

FAMILY DAY AND YOUTH DAY

Friday was family day. As in many carnivalesque festivities throughout Latin America, an adolescent girl was selected to be crowned *reina del festival*. With the crown on her head, she walked around the neighborhood from family to family accepting compliments and having her picture taken. A company had offered to sponsor a small prize to the young person who had done the most for the community, and that person was given an award in a small ceremony by a microphone stand at the edge of the park. Occasionally someone stood by the microphone to express the community's appreciation for a particular leader, or to sing a melodic tune, or to repeat the importance of sustaining the neighborhood that the "pioneers" had built. Indeed, throughout the weekend, at just about every large break between performances or events, someone would step to the microphone to express the community's appreciation for a particular leader, to repeat the importance of sustaining the sense of community, or to retell the glorious story of the neighborhood's birth. In the words of the (bilingual) program that year, the festival was a place to "affirm our past victories, strenthen [*sic*] our cultural heritage and recommit to maintaining a strong and united Villa Victoria."

On Saturday afternoon, a number of activities were set up for the young in O'Day Park. A DJ had set up turntables under a tree and was playing hip-hop, R&B, and reggae to a group of teenagers who had assembled by the speakers. Full-court games of basketball were taking place as part of a short league started earlier in the summer. Some kids were throwing shots by a smaller hoop behind the main court. The rim was bent down permanently by forty-five degrees from years of slam dunks. Soon, the audience began asking the DJ for more reggae. He complied with a fierce beat, to which two girls performed intense, elastic versions of "the butterfly," going lower and lower with every turn of the knee. Another girl followed, showing her skills, and then another, who could not have been more than ten years old. They drew a small crowd, which applauded with a mixture of surprise, amusement, and incredulity.

That day I helped one of the organizers of the festival with an arts and crafts program for children. On what was once a green path between the plaza and the park stood several *maceteros,* mostly devoid of plants, which had been neglected for years. The path had been fenced in on both sides years earlier during the height of drug activity. The organizer had given the *maceteros,* which were about a foot and a half high and several feet in diameter, a fresh coat of red base paint. The children's task, with our help, was to color in the flowers and *Taíno* symbols she had outlined over the base. Several children, with their mothers, aunts, and cousins, painted with us for a few hours. The children did not grow tired or restless, and they happily signed their names on the *maceteros,* proud of their work.

THE MAIN EVENTS

Saturday and Sunday were the most crowded days. Latinos from all over the city assembled at the plaza, including musicians, artists, professionals, and graduate students from the local universities. The crowds changed constantly during the day. A couple thousand spectators or participants attend on any given day, and around four or five hundred are visible at any given time during the most crowded hours.

Much of the attraction, it seemed, was the food. More than half of everything served was fried, greasy, and extremely delicious. Because of the heat, drinks sold quickly, even at a few dollars per small bottle, as did baked and fried pastries. Plates of rice and pigeon peas with roasted pork sold out early. I ran into Karina, an organizer who had met with a health inspector. She complained in Spanish that the inspector had demanded that the foods be frozen until the instant they were going to be cooked. She found this ludicrous. "Mario," she said, "do you know what happens when you deep-fry frozen meat?"

On Sunday, "Puerto Rican Heritage Day," the events began early in the afternoon and ran through the evening. About two dozen musical and dance acts were on stage, including national and local bands playing salsa, merengue, *bomba,* and *plena.* Puerto Rican culture was heavily represented in the program, but there were also Latin American and Caribbean acts, such as West Indian steel band performances and Honduran and Peruvian folk dance. One of the bands, composed primarily of present or former residents of Villa Victoria, was exceptional. During the show, they saluted several persons in the audience. A group of elderly *trovadores* competed in that improvised vocal medium from the hills of Puerto Rico, the *trova.*

Several dance performances, often well choreographed, took place in the middle of the plaza itself after residents widened a circle to give dancers the space to perform. For one of the shows, three adolescents role-played the entire story of *Pedro Navaja,* Ruben Blades's salsa classic, while the audience sang along the parts they could remember. The song tells the story of Pedro Navaja ("Peter Navaja" or "Peter the knife"), a gold-toothed New York thief who watches, stalks, and stabs a prostitute in the middle of the night. But the prostitute, accustomed to the danger of the New York streets, had been carrying a .38 Smith & Wesson, with which she shoots Pedro. The song's lyrics have become a hymn of sorts for a generation of Latinos from New York and Latin America. The teenager playing the prostitute had squeezed into a short, campy, pink rubber dress, to the amusement of the crowd. The presentation was funny, and it ignited the audience. At another performance, an Afro-Latino dance troupe, composed entirely of adolescents and children, performed three traditional pieces from Afro-Cuba or Puerto Rico. Their attire was traditional and tailored. After the performance, a woman who had led the dance group for over a decade was honored publicly and given flowers. Everyone applauded and greeted her with evident affection.

In many ways, the distinction between performer and participant was diffuse. Many of the performers lived in the neighborhood, performing a *trova* at one point, applauding the young *batuteras* at another. The shows themselves often involved call and response or some type of audience participation. One flamboyant, openly gay man wearing a cape drew as much attention as a few of the shows, as he avidly danced to the spicier beats, comically gesticulating in parody of an excessively effeminate, overly sexed woman. There were back-to-back shows all afternoon, and no way to withstand the heat to see them all, so most people half watched the shows, half hung around the food trucks, or strolled the sidewalks of the neighborhood. Throughout the afternoon, girls in their teens pushed strollers up and down the streets wearing backless tops and fitted jeans, asserting both their youth and responsibility, refusing to give up their sexuality for their children or vice versa. Small packs of boys wearing bandanas of the Puerto Rican flag followed them around, teasing, joking with, or superficially harassing them.

The evening ended with music and heavy dancing throughout. By early night, the plaza and streets surrounding it were full of people. All of the bands at the plaza played salsa, merengue, *plena,* or *bomba*—no reggae, hip-hop, R&B, or American rock music. It was as if the bands, selected by the adult organizers and performing at the plaza, constituted a different world from that of the DJ's, put together for the teens and setup at the park. Throughout the night, one man in the audience holding a cowbell marked the rhythm in accompaniment. Men and women had begun to feel the effects of alcohol, and a few middle-aged women made passes at the younger men in attendance. By the evening's end, I had a difficult time imagining anyone complaining they had not enjoyed their weekend at the Villa.

A Peculiar Institution

The size of its crowds, diversity of its music, and impressiveness of its artistic repertoire symbolize the uniqueness of Betances, an improbably large, stubbornly self-sustaining yearly institution operating from this tiny housing complex in the South End. It has been a hit every year, boisterous but family-oriented, carnivalesque yet culturally rich—a welcome celebration of Latino, and especially Puerto Rican, art and culture. Its importance to the Latino community in Boston is undisputed, despite the presence of another, much larger Puerto Rican Festival held yearly at Franklin Park. Former Villa residents from all over the city and the country mark their yearly calendars to attend Betances; large groups of Latino graduate students and musicians from the local universities flock to the plaza every year, almost religiously, clapping *la clave,* the basic salsa beat, to rhythms of the bands. The Betances is highly anticipated, class-diverse, and a near-permanent institution in the neighborhood. Yet it is also invisible from the vantage point of the surrounding South End.

Throughout the weekend, the festival did not spill out into the streets beyond Villa Victoria, except for the short Thursday parade, which curved tightly around the outside of the Villa on Tremont Street. There were no large crowds of Puerto Ricans on the opposite side of Tremont, or one block over on Union Park, or one block over in the other direction, on Rutland Street. Were it not for the blast of the speakers, one might have been forgiven for believing nothing was taking place at the Villa. Odd as it may seem, the estimated 15,000 attendees, mostly Puerto Ricans, who crowded the Villa over the long weekend stuck almost exclusively to the twenty acres of the complex, fitting in, one way or another, despite the sweltering heat. There were no fences, no blockades, no formal rules prohibiting attendants from walking throughout the neighborhood or around the South End's sidewalks, yet the attendees nonetheless kept to themselves. The festival, by the collective if unconscious will of its participants, was a geographically constrained event.

For their part, the residents of the wider South End were conspicuously absent from the festival (despite its having been advertised in the *Boston Globe*). Though free and open to the public, Betances did not attract residents from Union Park, Rutland or Worcester Squares, Columbus Avenue, or the St. Boloph section of the South End. That there could be 5,000 people on any given day of the festival is surprising not only because of the small size of the plaza and the neighborhood but also because almost all of them were Latinos. While at the festival I saw several families who could be African-American or dark-skinned Latinos; there were also some Chinese families, partaking in the festivities as everyone else was. But I saw almost no white attendees, at most a few dozen on any one day. The first year I was at the festival, I spent eight hours at the plaza one day; I saw fewer than fifteen white persons. The following year I ran a similar (subjective) survey over the course of a half day. I saw fewer than a dozen, which included a couple of police officers and a volunteer with IBA. The absence of local South Enders at the festival was particularly peculiar considering Boston's local culture, which supports dozens of yearly street, river, and park festivals, with hundreds of thousands of participants, as well as the current cultural popularity, throughout the nation, of Latino music, arts, and culture.

Indeed, although the festival celebrated life, equality, and the beauty of diverse musical and artistic cultures, the combination of inside and outside circumstances in that section of the South End gave the impression of an invisible fence, drawn neatly around the Villa, that kept residents (and Latinos) in and nonresidents out. Betances was at once public and intimate, consciously and honestly open to all yet practically limited, by some unspoken understanding, to the few. The festival, the years I was there, was a private public event.

Social Isolation

In many ways, public festivals represent a group's central attributes, capturing its core and enlarging it exponentially. For a brief time, they exaggerate multiple elements of the culture and display them nakedly in all their drama, their joyfulness, and their prejudices. This is particularly true at the Villa. The pattern of interaction between Villa residents and South Enders during the festival epitomizes and magnifies a central aspect of Villa Victoria: that it is a largely self-enclosed community, as disconnected from the surrounding South End as the latter is from it. The Villa captures, in one sense, what Wilson (1987, 1996) has referred to as the social isolation of poor neighborhoods, writ large: social isolation at the collective level.[2]

Though the Villa's isolation from the surrounding South End is not unimaginably extreme, it is unmistakable. A walk along Tremont Street will reveal the presence of Latinos only between the corners of the two streets that bracket the Villa. The hair salons, cafés, restaurants, theaters, bakeries, flower shops, boutiques, and other establishments in the surrounding South End rarely, if ever, see Latino clients, even though there are 3,000 of them within walking distance. Their absence is particularly striking at many of the restaurants on Tremont, where one sees a clientele through the windows that in no way resembles the population on the opposite side of the street. Good weather brings scores of Latino children out to play ball by "the humps" (a miniature square between Aguadilla and San Juan Streets). Young men bet on dice with fresh dollar bills by O'Day Park. Others stand along a cyclone fence chatting, looking for drug buyers. Adolescents ride their bikes around the park or in and out of the plaza. Women, with one child in a stroller and four or five others running around them, saunter around the park, sidewalks, greenery, taking in the fresh air. Yet one will rarely find any of them one block away from the Villa in any direction. Except for their time in school and occasional IBA-organized field trips, most of these adolescents spend nearly all of their time at the

---

2. The Villa can be characterized as being in a state of collective or community isolation, whereby the neighborhood, as a whole, is isolated from the outside, middle-class South End. Nevertheless, there is a great deal of variation within the Villa in terms of individual social isolation, i.e., the extent to which particular residents are connected or disconnected from the middle class in the South End or elsewhere. Indeed, many residents of the Villa are not socially isolated individuals, and chap. 7 will discuss what distinguishes those who are not from those who are. This chapter only addresses the factors affecting collective isolation.

Villa. Retirees and elders, along with a few alcoholics, longing for fresh air, spend long afternoons, especially on Saturdays and Sundays, chatting under the shade of the trees in the plaza and strolling up and down the Villa side of West Dedham Street. Yet they rarely, if ever, take promenades along the beautiful fountains and manicured greenery in Union Park, even though the latter is closer to Plaza Betances than the Villa's own less picturesque O'Day Park.

The Villa is notable in part for being so populated, overflowing with families on its streets and sidewalks. With 60 percent of persons age sixteen or older jobless in 1990, there are large numbers of idle adults in the neighborhood, and many of them are out in the streets and sidewalks when the weather permits.[3] Some of these are people too elderly to be employed; others are alcoholic middle-aged men and women taking shots from paper-bagged bottles; others are parents keeping an eye on the few dozen children who play in the plaza from time to time. Yet rarely, it seems, either for leisure or for business, do these people, individually or as families, break out of their self-contained enclave; they remain tucked within the boundaries of their hard-fought neighborhood. In fact, that first time when I came across the festival and could not tell, from looking in either direction of the street, that anything was taking place in Villa Victoria was not a rare circumstance; it was the norm. One resident, Oscar, captured the situation succinctly: "It's like two different worlds in one section of the city. There is the South End and there is Villa Victoria. . . . They do their thing, we do our thing." Villa Victoria is, in many ways, a small world unto itself.

Sociologists such as Wilson (1987) have argued that one of the effects of concentrated poverty is the social isolation of residents from middle-class networks. Many researchers have tested versions of this hypothesis (Fernandez and Harris 1992; Rankin and Quane 2000), but few have attempted to explain the mechanisms by which this would happen. A peculiar twist in this case is that a large middle-class is available within close proximity of these poor residents. Why do they fail to develop ties to it?

The question is not trivial. The potential networks located in the sur-

3. The figure refers to Latinos in the census tract encompassing Villa Victoria. The unemployment figure is 26 percent. This figure excludes people who are not in the civilian labor force, those who either cannot work or are unwilling to do so. The jobless rate includes all persons over sixteen years old who do not have jobs, regardless of whether they can or are willing to work. Also note that the available figures are, as of the time of this writing, for 1990. The nineties saw an economic boom that drove jobless rates down in Boston and also, probably, in the Villa. In the neighborhood, they do not seem to have decreased much.

rounding South End constitute avenues for mobility and influence (Lin 1999). The South End is one of the most politically powerful neighborhoods in Boston, as evidenced, for example, by its ability to secure quickly a highly reinforced police presence during a crime wave in the early seventies (Lukas 1985). Hundreds of influential members of Boston's political, cultural, and economic elite live in the South End. Access to these residents could have dramatic effects on the residents' ability to limit crime, attract funds for its community centers, control traffic congestion, and so on (Sampson 1999). Particularly curious is that the census tract in which the Villa is located is statistically highly integrated, only about 20 percent Latino. Judging from a census map, one might anticipate a high degree of contact between the poor Latinos of the Villa and the middle- and upper-middle-class whites of the surrounding South End, leading to the expectation of interaction and political alliances around neighborhood issues (Massey and Denton 1993).

Nor is it the case that cross-class or cross-race interactions with the South Enders are unimaginable. Many of the white residents moved to the South End deliberately wishing to live in an integrated city neighborhood, to escape the suburban upbringing that their parents' had foisted on them a generation earlier. As Lukas (1985) suggests, it was as if, having read Jane Jacobs's (1961) *Death and Life of Great American Cities,* they had decided to put her experiment to practice. Many of them sought integration, at least some version of it, to meet and get to know the poor, urban people who had seemed so distant during their own childhood; they sought to educate their children in a diverse society, having them attend school with children of other races and backgrounds. In the words of Vicky, a white South End resident for six years, living with her fiancé: "We fell in love with the South End, [with] the diversity of the culture." Yet despite her casual friendliness and integration into the neighborhood, she knows almost no residents of Villa Victoria.

From the perspective of the Villa the situation is just as perplexing. Had the neighborhood been tucked away several miles from the nearest highway or separated from the rest of the city by a railroad yard, the community's self-containment and its residents' tendency to remain within its boundaries might have been less perplexing. But the Villa is located in the middle of one of the most central neighborhoods in a densely populated, geographically small city, with no physical barriers of any kind between itself and the surrounding community. There are no gates, no markers obvious to a first-time observer, no train tracks to cross. Why, then, do the denizens refuse to cross a line that exists only in their collective thoughts?

Addressing a Social Phenomenon from a Sociospatial Perspective

Two different sociological traditions, stemming from camps that rarely discuss one another's work, provide a partial answer to this question: the Chicago school's work on ecology and space, and the cultural sociology work on boundary drawing and distinction. Much of what takes place in the Villa results from what may be termed the ecology of group differentiation, by which the spatial characteristics of the region become inextricably linked to its class and racial ones, reinforcing, rather than undermining, the differences between residents and nonresidents of the Villa and spatializing, and therefore concretizing, what cultural sociologists, among others, have called boundary work (Barth 1969; Gieryn 1995; Lamont 1999). A different spatial configuration of the region might have resulted in less isolation of the Villa's residents from their surrounding middle- and upper-middle-class South Enders.

URBAN ECOLOGY

The "ecological" conception of the city and its neighborhoods is part of the rich legacy of the Chicago school (Park, Burgess, and McKenzie 1925). Borrowing tropes from the field of biology (Gaziano 1996), Park argued that the composition of the city was the natural result of the free-market competition for space among groups, businesses, industries, and institutions (Park 1952). Burgess, building on Park's work, developed the theory of "concentric circles" to explain the natural growth of the city. He argued that cities expanded organically from an industrial and economic core in increasingly wider circles. In the areas immediately surrounding the core lived the poor and immigrant laborers; radiating out were the working class, then the middle class and commuters. As each group moved up the economic ladder—and they all eventually would—it would move farther away from the industrial core (Park, Burgess, and McKenzie 1925; see also Stein 1960; Fischer 1976; Sampson and Morenoff 1997). The school has been criticized at length. Most criticisms can be subsumed under the statement that it incorrectly assumed the various ecological processes it observed in Chicago were universal, regardless of regional variation, politics, racism, economic policies, or history (see Sampson and Morenoff [1997] for a review).

The most general contribution of the Chicago school to urban sociology is the notion that social relationships are spatially embedded—that to understand society one cannot neglect space. This principle becomes manifest in Villa. The region's spatial configuration accentuates differences and contributes to what might be termed group homogenization: the differentiation of a heterogeneous collective of individuals into two groups and the ensuing homogenization of each group. This homogenization takes place not just by eliminating within-group differences but also by identifying a set of new traits that become indicative of the group (see McPherson, Smith-Lovin, and Cook 2001).

CULTURAL BOUNDARY WORK

The differences, resulting only partly from racial and class composition, become group identifiers through a process of boundary work. With roots in the study of ethnic relations (Barth 1969) and the sociology of science (Gieryn 1995), the term "boundary work" refers to the process by which collectives of individuals create symbolic lines between themselves and others for the purpose of either accentuating their own identity or concretizing a new institution (also Small 1999). For Bourdieu (1984), cultural boundary work was the principal mechanism by which individuals distinguished themselves from others in society—and their very tastes and consumption practices exemplified this distinction. Studying American upper-middle-class males, Lamont (1992) uncovered that Americans drew boundaries differently from Bourdieu's French. The Americans drew looser cultural boundaries than did their French counterparts, but they drew sharper moral and economic ones. One might expect, then, for the affluent South Enders instinctively to draw boundaries between themselves and poor Villa residents.

But the white upper-middle class that Lamont studied, living mostly in suburban sections of New Jersey, is not quite the white upper-middle class in the South End. The latter are highly urban New Englanders, more likely to draw cultural distinctions than their New Jersey counterparts, yet more interested in the grittiness of urban life, and probably, as most Bostonians are, more left of center in political persuasion. Would they be more or less prone to engage in boundary work to distinguish themselves from the poor? The limitation of the works of Lamont and Bourdieu is that, by relying on representative samples of a larger population (a welcome, desperately needed contribution to qualitative work), they are forced to despatialize their analyses. They do not discuss "the home" as part of a specific type of neighborhood, but the home as home. Among this group of South Enders, however, buying a home in the city, and in the

South End in particular, was more often than not a deliberate act, one that colors and affects the boundary work they engage in, as we will see.[4]

A SYNTHESIS

Below, I explain the social isolation of the Villa as a function of the spatial configuration of the area and the boundary work between residents of the Villa and surrounding South Enders. The particular combination of spatial, racial, and class configurations at the Villa deters residents from crossing the "invisible fence" by exaggerating, rather than undermining, the differences between residents of the Villa and the surrounding South End; it contributes to the perception that there are two mutually exclusive, internally homogeneous, and—to an extent—diametrically opposed groups of people, rather than simply heterogeneous residents of different incomes who happen to live in different parts of the South End. This differentiation, in turn, discourages Villa residents from interacting with their surrounding middle-class neighbors and vice versa. The discussion will focus on each of the factors composing the differentiated ecology: the spatial configuration of the neighborhood, the quality of the landscape in poor and nonpoor areas, the spatialization of crime, and the class and spatial organization of race.

The Ecology of Group Differentiation

THE ROLE OF THE REGION'S SPATIAL CONFIGURATION

Neighborhoods are constantly in flux, as waves of institutions and populations enter and depart them. When a narrow geographic space, such as the area in and around the Villa, is populated by both poor and affluent residents, one of two dynamic processes are typically in place: gentrification (Anderson 1990) or middle-class flight (Wilson 1987, 1996). Anderson (1990, 1999) has written extensively about how these conditions affect interactions among poor and nonpoor in public space. One of the central features of neighborhoods experiencing either middle-class flight or gentrification is the fluidity and imprecision of the boundaries between where

---

4. Many researchers on this topic, trickling down from Bourdieu's work on distinctions, have inadvertently followed on one of his critical weaknesses: the assumption that it is the upper, not the lower, class that does all the boundary drawing, that the poor are neither interested in nor able willingly to differentiate themselves from the wealthier. I have found, however, that boundary drawing works both ways.

each group lives (see fig. 4, *top*). In these regions, which Anderson (1990) has called "marginal areas," any house in a given street may be inhabited by either poor or nonpoor people. By the same token, any street within such areas may be overwhelmingly poor or nonpoor. An interesting corollary of this fact is that, in marginal areas, class differences are not spatially delineated, so that one cannot necessarily tell which house on which street is inhabited by which class member (unless a dwelling is conspicuously rundown or restored). In these conditions, although poor residents may be discernible from the nonpoor because of their race or (perhaps) personal appearance (clothing, etc.), they are not discernible in space. Thus, neither group can avoid the other group's region, and interactions between the poor and nonpoor become inevitable. Although these interactions, as Anderson (1990) has shown, are often governed by a "code" of deference and distance, the conditions at least allow for the possibility of cross-class connections (see also Schwirian 1983, 90).[5]

The poor and nonpoor residents around Parcel 19 at this past century's end lived under markedly different circumstances. Here, class differences were sharply delineated in space. The poor lived almost exclusively in Villa Victoria; the affluent lived exclusively in the area surrounding it.[6] The boundaries between the two groups continue to be precise and fixed, marked clearly by the architectural design of the two groups' set of houses and by the clear designation of the poor groups' sets of residences as subsidized (see fig. 4, *bottom;* also Suttles 1968, 1972). The Spanish-style townhouses of Aguadilla and San Juan Streets are not in the process of changing hands to affluent residents, as houses might be in a gentrifying neighborhood. Nor is it likely the houses in the surrounding South End will change hands to poor residents as they might in a neighborhood experiencing middle-class flight, at least in the short-term future and barring drastic policy or economic changes. That is to say, there are poor streets, and there are nonpoor streets.

Moreover, the two sets of streets are distinctively clustered: the houses of the poor and those of the nonpoor in that section of the South End constitute two geographically separated, class-divergent areas. It is easy for an

5. Anderson's neighborhood is reminiscent of many aspects of the South End of the 1950s and early 1960s, in terms of if not class then race. The South End also contained a mixture of diverse groups, as if the entire neighborhood were a constellation of marginal areas. Different ethnic groups inhabited roughly different sections, but the latter were diffuse, loose territories.

6. The following discussion does not address the entire South End, in which there are a few other (clearly designated) housing projects; it address only the area around what is known as Parcel 19, since it is the point where the Villa's poor and the nonpoor meet geographically.

FIGURE 4. Two types of boundaries between affluent and poor neighborhoods

individual in either class to avoid the other region. Sociologists have written of the importance of random, accidental, informal contacts among individuals to the development and sustenance of social capital. When spatial conditions reduce those opportunities, they decrease social capital and the opportunities for cross-class networks drastically.[7]

7. When the members of ETC worked with the architectural firm to design the neighborhood's basic landscape, they deliberately constructed a space that could create community. Several of the cross streets between Tremont and Shawmut were broken off. Recall that the two local streets, Aguadilla and San Juan, were designed to be U-shaped, so cars not going to the Villa had no reason to drive through it. Without through streets, alien traffic was kept at bay. Ironically, this structural differentiation was one version of the upper-class gated community, a persisting remnant of the neighborhood-as-self-enclosed community philosophy that Jacobs (1961) attacked.

The ecological effect, however, runs much deeper than the failed opportunities for interaction. At issue are the transformations the two areas have experienced over time. Spatial differences may help create and constitute social groups by homogenizing sets of individuals and exaggerating differences between them in the social imagination of residents, poor and nonpoor alike. The crux of the process is the homogenization of groups, a process partly constituted and certainly sustained by the very ecological conditions that make up the physical landscape of the area. How does this happen?

URBAN ECOLOGY AS A HOMOGENIZING FACTOR

At the end of the construction of the Villa in the mid-1970s, the neighborhood had become an improbably clean and attractive area in what had been one of the dirtiest and most deteriorating sections of the South End. The Spanish-style houses were designed, to be sure, to fit with the cultural and historical roots of the neighborhood's Puerto Rican residents; but they were also aimed at reimagining an older vision of the housing project as the large impersonal high rise. The high-rise project was the utilitarian outcome of a modified and somewhat patched-up policy designed to house at first young veterans and then poor families living there temporarily—people on their way, it was expected, to a better residence. Villa Victoria was an experiment designed by a group of idealists intent on not just servicing the poor but also creating a new type of subsidized housing project, one with a sense of neighborliness and community. The Villa was built to blend in, rather than clash, with what the city encouraged and expected to be an increasingly affluent community in the surrounding South End. Over time, the new housing project and the surrounding South End would fit together, if not perfectly in architectural style then definitely in attractiveness of landscape, creating a new type of urban residential district where rich and poor sections were indistinguishable to all but the most informed observers. This modified utopian vision, resulting from both the original plan of the BRA and the forced revision resulting from the mobilization of ETC, did not materialize. Over twenty-five years, as the landscape has evolved, it has not blended into a new type of urban community. The differences between the two areas by and around Parcel 19 have not diminished; indeed, the differences have increased in starkness, for as one area has improved in appearance and prestige, the other has deteriorated on both fronts.

In the area surrounding Villa Victoria, most of the last remaining working-class families have been replaced by increasingly middle-class and wealthy residents, homeowners whose primary housing concern is increasing the value of their properties. For visitors from the rest of the country unfamiliar with cities in the Northeast, Boston has always seemed "European," probably for its extensive layering of sidewalks in red brick and its well-preserved urban Victorian townhouses. The South End, as the city's, and one of the nation's, largest concentration of Victorian residences, exemplifies this landscape. The newer residents have invested in the upkeep and restoration of their nineteenth-century houses. They have repaired and refurbished their brownstones and three-story brick dwellings; they have patched and painted over the high front stoops, recasting the sense of homes high above the grittiness originally designed to impress the genteel upper-middle class of the nineteenth century; they have reset the low iron gates at the front of the townhouses, replicating missing bars from the original design; they have replaced decaying entrances with grand, carved doors in oak; they have even reconceived the former servants' quarters below the stoops as high quality, at times luxury, ground-level condos. Gardens are a source of pride for many of the new residents, and local neighborhood associations run garden tours where homeowners compare and compete for the most attractive yards. The squares, parks, and avenues throughout the neighborhood have also received continued maintenance. Birds and squirrels have returned to the parks' fountains; rats and mice, at least from some areas, have disappeared. Several of the sidewalks have been reset in handsome red brick and outfitted with elegant lamps, and a few streets have been stripped to expose attractive cobblestones. Many of the streets, reflecting the tastes and incomes of their new crop of owners, are now lined with late-model German and Swedish automobiles and sports utility vehicles. Late evenings in the fall reveal the lasting allure of the South End, as a slight fog settles over the streets and the diffuse light of the low-set lamps betrays a sense of tranquility, discretion, and privilege.

Homeowners in the South End are meticulous, property conscious, and fussy. Houses experience continued refurbishing, and purchasing a house there carries the unspoken—or sometimes quite explicit—responsibility to maintain the historical charm of the neighborhood. The new South End is, in fact, a source of city pride. It is the site of several urban tours. The South End Historical Society runs lectures and events, many with the subtext of the joyful return of the South End to its old, if short-lived, affluent glory. Everything works here. Indeed, to judge from the electronic mailing list servers to which residents subscribe, the most pressing problem in the neighborhood is often not crime or poor plumbing or even the maintenance of property values but finding enough spaces to park. The new South End is highly coveted in the city, making several sections of the neighborhood, including some across the street from Villa Victoria, extremely expensive. The South End weekly newspaper routinely lists two-bedroom condominiums in the neighborhood on sale for more than $500,000. Studio apartments rent for more than $1,000 a month. In the summer of 2000, several condominiums reached the million-dollar mark.

The transformation of the South End is in stark contrast to the Villa of the late 1990s and as recently as the year 2000.[8] Photographs of the Villa from the late 1970s (see Bond 1982) reveal a clean, fresh housing complex with budding greenery and buildings painted in attractive pastels. By the end of the millennium, after twenty-five years of limited budgets and regular wear and tear, the houses and apartment buildings, many of which were in need of paint, no longer radiated the optimism of the dwellings of the past. The small street surrounding the plaza, once layered in attractive cobblestones, was patched in several large spaces with unsightly asphalt and concrete. While some of the modest gardens in front of the houses were attractive and well cared for, many of them were neglected, devoid of greenery, eroding, used for haphazard storage, littered with broken supermarket carts and lawn chairs, or crawling with the mice and rats that seemed to have rediscovered several streets of the neighborhood. It was no accident that dozens of residents owned cats, even taking in strays. The crew cleaning the public spaces around the plaza and park never managed to keep the area litter free for very long. There were times when the neighborhood was relatively tidy, but there were also times when, contrary to the wider South End, there was trash strewn about the parks, plaza, and sidewalks. Much of the greenery was left uncut for weeks at a time and, in any case, was not nearly as carefully manicured as the parks in other sections of the South End. The small, Spanish-influenced iron fences throughout the neighborhood were in need of paint, and many of the spikes were bent out of shape. Every summer for the past few years, IBA mounted a beautification campaign with the aid of residents and volunteers from outside corporations. Between the morning and midafternoon of one day in July, the campaign planted trees and flowers, picked up litter, and painted a few public spaces in the neighborhood. Yet their efforts produced only ephemeral changes in the appearance of the landscape. At times, the differences between some parts of the South End and some parts of the Villa have been, indeed, striking.

8. A massive renovation project was begun in the summer of 2001.

What is striking about the streets bounding Villa Victoria is not merely their fixed nature; it is the way they differentiate areas marked by visibly identifiable class markers. That is, the streets do not just separate different areas of a larger neighborhood—they separate areas that look different, areas whose differences, furthermore are not arbitrary but highly tied to class-specific identifiers: elegant cast-iron gates, carved front doors, manicured flowerbeds, and renovated brownstones versus tipped-over supermarket carts, plastic lawn chairs, moldy wall bases, and aluminum front doors. In this section of the South End, knowing where a person lives means attaching to them a set of physical and spatial markers with which different classes are associated. And since the differences between the two areas have grown over time, it also means assuming that class differences are getting wider, that those residents of each "side of the fence" are increasingly different groups of people. The radical spatialization of class exaggerates the existing differences between the two collectives of individuals, reducing, perceptually, whatever similarities in arenas independent of class—such as an interest in reducing crime, an appreciation for diversity, the desire to reduce traffic or noise—there might have between them.

BUSINESS

This differentiation is both exemplified and exacerbated by the management of businesses and organizations, which, being on either side of the boundary lines, are forced to adopt the class-specific character of their surroundings, but also, adjusting their business practices to a neighborhood ecology, tend to cater their services to one class group or the other. The South End is overrun with tiny shops and boutiques, offering services both commonplace and hard to find, of general interest and esoteric. There are dozens of small grocery stores selling newspapers, drinks, canned food, and pastries along Tremont and Washington Streets, as well as scores of what are often referred to as specialty shops. In one small store, one can purchase an unfinished, plain clay cup, plate, or bowl, decorate and paint it, and have it baked in a kiln overnight. One tiny store, the size of the ground floor of a brownstone, sells beautiful oriental-style carpets; another, luxury real estate in the South End and Back Bay. Real estate and travel agents abound, helping people settle into the neighborhood and, altnernatively, leave town as frequently as possible. A small bookstore specializes in anarchic and feminist literature and radical social thought, offers occasional movie nights, and sponsors small-scale events and public lectures by leftist speakers. One Thai restaurant serves some of the tastiest *pad thai* in Boston, in a richly decorated, cozy location suggesting less a restaurant than a café. Another restaurant offers Brazilian fish in peppers and onions, nectars, flan, and flattened fried green plantains with a sweet carrot dip. Pizza, by the slice or by the pie, is easy to come by. A small café on Tremont, decorated in a fierce modernist style, offers large cups—bowls, really—of coffee or hot chocolate, pastries, sandwiches, and fresh-squeezed juices. There is, now, a Starbucks. There are several video stores to be found, as in most Boston neighborhoods, and several bars attracting either the martini crowd or the few working-class locals. One supermarket offers fresh produce, in addition to its own homemade brand of lemon-ade, root beer, and cream soda. A small eatery serves fried codfish cakes, *alcapurias,* sweet plantains filled with ground beef, Jamaican patties, Puerto Rican *pastelitos,* and other baked and fried goods.

The small stores and restaurants are scattered along the South End's main streets, but they are sorted by class. Small businesses in the middle of the Villa see few middle-class South Enders, making them, by default poor- or Latino-oriented stores. Stores deep in affluent South End "terri-tory" (Suttles 1968, 1972) rarely see Latino patrons. As Villa residents say repeatedly, they would "not feel comfortable" going there. Stores one short city block away from the Villa in three of the four directions from it—dozens of restaurants, cafés, bars, and boutiques—have an almost completely white clientele. Much of the discomfort, related to class differ-ences, would be evident regardless of where the restaurants were located. Restaurants that cater to an affluent clientele dictate norms of dress and behavior that may seem culturally alien to poor Latinos raised in rural Aguadilla or Dorado. Yet even several of the more "democratic" establish-ments (e.g., video or grocery stores) in the heart of the affluent South End see few clients from the Villa. Since its location partly defines a store's class status, it also defines its clientele.

At the same time, business owners and organizations tend to cater to the clientele that surrounds them. The restaurants one block away from the Villa do not offer menus in Spanish; the hair salons do not (for the most part) have Spanish-speaking staff; the Laundromats do not advertise in Spanish; the cafés do not serve *café con leche.* Many of the stores have "rainbow" stickers on their doors signaling that gay and lesbian patrons are welcome, but few, if any, have stickers stating "Se Habla Español" to signal that Spanish-speaking patrons are welcome. Many of these stores' owners have hired decorators specializing either in sparse, modernist designs or in artful, young-urban motifs, both catering to slightly different subgroups of the same educated class, which Brooks (2000) recently labeled "bourgeois bohemians."

Foot traffic matters. The majority of these small establishments, especially those offering specialized services, depend, by and large, on foot traffic, on a large volume of walkers passing by the front of the store who might find an interest in buying their particular product even if they had not planned to do so. Storeowners offering a product likely to be bought by one group would be suicidal to lease a lot within the other group's "territory," since the proportion of foot traffic of potential purchasers would be low. For an entrepreneur planning to sell and rent real estate in luxury condos, opening a store on San Juan Street is economically irrational; for one planning to specialize in pigs' feet, *alcapurias,* and deep-fried codfish cakes, opening on the corner of Dartmouth Street and Columbus Avenue is a waste of time. Storeowners are both responding to the ecology as they see it and contributing to the differentiation of the groups by serving as class-specific markers. Neither process logically precedes the other; they feed each other dialectically as the neighborhood grows and its internal boundaries become increasingly fixed in space.

Particularly instructive are the stores located directly on the boundary line between the Villa and the rest of the South End, especially on the more commercial Tremont Street. A researcher might predict that stores here would cater to diverse, English- and Spanish-speaking, Latino and white clienteles, since, in economically rational terms, the greater the clientele base the better.[9] However, with some notable exceptions, the opposite is true. Businesses located on the boundary between the poor and nonpoor sections of the South End—where their location makes their clientele potentially ambiguous—quickly define themselves as "belonging" to one or the other class group, effectively construing their clientele and implicitly, if unconsciously, excluding those of the opposite class. An illustrative case is one of the several Laundromats located at the edge of the Villa. The Laundromat in question, which is outside of the Villa, is actually closer to many Villa residents' houses than the Villa's Laundromat, which borders the central plaza. A business owner recognizing this situation might, thinking in strict economic terms, advertise both in English and Spanish, thereby appealing to the clientele from both the Villa and the

9. Unless, of course, a business-owner believes catering to both groups would drive one of them away.

nonpoor South End. However, the owner does not. One day a large sign reading "Free Soap" was posted in the Laundromat, which suggests that the owner was probably seeking more business. "Jabón Gratis" could easily have been added to bring in additional clientele but wasn't. (By the same token, residents from the Villa, even those near the business, rarely use that Laundromat. Just as businesses conform to class-bound differentiations, so do individuals.) A similar case is another business located on the boundary line, on Tremont Street. Zapatería el Amanecer, a shoe store, does not also give its name as "Sunrise Shoe Shop," even though doing so would be economically rational, for it might attract English-speaking residents who need shoe repair.[10] When social worlds are constructed and delimited by clear and visible boundaries, businesses, like individuals, conform to them, even if unconsciously (see Suttles 1968).[11] There are notable exceptions to this overwhelming pattern, such as a local store that advertises all its services in English but has Spanish-speaking staff and a company whose masthead, high above the door, is painted in bright blue letters in both English and Spanish.

Businesses are subject to the differentiation of the two areas by responding to the expected foot traffic in their location. Yet they also contribute to that differentiation by characterizing themselves according to their site-specific markers and orienting themselves either to affluent or to low-income and Spanish-speaking or Latin-American clients. The result is resource-segregation by location. The process, however, is exacerbated by a critical factor I have so far not addressed: race.

Race

Gerard Suttles (1968) has called the territorialization of race "ordered segmentation," whereby territorial boundaries marking the turfs of different or antagonistic racial groups both perpetuate the mutual exclusiveness of

---

10. Names, such as Zapatería El Amanecer, and minor details have been changed to protect anonymity. The changes do not affect the conclusions.

11. The word "unconsciously" cannot be emphasized enough. Sometimes, business owners do not want clients from a particular class or racial group. But other times they simply did not think to do anything in particular to bring in the other group. The Laundromat's owner, e.g., does not speak Spanish. Indeed, although his clientele is about 80 percent white, 10 percent black, and 10 percent Latino, he said when he first opened the store, "I expected to have more people of different backgrounds."

the groups and maintain order by minimizing opportunities for contact and, therefore, conflict. Suttles focuses on territorial relations among different ethnic groups; however, his work can also help in contemplating the process of class differentiation and social isolation in the Villa. There are important differences. Whereas the various ethnic groups in Suttles's Addams area were more or less equal groups competing for turf, the two ethnic groups in the South End are sharply unequal—one, among the poorest in the city; the other, among the most affluent. Whereas the Addams' area experienced overt geographic contest over turf, this section of the South End experiences little overt contest, for boundary lines are fixed and well understood. However, as in the Addams area, the spatial delineation of groups serves both to (*a*) perpetuate the notion that they are, indeed, separate groups and (*b*) minimize the opportunity for contact. When applied to the problem of social isolation, a mechanism that minimizes the opportunity for contact is one that increases social isolation.

The ecological and class-related processes described above work hand in hand with racial factors to perpetuate the notion that the residents of the two sections constitute groups and that the groups are separate, internally homogeneous, and mutually exclusive. The provocative fact about class and spatial markers is their ability to function in the absence of any actual persons. On a perfectly deserted Sunday dawn, this section of the South End would still betray its near-geometric spatial segregation of class markers to a careful observer, for tipped-over supermarket carts could only be in one location, and majestic front doors in carved oak, in the other. Ethnic differences, then, materialize and concretize an ecologically embedded process already in place.

Latinos walking on the predominantly white South End (e.g., Rutland Square, Union Park, and West Brookline Street, all one block away) are conspicuous. Anyone would assume, after living in the neighborhood long enough and appropriating its particular unspoken understandings of social relations, that the Latinos are passing through on their way elsewhere (probably the Villa), that they live in some other location and are, therefore, out of place. Similarly, whites on San Juan Street or Aguadilla Street—or anywhere within the Villa's rectangular plane—are conspicuous and thought to be either on their way somewhere else or looking to buy marijuana or heroin (see also Bourgois 1995). Race is an automatic signal. Two of the Villa's border streets, relatively commercial, highly congested streets with heavy rush-hour traffic, are a sort of neutral territory where no ethnic group necessarily dominates.

But race does not just work as a signaling mechanism; it also, of course, brings about prejudice. Within this context, the significance of race is not merely the discrimination faced by residents of the Villa—at different times enraging, humiliating, or simply "unbelievable"—but also its effect on the homogenization of South Enders in the minds of Villa residents. Given this spatially differentiated setting, when emotionally charged or highly contentious patterns of behavior occur with greater frequency among a group on one side of the boundary line, they come to be perceived, in the minds of the other group, as inherent to the first—as endemic characteristics of the entire group. As Villa denizens experience acts of discrimination from whites in the surrounding area, those acts become emblematic of the group, which is then, collectively, met with increased suspicion.

It is not surprising that many Villa residents described incidents of racial discrimination, both overt and subtle, with residents of the wider South End. Once, Laura, dark olive-skinned and in her twenties, was quietly escorting a group of about fifteen children from an after-school program across West Dedham Street during rush hour. Since the children were young, crossing the street to the Villa took a few seconds and traffic was temporarily halted. Finally, a white woman waiting behind the wheel of a waiting car leaned out the window and yelled an ethnic slur at Laura, adding a comment that it was Laura's attitude that kept her stuck in poverty.

One summer, Daniela, a light-skinned woman whose English betrays a heavy Spanish accent, was trying to organize a tour of the South End and the Villa that would involve both residents and voluntary neighborhood organizations from the greater South End. Trying to put into words the covert prejudice she sensed, she explains in a combination of Spanish and English:

> You know how many doors I knocked on? I'm talking about the South End. I went to the neighborhood association, to the "neighborhood associations," the neighborhoods right down there [*she points*]—let me not mention any names. . . . Do you know how many doors I knocked on to get help, to have people even just sit with me? . . .
>
> We had some contributions, but no one wanted to get involved. Why? OK, maybe we were poor. "But we had the willingness to improve our community," at least. . . . When I went to knock on the doors of these [neighborhood] associations, I swear to you it was like a "slap in the face." Like, you now, I'm so puny, I'm too poor, I live in Villa Victoria. So I felt offended. There was a time when I felt—look. [*She sighs loudly.*] Who do these people think they are? [They think that] since they have more money

and live in nicer apartments that we don't have a right to improve ourselves
. . . ? Look . . . let me tell you . . . that was. . . . I felt so, so, so small, because
these are people who have their . . . you know . . . people who don't believe
you are at their level. . . . They look at you, and its either your skin is a
different color or your eyes are a different color or you don't have a purse of
the right brand or shoes of the right brand—well, they look at you over
their shoulders. I felt humiliated. I tell you, I was not doing well.[12]

In this environment, ambiguous interactions of disrespect are easily read
as racially tinged (and often are).[13] Gloria, who was organizing a dinner to
launch her all-girls after-school program, went with a helper to several
restaurants and businesses along Tremont Street to ask for donations. At
one chic restaurant, she remembered feeling particularly conspicuous, as
she and her helper were the two only nonwhite people there. When she
approached the manager and politely asked for donations (of food or
money), "that lady just started *yelling* at us," she remembers. Gloria recalls
with indignation that the manager would not have addressed in the same
tone someone whom she did not consider her inferior, someone, Gloria
thought, who was white.

For a few months, Melissa worked in an office building on the edge of
Chinatown, just east of the South End, so she routinely walked to work.
Her walk took her through the more affluent sections of the South End.
One morning she ran into an attorney for the company as he stepped out
of the brick townhouse where he lived. "Even though I really didn't want
to walk with him," she said, they walked together. To make conversation,
she asked him, "How do you like living in the South End?" He replied,
"It's nice. But it's a little too colorful for me." She recalled: "I was too

12. Phrases uttered in English are demarcated with quotation marks.

13. As many researchers have noted (e.g., Schuman, Steeth, and Bobo 1985), racial discrimination has become increasingly subtle, and many comments or incidents not recognized as dis-
criminatory by outsiders are recognized as such by people who have dealt with them all their
lives. In addition, it is often difficult to verbalize discrimination when the latter manifests itself
in interpersonal gestures and subtle behavioral cues. Consider a parallel from a very different situation: Most young women can tell when a man staring at them is doing so with sexual/mali-
cious intent or not, even in the absence of overt statements or gestures. Yet any such woman
trying to explain that situation to an outside party will likely have a difficult time stating what
specific characteristics of the man's look made it seem sexual or malicious. In all likelihood, her
only recourse (other than stating that it seemed sexual) would be to state that her experience and
intuition made it obvious to her that the man was staring at her in a harassing manner. Similarly,
many residents' statements might be difficult to recognize as racial to someone who was not present in the situation or who has not experienced racial discrimination over an entire lifetime.
And, in truth, no one but the perpetrator will ever truly know. More often than not, however,
the residents' life experience with discrimination (as any woman's life experience with harassment) makes them the best judges (other than the "offender") of what took place.

young to really process [right away] what he said. It wasn't until I reached the office that I thought [wait a minute]!" She wondered whether she—a brown-skinned Puerto Rican—was supposed to contribute to the neighborhood's undesirable "colorfulness." Whatever the intent of the other party, the residents' interpretations of negative interactions as racially tinged affect their interactions with the wider environment.

These experiences, localized as they are in the South End, are retold within the Villa community and serve to reinforce the notion of the surrounding South End as alien and, to an extent, hostile, encouraging the community's enclosure within its protective boundaries. Such experiences serve, that is, as one mechanism to sustain the symbolic boundaries through which Villa residents differentiate themselves from South Enders. That not all white South Enders are racist is well known to residents but is, in this particular respect, sociologically irrelevant. The spatial and racial characteristics of the area do not just operate by differentiating the poor from the nonpoor. They also function by substantiating the notion that these are internally coherent and homogeneous groups, that singular experiences with individuals are representative of the whole. In this sense, race bears a curious parallel to another highly contentious issue: crime.

Crime

In the current literature on neighborhood effects, the question of crime is usually discussed within the context of social organization theory (Shaw and McKay 1942, 1969; Sampson 1999), whereby neighborhoods high in social capital are expected to be capable of reducing the incidence of crime by maintaining social control. This particular conception of the relationship between crime and social capital is addressed in the following chapter. The interest in the present discussion is how crime, when localized in the spatial context discussed here, contributes to the homogenization of groups. In this sense, crime is a sort of behavioral marker, one that, when attached to a location in a highly differentiated setting, becomes attached to the collectivity associated with that location.

Villa Victoria has a notorious reputation locally as a crime-ridden neighborhood (see Lukas 1985; e.g., also Brand 1987). For years, O'Day Park, on the West Newton side of the Villa, was known as the center of the local heroin trade (Lukas 1985, 424 ff., 624 ff.). The early nineties witnessed a vicious feud between a gang of teenagers in the Villa and another gang at a nearby housing project, which brought violence to the neigh-

borhood, especially to the park, where several adolescents died or were seriously wounded as a result of drive-by shootings (see e.g., Manly 1992).
Young people frequently smoke marijuana in and around the park, and in
the evenings, the park becomes deserted except for the occasional group of
young men and for the still-active trade in marijuana, cocaine, and heroin.

O'Day Park is often perceived in the wider South End as emblematic of
Villa Victoria; since it is within the bounds of Villa Victoria, O'Day Park
"belongs" to the complex and, therefore, is conceived of as representative
of the entire neighborhood: if O'Day Park is dangerous, so, in outsiders'
minds, is the Villa. Speaking in Spanish, one Villa resident shows her per-
ceptiveness about this fact: "There are lots of people around here who do
a lot of mischief [*que son tremendos*], who don't set a good example. And
often that affects all of us in general because people look at us through the
same lens [*con los mismos ojos*] that they use to look at these people. If a person is selling drugs down there, well, they see us the same way." She ties
this perception directly to South Enders' reluctance to enter the neighborhood: "That's what I've wanted to change, that image. And maybe changing that image I could get people who walk around Washington [Street, a
block away from the Villa] but who could walk through the neighborhood—who walk down there so they don't have to walk through Villa
Victoria—maybe I could get those people to stroll through the streets of
Villa Victoria and [its] sidewalks." Though crime has dropped markedly
in the Villa over the past eight years, the perception, as this resident cor-
rectly notes, remains.

In many predominantly white circles, the Villa is known as a "bad" area
or a ghetto (Brand 1987, 183). Indeed, a local publication recently called
Villa Victoria "the South End's drug store." One afternoon, during one of
my first visits ever to the neighborhood, I rode in a van into the neighborhood with about a dozen students from a local university who were there
to run an after-school program for elementary school children at the
Blackstone School, across the street from the Villa. The children were
picked up at "the Blackstone" and walked a few blocks along the edge of
Villa to another school, where the program was run. Even though the program took place in the middle of the afternoon, in broad daylight, in one
of the busiest streets in the area, the college students only walked around
in pairs, fearing that if they walked alone in the Villa, even if merely between the place were the van was parked and the Blackstone, they might
be assaulted. About ten years ago, a professor at a local college purchased a
house on a street just off Tremont, near to but on the opposite side of Villa
Victoria. After the closing, the professor recalls, the real estate agent

pointed in the direction opposite the Villa and said, "By the way, when you go for a walk around the neighborhood, walk *that* way." In his book *Common Ground*, journalist Anthony Lukas (1985, 628) describes what went through the mind, years ago, of Colin Diver, a white South End resident, who was chasing a thief from his house on West Newton Street into Tremont Street in the direction of Villa Victoria: "Colin hesitated for a moment. Tremont was a significant boundary to his world, the southern border of the gentrified South End. Beyond it stretched a row of tenements, occupied principally by Puerto Ricans, Dominicans, and Cubans. The O'Day Playground halfway down the block was the center of the South End's heroin trade, a dangerous place at any time of the day or night." Although he had lived just across Villa Victoria for months, Colin rarely, if ever, crossed Tremont.

The belief that O'Day Park is "a dangerous place at any time of the day or night" may have come from either Colin or Lukas, but it captures, in either case, a widely shared if inaccurate sentiment. The Villa, in the imagination of much of the surrounding South End, is a crime-ridden neighborhood, and its residents, by extension, are potential criminals. That not every Villa resident has committed a crime is well known to South Enders, but, as with racism from the perspective of Villa residents about white South Enders, sociologically irrelevant. That a preponderance of highly publicized crimes have occurred on the opposite side of the boundary contributes to the homogenization of the individuals making up the neighborhood; criminal acts become a behavioral marker of the collective, and all associated individuals become suspects.

Many South End residents living on cross streets between Tremont Street and Columbus Avenue see Tremont as a natural border not to be traversed. When advertising for events that take place in public areas, such as South End's Sparrow Park, which hosts outdoor jazz in the summers, middle-class volunteers stick leaflets in the windshield-wipers of cars parked throughout the South End, yet the leaflets rarely seem to make it past Tremont, into the Villa. Ulysses, a young, educated white resident of Rutland Square, just off Tremont Street, never crosses Tremont when he walks his dog. He says, "I pretty much walk by here [Rutland Square], down Tremont, down one of the [side] streets [parallel to Rutland, away from the Villa] then back on Columbus and back here." In fact, as recently as ten years ago, Villa resident Gloria recalls, "you wouldn't see white people on Tremont Street" (at the time there were also a few more Latino-owned properties on the non-Villa side of the street). Ian, a white, bespectacled attorney, and a South Ender of several decades, loves his neighborhood. "You can find everything here," he explains. But he has reservations about the Villa. First, he does not like the way it looks: "[Villa Victoria] looks suburban. . . . Like it belongs in Acton or something." About its residents, he says: "It's a huge concentration of people who can't [afford to] live anywhere else." For him, the high concentration of poor people living in the Villa makes it more difficult for him to live in the neighborhood. "Everybody [in the South End] feels comfortable [about it] because there's enough of everyone else [i.e., nonpoor people]. . . . But it's very isolated." Thus, although he proudly explains he knows almost all of the neighbors on his West Brookline block at least by face, he never ventures into the Villa, just across the street from his block.

Neither group, therefore, crosses territories unless they have to. As one resident put it, "you can feel the tension. There's a great tension between both communities."

At times, minor events elucidate unspoken understandings of the relationship among race, class, and place in a community. This is particularly true with respect to the presence of whites in the Villa, a situation that, since I am not white, I had only observed but had never experienced. Once I had the rare experience of being treated as a white person might in the Villa, a microinteraction that took me by slight surprise.

In the spring of 2000, I was visited by an old college friend who would be in town for the weekend. She had never been to Boston before, so she wanted to experience its nightlife. We went to a few bars in downtown Boston. On the way back, after having a difficult time finding a cab, we walked back to the South End via Tremont Street. The night was crisp, clear, and just under seventy degrees. As we neared the far edge of the Villa, she asked whether this was the neighborhood I had been studying. I said it was and offered to show her the plaza, an indicator of how this housing project, though not without its problems, looked nothing like the typical high rises of Chicago and New York. The time was three a.m. The streets were deserted, eerily calm. Uncharacteristically (for being in the neighborhood), I wore a pair of gray wool slacks, a fitted black dress shirt, an elegant wristwatch, lace-ups; my friend, a Midwesterner of Norwegian descent, wore dark club gear. My friend stopped by a plaque affixed to a column at the edge of the plaza, a marker awarded by the Bostonian Society designating the neighborhood as a historic location. As she was reading it, about six young men, possibly teenagers, whom I did not recognize in the darkness, sat on bicycles at the far edge of the plaza. Within seconds, one of the young men approached me and nodded,

"Whassup?" I nodded back, "Whatup," still not recognizing him. He raised his hand as if to shake mine, and I complied. In his hand, I felt a small bag of marijuana held against the palm by his pinky and ring fingers. I did not expect it; in fact, I was surprised. We shook for a few seconds, but I did not take the bag. He took it back, angered, and returned across the plaza to the group.

I was surprised at my surprise. After more than a year doing research in Villa Victoria, I had never been in the Villa with a white person, much less while I was wearing slacks and a dress shirt. As I well knew, on a regular day, white people only walked into the Villa when they were heading somewhere else; at that time of night, they only did so when they were buying marijuana. There could be no other realistic interpretation of what we were doing there at that time because the constellation of social interactions that had been built over time in that space dictated it. One of us was white; though neither of us is affluent, we were wearing the attire of the northeast urban middle-class, attire peppered with class markers; we were on the "wrong" side of the boundary line, not just beyond Tremont, but in the plaza itself, the neighborhood's most private public space. Anyone not anticipating or expecting that drug-related interaction would have been either highly naive or a newcomer. In a strange way, the experience concretized what I had observed for months; being dark-skinned, I could not experience first hand the collection of attributes I knew to be associated with whites assumed to live in the South End. Late at night, looking as I normally look and walking by myself (as I often was), the young men, if they did not recognize me, might have wondered what I was doing there, but their first assumption may well not have been, "buying weed." And the drug dealers I knew would have known I never buy any marijuana. The fact that my friend and I were not intoxicated did not matter: the man who approached me must have thought we had to be drunk for a white woman to be walking around there just to take in the evening breeze. After a few minutes, we left, my out-of-town friend still pondering the significance of the plaque on One Paseo Borinken.

How to Create an Isolated Neighborhood

The particular type of social isolation Villa residents experience—isolation from surrounding middle-class neighbors in the secondary neighborhood (the South End)—results partly from the ecological, class, and racial characteristics of the neighborhood, which differentiate poor from nonpoor and homogenize each group in the minds of those not in it. If, based on the Villa, one could imagine willingly creating a neighborhood such that the poor and nonpoor did not interact, one would do the following.

(1) Ensure that the boundaries between the residences of the poor and those of the nonpoor are not fluid but fixed, as shown in figure 4 (*bottom*), with such markers as streets, train tracks, or hills, and likely to remain fixed in the foreseeable future. (2) Make certain that the landscape on either side of the boundary line is different enough from that on the other side so that identifying it is as simple as knowing the characteristics of the houses, streets, apartment buildings, sidewalks, parks, cars, front gates, and so on—as well as the characteristics of businesses, organizations, and service providers. (3) Ensure that these differences are not arbitrary but tied to specific class markers, such as ornate gas streetlamps, elaborate front doors, makes of cars, water fountains, leaking roofs, broken windows, garbage piles, and so on. (4) Make sure that a visible proportion of residents on each side of the line is of a particular racial background that is scarce on the other side. (5) Ascertain that a highly contentious set of practices, such as dealing drugs, engaging in violent crime, or discriminating on the basis of race, occurs predominantly on one side, even if it is only by a minuscule portion of residents or in a small, easily identifiable section of that side. The result is an isolated neighborhood.

In the Villa, the passage of time has cemented these processes by increasing the differentiation between the two areas and adding experience upon experience, either racial or crime-related, to the collective understanding and cultural memory of residents on each side of the line. Spatial configurations, and the passage of time, affect significantly the relationship between the Villa's neighborhood poverty and social isolation. The following chapter addresses social capital—specifically, again, the question of isolation—from a wider perspective.

SIX

Social Capital and the Spatialization of Resources

You know . . . everything is around me. I don't have to leave my community very far to be able to get something. — OSCAR

The Rest of the Middle Class

In chapter 5 I demonstrated why the Villa's residents, though surrounded by a rich pool of middle-class people, still maintained little or no contact with that society, behaving in ways we might anticipate from a community miles removed from the nearest middle-class household, not mere steps away from hundreds of politically liberal intellectuals, artists, and professionals. Nevertheless, not all poor neighborhoods are surrounded by middle-class residents. Nor is my interest in the external social ties of the poor limited to those individuals who happen to live in the immediate physical surroundings of poor neighborhoods. I seek to understand their connections to the mainstream at large, with any middle-class network that may provide role models and information about resources for upward mobility (Fischer 1982; Wilson 1987, 1996; Fernandez and Harris 1992; Rankin and Quane 2000). One of the most perplexing questions is precisely what it is about poor neighborhoods that limits the residents' interactions with the middle class. Here, the original hypothesis bears repeating: the poverty of the neighborhood, independent of the individual's poverty, results in this disconnection from the mainstream.

The relationship is by no means obvious. Many social scientists conduct their work as if neighborhood poverty automatically implied isolation from the middle class; some even measure a neighborhood's "isolation" by its concentration of poverty. This hardly seems sensible, unless we are prepared to assume that the poor spend all of their time in their own neighborhoods.

We know they do not, for at least one easily discernible reason. As New-man (1999) reminds us, many residents of poor neighborhoods work, and few of those who do so work in their own poor neighborhood. In the Villa, only a minuscule portion of all employed adults work within the twenty acres that make up the neighborhood. The rest work elsewhere, including locations where they come into contact with middle-class people. Do they not make acquaintances there? If not, why should the poverty of the Villa affect the possibility of those acquaintances? What is the appropriate way to think about this relationship? How work affects social capital develop-ment will occupy much of chapter 7, where, by means of case studies, I disentangle some of the conditions under which these relationships man-ifest themselves (or not) as expected. The current chapter addresses an equally important realm.

Social life is not limited to work and home; we do much more than la-bor and sleep. We clip our hair, paint our nails, pray, eat out, dance and drink, wash and dry laundry, drop off mail and pick up stamps, cash pay-checks, buy the local paper, purchase groceries, and shop for clothing, shoes, makeup, tampons, tools, music CDs, and school supplies for chil-dren. More than work and rest, contemporary social life involves an addi-tional, heterogeneous realm comprising all those mundane activities without which we simply do not function. Complex theories about the poor have examined where they live (Wilson 1987) and where they work (Kain 1992), but few have examined where they conduct this third realm of everyday life; even fewer have studied its relationship to neighborhood poverty (but see Brooks-Gunn, Duncan, and Aber 1997a; Pattillo-McCoy 1999). To the student of social capital, this realm is indispensable. Where do residents of poor neighborhoods—where do the Villa's residents—conduct the multiple affairs persons do simply to go on living? Do they do so in their own poor neighborhood? Does neighborhood poverty in some fashion reduce these opportunities to interact with other social classes?

One of the effects of how fieldwork has been approached in social sci-ence about poor neighborhoods may be that we have studied them as pe-culiarly sociological but nonsocial worlds where the urban poor do every-thing except the ordinary things ordinary people do. They dodge bullets, one would think, but they do not visit the barbershop; they negotiate complex interactions with violent thugs and harassing cops, but they never patronize the post office. Rarely do sociological treatises suggest that the urban poor live in any way other than under a permanent cloud of vi-olence, fear, distrust, or alienation, that they also manage to live a quotid-ian existence, to conduct the unspectacular affairs of everyday life without which few in modern society could function. These ordinary elements of social behavior represent one of the richest sources for capturing the relationship between neighborhood poverty and the generation of social capital, for social ties often result not from planned or controlled compacts or exchanges but from random and informal interactions (Jacobs 1961). The Villa's case makes clear that the relationship between neighborhood poverty and cross-class networks depends—once the realm of work is accounted for—on the location of the resources the poor need to conduct their day-to-day lives.

This chapter suggests that the relationship among neighborhood poverty, resources, and social capital in Villa Victoria is governed by two paradoxes—or, more accurately, this chapter analyzes two relationships that appear paradoxical based on how we typically picture poor neighborhoods and how we generally believe their problems should be solved. The first of these is the relationship between neighborhood poverty and the prevalence of resources; the second, between the prevalence of resources and social isolation.

In his vivid depictions of the transformations taking place in Chicago, Wilson (1987) presented a neighborhood in which the departure of the middle classes had deprived the neighborhood of critical institutions and businesses. These resources, such as functioning churches, supermarkets, schools, and community centers, had helped sustain the viability of these mixed-income communities in the past. In much of the subsequent research, the relationship between high poverty and resource deprivation has been taken for granted rather than tested empirically. This was aggravated by the scarcity of large-sample data on the prevalence of such resources in neighborhoods. Many researchers simply assumed, implicitly, that most poor neighborhoods resembled Wilson's Chicago ghettos, that they were resource-deprived, desolate areas where concentrated poverty had eradicated all signs of organized life (e.g., Brooks-Gunn, Duncan, and Aber 1997a, 1997b). The case of Villa Victoria questions the wisdom of this approach. The Villa, we shall see, is a high-poverty, high-resource neighborhood, a relationship that is far from being an artifact of chance.

Furthermore, this very prevalence of resources has the paradoxical effect of limiting the opportunities of Villa residents to interact with the middle class. When we consider the plight of poor neighborhoods, most of us assume that improvements in one dimension will generate, or at least not retard, improvements in all other dimensions, such that more resources may well result in more cross-class contacts and certainly not fewer of them. The case of the Villa also questions this assumption. As we shall see, at least with respect to certain resources, the positive attribute of greater resources contributed to the negative outcome of social isolation.

I will define a resource, broadly, as any business, government agency, nonprofit organization, or public space that serves a resident's need. I ask how the prevalence of resources manifests itself. What do these resources look like? And how do they affect whether residents generate and sustain social ties with people outside of Villa Victoria?

Resources in Villa Victoria

In the 1970s, when ETC and its architects conceived of the neighborhood, one of the their guiding principles—a notion prevalent among the grassroots and political activists of the time—was self-reliance. As we saw, residents of Parcel 19 had asked for "stores in or close to the area: grocery and meat market, delicatessen, laundrymat, hardware stores" (NU, box 3). Having wide-ranging freedom to decide the spatial makeup of the new housing project, the group allocated lots for small businesses and organizations that would provide services for the local community. (It did not hurt that several of these lots were already zoned as commercial.) Most of these lots were located along a small commercial stretch bordering the plaza. By the spring of 2001, the few lots in and around Villa Victoria had been filled. At the time, the Villa impressed me as being especially rich in resources. This is what I saw.[1]

At the far end of the stretch was the South End Credit Union (SECU), established to help residents secure loans, repair credit histories, and cash checks without resorting to expensive check-cashing operations. One imagines several of the early professionals involved in the birth of the Villa conceiving of the SECU as part of the general plan by which residents would presumably live in the Villa temporarily, all the while setting money aside until they could afford a place of their own. In hindsight, the notion that poor residents, whether unemployed or not, could save money while paying 25–30 percent of their wages every month to the housing office seems hopelessly idealistic. Residents used the SECU sporadically. It maintained irregular hours, was often closed for what appeared to be days at a time, and suffered repeated reprimands from residents for often being out of cash.

---

1. There have been changes since then. The Villa, and the rest of the South End, is in continuous flux. Several of these changes are described in the epilogue.

Next door was the Batey Technology Center, an innovative nonprofit program funded generously by a large technology company. It housed two dozen state-of-the-art desktops with word processors, spreadsheets, high-speed Web access, and more.[2] "The Batey," as it was called, offered free and bilingual courses in introductory computing, word processing, spreadsheet management, and more advanced topics such as HTML programming and networking.

A next-door office once served as headquarters for ETC's neighborhood meetings in the late sixties and early seventies. It was now the security office, staffed by guards hired by the management office to oversee the Villa. There were maybe three or four guards on staff at any time, though I hardly saw them. Over the late nineties and into the early part of the new millennium, several companies that had been hired to provide security were replaced, as residents complained of one or another mishap or infelicity: that the guards were improperly trained, too old to chase drug dealers, scared, unable or unwilling to enforce drug laws, or too flirtatious with the neighborhoods' young women. Eventually, ETC settled on a competent company.

Next to the security office was a small, privately owned Laundromat with several large washers and driers, a particularly important resource since most apartments did not have their own. Next to the Laundromat was the twenty-five-year-old Escuelita Borinken. The first time I visited this child-care center, I saw scores of children, mostly Latino and African-American. Their names were written on the floor, in circles, to note their position during specific activities. Large plastic cushions in bright colors were stacked against a wall; these were laid across the floor for naptime. The director boasted the progressiveness of the children's curriculum, which dictated personalized learning geared, in part, to the child's strengths, and offered English speakers the opportunity to learn Spanish and vice versa, which seemed to please many of the parents. Some parents were unable to teach their children English; others, second- and third-generation Puerto Rican migrants as well as African-Americans, wanted their children to learn Spanish. During meals, children were sometimes served rice and beans and plantains, while at other times they ate macaroni and cheese and broccoli. The school had room for fifty-three children, with thirty-four of these slots subsidized by the Office of Child Care Ser-

2. Even though the so-called digital divide persists, Internet access is no longer as inaccessible among poor neighborhoods as it used to be (see, e.g. Famuliner 1999). Several of Boston's poorest neighborhoods have received computer donations (as the Villa has) from large computer technology companies.

vices and about eighteen of them taken, at any given time, by mothers on Temporary Assistance for Needy Families (TANF). All of the center's children either lived in the Villa or were associated with someone who did.

Across the street from the plaza, below a row of Villa apartments, was a small, Latino-owned grocery store. The store offered a wide array of Latin American canned or bottled or boxed foods (mostly produced by Goya Foods), soft drinks of all kinds, fresh coffee, and cheese Danishes. The market also sold an extremely wide array of lottery tickets, ranging from the scratch-and-win variety through the multimillion dollar state jackpots. Nearby was a local post office, and next to the post office, a Brazilian restaurant capable of attracting a large, non-Latino clientele, one of the few establishments on one side of the "boundary line" able to attract clients from the other. Further down the street, the Blackstone Elementary School, one of the city's major bilingual institutions, served many of the Villa's grade-school children.

The few establishments in the small plaza and adjacent to it attracted a great deal of foot traffic. Their walls and columns were often covered with posters by service-providers and companies or individuals offering services. Once, for instance, several posters on the columns read "Bethel Food Pantry—Today." The pantry was offering free food to whoever could provide proof of living in the 02118 zip code and of being under public assistance. Another time, taped to the window outside of the technology center, a poster contained a letter by the Boston Police Department advertising openings for traffic supervisors (people to direct traffic in front of schools during rush hour) and 911 operators. According to the letter, whereas in years past the waiting list for these positions was in the "hundreds," the department was now "struggling" to fill the positions. This was late 1999. The letter also reminded the reader, in a separate sentence highlighted in bold letters, that all applicants would be screened for a criminal record and drug use.

On the opposite side of Villa Victoria, next to O'Day Park, was the Jorge Hernández Cultural Center, a cultural performance center converted from an old church. The church was named after a former director of IBA, a much beloved Harvard graduate who had managed to secure the church for IBA shortly before his death. High on the church's facade was a mural of two large, cupped, open hands supporting the faces of the Villa's pioneers and former community members and several emblems of the struggle to create Villa Victoria. The church once boasted stunning stained glass windows, some of which were still intact. After several rehabilitation projects, during which volunteers and community leaders repainted and refurbished much of the inside of the church, it captured much of what one assumes was its original beauty. A parish house attached to the center was boarded up with plywood, soot-ridden, and seeming generally abandoned. A few years earlier, someone had painted colorful flowers and plants on the planks of plywood covering the parish house's windows, giving the scenery a somewhat incongruous but welcome appearance next to the aged somberness of the church.

Sprinkled throughout the neighborhood were small stores and organizations offering various other services. One establishment sold beepers and cellular phones; another was a hair salon. One tiny eatery—with four tables for two or three and a minuscule counter section flat against a wall with three stools—was very popular. A television at the far corner was constantly on. No alcohol was served. A young woman of Dominican descent took orders from behind the counter, on which sat a glass-and-aluminum heater displaying roasted pork ribs, fried codfish cakes (*bacalaito*), Puerto Rican *pastelitos,* and Jamaican beef patties, baked sweet plantains, deep fried stuffed potato dough (*papas rellenas*), and chicken in tomato sauce. One could order Cuban sandwiches, rice dishes, stewed beef, fried green plantains (*tostones*), *maltas,* juices, and fruit shakes.

An Episcopal church, housed in an unassuming brick building at the edge of the neighborhood, still held community service meetings and the mass in Spanish. The church's pastors had been involved with the community for years, from the time they helped organize against the residents' relocation from Parcel 19. Several of ETC's early organizing meetings were held in its basement. The parish was tiny, but several residents, including Catholics, attended out of habit or loyalty. Another even more unassuming brick building in the Villa was a nondenominational "community church." Two blocks away was a large cathedral, a stunning edifice with stained glass dating to the nineteenth century. This church was also active in the South End community; for its volunteers, it produced a regular publication, "Making A Difference: A newsletter about the Donors, Recipients, Volunteers and Staff Who Are Making a Difference in the Archdiocese of Boston." It hosted a local Catholic school, which some of the Villa's residents attended, and held mass in English and in Spanish. Across the street from the cathedral was the Cardinal Cushing Resource Center, which sold second-hand clothing, textiles, lamps, and old appliances, canned food, rice, and pastries wrapped in plastic.

Directly across from the IBA offices was, during my first year of research, the South End Community Health Center (SECHC). It was a large concrete structure, resembling more a warehouse with windows than a health center. Immediately in front of the door was a long black stairwell leading to the second floor, where three receptionists sat. Directly behind them were long rows of files neatly organized. The second floor was clean and well kept, the staff, efficient, professional, and organized. A bilingual information booklet, *South End Community Health Center,* contained photographs of nurses and doctors tending to patients, most of whom were children, and almost all of the people photographed were African-American or Latino. The first page, under the heading "Philosophy," had the following passage: "High Quality health care is the right of all people, regardless of ability to pay. High quality health care is comprehensive, preventive and accessible." The SECHC was affiliated with many of the major hospitals in Boston. According to the publication, the health center "was established in 1969 by a community health committee [that was concerned] about the lack of preventive and sensitive medical care for Spanish-speaking and black residents of the South End." The center provided physical and mental health services; it also ran a WIC program, health education, and dental services. The dental clinic, across the street, offered all basic procedures; if a patient required specialized treatment, he or she was referred to the Boston University Dental Clinic. Next door to the SECHC was another community center. That center ran a summer program, sometimes in cooperation with IBA, and it boasted a swimming pool and outdoor basketball courts.

Within the Villa or directly on its geographic borders, there are at least four bodegas, two small Latino-owned restaurants, two pharmacies, three small churches, a public garden, a basketball court, a swimming pool, a park, a Latino-owned moving business, a bilingual elementary school, a day-care center, a hair salon, the community health center, the dental center, a technology center, and a credit union—all of which provide services in Spanish. In addition, another community center, another park, and the neighborhood library are only one block away; a supermarket is two blocks away; and the Boston Medical Center, as well as several more churches, are three blocks away. This list, furthermore, excludes the dozens of restaurants, cafés, and boutiques within blocks of the South End, which Villa residents rarely patronize. The Villa, though poor, is by no means poor in resources.

The Villa's high-poverty, high-resource status is neither odd nor illogical. In fact, though the Villa's density of resources is unique given its small size, its abundance of resources is by no means extraordinary for a Boston neighborhood. Boston is a service-rich city with a wide and healthy base of nonprofit organizations, volunteer-dependent associations, and community-service providers, sustained partly by a liberal political culture and by a preponderance of college and university students. In Boston, services catering to the poor tend to cluster around poor neighborhoods, for this is where those services are needed most. Poor neighborhoods such as the Villa in the South End, Hyde and Jackson Squares in Jamaica Plain, and Dudley Square in Roxbury all contain more resources targeted at low-income people than do affluent neighborhoods such as Harvard Square, Beacon Hill, and the Back Bay, or even middle-class neighborhoods such as the Fenway and Porter Square. By the same token, specialized businesses, in this case bodegas and other services aimed at Latinos, abound in locations where demand is high: Villa Victoria; Hyde and Jackson Squares, which have a high concentration of Dominicans and some Puerto Ricans; and East Boston, which has a high concentration of Central Americans.

Betraying the scarcity of ethnographic studies on this particular issue, Wilson's depiction of resource deprivation in high-poverty Chicago neighborhoods is often taken as indicative not merely of Chicago but of all poor neighborhoods (e.g., Brooks-Gunn, Duncan, and Aber 1997a, 1997b). Though in theory it might seem reasonable that poor neighborhoods will also be poor in resources, in practice, on careful observation, it becomes clear that the opposite is just as plausible (see also Schwirian 1983, 90–91). In cities with a preponderance of such services, the services will probably target the poor. The differences between the Villa and Wilson's neighborhood force us to question the automatic link between neighborhood poverty and resource deprivation.

How Resources Affect Social Capital

The second, and perhaps more central, issue at hand is how this prevalence of resources affects the capacity of residents to generate middle-class ties. Paradoxically, this prevalence of resources, by multiplying the services residents can obtain with little mobility, increases the likelihood that their social worlds will be limited to the few blocks in and around the Villa. That is, this resource prevalence increases "bonding" or within-class social capital and decreases "bridging" or between-class social capital (Granovetter 1973; Putnam 2000).

The creation of social ties of any type depends on what Huckfeldt (1983) has called "associational opportunities." The appeal of Huckfeldt's term derives from the issues to which it directs our focus: rather than asking who will have what type of network, it asks who will have the opportunities to generate what type of network. Studying whether an individual makes friends of a particular type is difficult (though not impossible) to carry out sociologically, for it depends on nonsocial attributes such as the individual's gregariousness, agency, self-confidence, and extroversion. Studying whether an individual will have the opportunity to make friends of a particular type is more amenable to an analysis focused on neighborhood-level attributes and ecological or spatial conditions.

After the poor's place of rest and place of employment, their associational opportunities will depend on where they conduct most of the day-to-day business necessary (or helpful) for survival—shopping for groceries, washing laundry, dropping off the children at school. In the Villa, the Laundromat served as an ideal place for random interactions with neighbors, conversations about the weather, children, drugs and crime, IBA, and the neighborhood, since washing and drying even one load required up to an hour and a half of idle time. A local beauty salon served the same function for similar reasons. The park and plaza were specifically designed for leisure time. The child-care center, swimming pool, community center, local school, and churches were designed for other functions but allowed ample time for parents (and the young) to mingle. Grocery stores, pharmacies, check-cashing shops, the post office, and other places where residents wait in long lines allowed comparatively fewer chances for generating new relationships but ample opportunity to sustain existing ones, as residents ran into friends and acquaintances.

That such activities could be conducted within steps of the house meant that local networks were strengthened. But residents' chances of meeting persons of other classes were also dramatically diminished. This relationship is particularly strong because many of the services the community needs, Latin-American cultural products and services for the Spanish speaking, are specialized. A Villa resident needing Latino groceries such as *malta,* pigeon peas, plantains, and pork fat; a day-care center with Spanish-speaking instructors; a bilingual elementary school; a bank with Spanish-speaking staff; prescription drugs from Spanish-speaking pharmacists; dental or basic health service from Spanish-speaking doctors; religious services (Catholic or Protestant) in Spanish; a restaurant serving Latino foods; a copy of local Spanish weeklies; free bilingual computer instruction; ESL classes; or live Latin entertainment need not leave the few blocks composing Villa Victoria. All of these services are offered within that small, twenty-acre area. In fact, the overwhelming majority of these services are not offered in the surrounding South End, and, beyond that, are offered only in certain neighborhoods in Boston.

Oscar, a young and somewhat restless man who has developed a fondness for Villa Victoria, is particularly pleased with the availability of resources in the neighborhood, despite the fact it may limit his opportunities to interact with residents of other neighborhoods. As he explains,

> I have a corner store right there. I have a day-care center in case I have a child. I have a credit union if I wanted a little bank. I have a post office right there. I have little restaurants all around. I have a security force here. I have my home. . . . I have an elementary school right down the street from me, I have a community center which has a pool. I have everything around me. I have a church that's right around the street if I wanna go to church. You know, like, everything is around me. I don't have to leave my community very far to be able to get something.

Residents needing these specialized services, especially residents pressed for time, are likely to seek them—and, in the case of rare goods and services, are forced to seek them—right in Villa Victoria, reducing their need to spend time in other sections of the city and their opportunities to interact with residents from middle-class neighborhoods. Busy individuals are unlikely to travel long distances to obtain services they can obtain near home.

A high-resource neighborhood, therefore, makes quite convenient what turns out to be social isolation. In a classic article, Breton (1964) reported a similar pattern not within neighborhoods but within ethnic groups; he has found that a group's "institutional completeness"—the number of resources the ethnic group can provide—increases the proportion of within-group ties, decreasing the proportion of ties with members of other ethnic or racial groups. The Villa represents the spatialization of institutional completeness. As resources rise, so will internal social capital, and so will social isolation.[3]

Notes on the Use of Noncritical Resources

All other factors held constant, the greater the number of resources we add to poor neighborhoods such as Villa Victoria, the more likely residents will be to remain within its bounds, duly affecting their possibility to in-

3. It is important to note that this discussion of resource availability differs in one important respect from Wilson's social isolation thesis. A number of the institutions described in this chapter (such as the South End Health Clinic) are run by people who do not live in the Villa. When individuals interact with people at these institutions, Wilson would argue, and I would agree, they are having contact with the middle class.

teract with the middle class. This point is critical, for it questions our common expectation that "all good things go together." Indeed, what is considered an improvement in one dimension may well harm progress in a different dimension.

Nonetheless, this proposition depends on all other factors being constant, and in social life they are not. In the next chapter I discuss the importance of individual biography and individual contextual effects in mediating whether and how higher resources—and neighborhood poverty in general—constrain external social capital. But several contextual effects depend on the characteristics not of individuals but of the neighborhoods themselves. Neighborhood-level attributes may affect whether the straightforward postulate presented above manifests itself in actuality. Furthermore, residents' use of resources will be highly conditional on how they perceive both the resources and the neighborhood—that is, on the interaction between neighborhood-level characteristics and individual-level perceptions.

To address these conditional factors, it is useful to distinguish between critical and noncritical resources. The former refer to those resources serving sustenance needs, such as grocery stores and health-care centers, as well as post offices and elementary schools—those services that individuals would have to obtain one way or another in order to go on with their lives. Noncritical resources are those serving nonessential ends, such as recreation; these resources would include parks, plazas, recreation or community centers, swimming pools, and the like. The positive relationship described above between resource availability and social isolation refers, I suggest, to critical resources. Residents are unlikely to travel far distances to obtain services they can obtain—in equal or better quality at an equal or lower cost—near home. For example, the mother of a three-year-old in the Villa will only seek a child-care center other than the Escuelita if there are no open slots or she is dissatisfied with the center's cost or quality. Thus, the use of critical resources can be modeled largely based on an assumption of rationality.

The use of noncritical resources, however, cannot be modeled so easily on that assumption. Since residents can live content and productive lives independent of their use of noncritical resources, such use will depend on the effects of intermediary circumstances. Consider one noncritical resource, the Batey Technology Center, which struggled in its early months. The center's machines were cutting-edge and residents had free and open access to them during most of the day and part of the evening. But during the bulk of my research period, most residents did not patronize the Batey.

In addition, there was a clear stratification of users. Most users were children and teenagers, and, indeed, the heaviest usage time was shortly after classes ended for the day, sometimes as part of an after-school program hosted by IBA in conjunction with other agencies. Most adults were simply uninterested in the center, and those who were interested only used it sporadically. Naturally, part of the issue was their lack of familiarity with technology. I taught a few courses on introductory and intermediate computing for adults, classes I ran in both English and Spanish. Most of my students did not know how to type, how to turn on the machines, what a mouse did, or what e-mail or the Internet were. Yet my students appeared to prefer not being there when adolescents and children were in the center in large numbers. In addition, during its first year or two, residents did not know when the center was open or exactly what was in there. At the time, a scarcity of volunteers and paid staff undermined IBA's efforts to stabilize and normalize the young center. The computer courses were sporadic; the schedules were continuously changing; the center would close unexpectedly for no apparent reason. In short, the use of this resource was not predictable and stable, as that of the Laundromat or post office; it was haphazard, and as such its utility to residents—and, consequently, its effect on network generation—was questionable. What are we to make of the haphazard use of noncritical resources?

The case of the technology center suggests at least two sets of issues that affect whether a resident makes use of a noncritical resource: the characteristics of other persons who are using it and the way the resource is run, maintained, or organized. Most of us implicitly assume all poor residents will respond to their conditions similarly—that is, with either most residents making use of a resource or most not and with any resident as likely as any other to make use of it. However, poor neighborhoods may stratify themselves internally in such a way that some noncritical resources become attached to one group rather than another—"property" of one group and not the rest. Thus, a particular segment of residents may refuse to use or patronize a noncritical resource not because there is anything missing in it but because it is associated with another segment. In addition, since noncritical resources will not generate automatic demand, the way the resource is run or maintained or organized will probably affect who makes use of it and to what extent.

The rest of the chapter will expand on this issue, adding some flesh to our skeletal outline of the relationship between resources and social ties among residents in poor neighborhoods. The discussion will center on three noncritical resources that reflect these two effects in varying degrees:

the Jorge Hernández Cultural Center, the Plaza Betances, and O'Day Park.

THE JORGE HERNÁNDEZ CULTURAL CENTER

How is one resident's use of a center affected by who else makes use of it? And what about the management of the center would play a role in this relationship? In the Villa's Jorge Hernández Cultural Center (JHCC), the answer to these questions revolves around class-based cultural tastes.

The JHCC, based in a converted church on the western edge of Villa Victoria, sponsored most of IBA's indoor activities and its own artistic series. One of these, El Bembé, was a series of live salsa band dances in the fall and winter; the other, Café Teatro, was a shorter series of live Latin and Latin jazz musicians, poets, and vocalists. The series have been wildly successful in Boston, attracting thousands of young professionals and college and graduate students and inspiring the local papers to produce several feature articles on events taking place at the center.

Surprisingly, however, the series have had difficulty attracting local residents. Scores of residents complained they "don't feel comfortable" at the center's events and that "it doesn't feel like it's [their] place." The JHCC was a local resource that, except for events organized by IBA directly for the community, such as Three Kings Day, remained unused by locals. This did not result from the center's management during my time there, for residents' use of the center seemed to have been scarce for over a decade. It reflected, instead, both the center's fundamental goals and the groups with which it was perceived to be associated.

The JHCC was conceived in the mid-1980s as a way to showcase Puerto Rican arts and music, to help people from the community interact with people from different classes and backgrounds in Boston, and to bring in revenue for IBA, all under the umbrella of "Latino culture." "This community," said the first manager shortly after inauguration, "has been excluded from cultural events in the city" (quoted in Garelick 1986). Latino culture would serve as the bridge between communities, both reducing the isolation of Villa residents and dismantling New England's stereotypes about its Puerto Rican poor. But the term "Latino culture" meant one thing to white, middle-class New England and another thing altogether to Puerto Rican, poor Villa Victoria. In fact, it often meant different things to the Latino graduate students of Boston who also patronized the center and to the residents of the Villa.

To the organizers of JHCC cultural events, and to the white and Latino middle-classes who came to patronize the events, the term "Latino culture" invoked a pan-American amalgam of Nuyorican poetry, avant-garde Latin jazz, salsa-cumbia, flamenco, and Argentine tango, Chicano alternative music, and West Coast Spanish rock spiked with Andean rhythms and beats. But the Puerto Rican residents of Villa Victoria were neither familiar with nor interested in the esoteric Latin jazz of Danilo Perez or the erudition of the Ramon de los Reyes Spanish Dance Theater. These events, for all their Latino influence, were as culturally relevant to most residents as a New England "spoken word event." The fact they were in Spanish and that the artists were of Latin American descent did not change their membership in an educated artistic setting developed among an international Latino cultural elite very much in tune to a wider audience. It was Latin American culture, to be sure, but a new, amalgamated culture very much attuned to an interest in diversity of the American educated class, Latino or otherwise. Thus, when residents saw advertisements for a Café Teatro event featuring an Argentine tango performance or a jazz workshop, they expected not a familiar Puerto Rican event but an alien, upper-middle-class one. Thus, they complained that the center was "mainly for high-class people."

Their complaints should not have been surprising. Consider that the very notion of a "café theater," of café society in general, is a French import to the United States, a society thousands of miles removed, both in fact and in the cultural imagination, from either the streets of Aguadilla or Aguadilla Street. Aguadilla, where many of the first generation migrants were raised, did not have French cafés. Nor did Aguadilla Street, where the children and grandchildren of those immigrants lived. To be sure, the people of the two Aguadillas differed from each other. The first generation was musically attuned to the *trova*, to Puerto Rican guitar trios, to the early salsa of Yomo Toro and Willie Colón—it was no accident that the single JHCC event most consistently attended by local residents was the yearly *trovadores* competition. The second and third generations, ranging from the teenagers to those in their early thirties, were attuned to "beats" and freestyle, reggae, Spanish reggae, hip-hop, and R&B. Yet despite these differences the generations shared their alienation from the wave of pan-Latino and multicultural artistic culture prevalent among the educated classes.

The case of JHCC demonstrates how cultural practices may appear endemic while being in fact alien to those to which they are ostensibly catered. The JHCC came to evince many of the characteristics of wider South End businesses most residents fail to patronize. The center's cultural cues, though apparently "Latino," were in fact tied to an elite, educated class with which the lower-income Puerto Ricans could not identify. They found it "high class," they did not feel comfortable there, so they did not patronize it or did so only rarely. As a result, this resource neither exacerbated nor lessened social isolation. Though it was originally intended, among other things, to bridge social classes, it could not accomplish this task.

PLAZA BETANCES

When asked about institutional resources in neighborhoods social scientists often think of cultural and community centers, not parks and plazas. The former have a visible staff, budgets, office space, and open and closed hours; they are organizations, as public spaces are not. But parks and plazas are local resources in the context of this study because they serve to reinforce internal social capital by providing opportunities for interaction. Moreover, as we saw previously, they can be and often are explicitly designed for such purposes. In this respect, they are subject to patterns similar to those of other noncritical resources, such as the JHCC, in that residents may fail to make use of them if they are associated with groups the residents would rather avoid.

Once, while walking across Plaza Betances and having a conversation with Melissa, a young, nearly lifelong resident of the Villa, I was approached by a man in his sixties. He wore a dark brown overcoat to ward off the autumn chill, khaki pants, and a loose backpack, and in his hand he held a brown paper bag containing a bottle. With glassy, opaque eyes, he stared straight at me—or maybe straight through me—and mumbled something I did not understand. He smelled of alcohol; he looked high. He mumbled it again, this time looking serious: "You better take care of my girl." Melissa pulled me away, saying, "Don't worry about him. That's my [cousin]. . . . Ever since he got shot he hasn't been the same."

The men and women who spent hours at the plaza had diverse life stories—one had been shot, another had lost use of an arm, another had lost a finger at work decades ago, many had simply retired, others had succumbed to depression, some were homeless, one or two seemed to suffer from Alzheimer's—but they were all, the regulars, over forty or fifty, and several of them, men and women, smelled of alcohol. Melissa, in contrast, never hung out at the plaza. Younger women and men rarely spent extended time there, except on the Villa edge of the square, and late in the evenings, when most of the elders were gone. Children often played there, but almost always under the watch of an adult. The use of the plaza was definitely age sorted.

The public areas in the Villa, the plaza included, were designed to build community, and, indeed, they served that purpose in many ways. A beautiful mosaic mural to the side of the plaza depicted the self-perceived history of the neighborhood, running from the sixteenth-century Taínos in the island before the Spanish invasion through the construction of the Villa's quaint houses, of which there were several representations. Children's names dotted the bottom of the mural. The mosaic represented historical continuity and, thus, community, and, as part of the plaza, it also helped sustain community. My very first time there, about fifteen or twenty girls, maybe nine or ten years old, were playing outside under the watchful eye of two women who glanced at me with a mixture of suspicion and anxiety. It was conspicuously clear that everyone knew everyone else and that no one recognized me. When residents hung around the plaza they drank, gossiped, played dominoes, complained about IBA or the security offices, talked politics, and, not insignificantly, ran into other residents on their way to one of the many businesses and establishments surrounding it. These random interactions are in many ways the crux of the sustenance of internal or "bonding" social capital, for residents sustain ties to one another with no real effort. The plaza, it was clear, helped maintain community.

But by far the most prevalent use of the plaza was by people over fifty, who, to the chagrin of many of the younger residents, had taken over the territory. That is to say, there was not mere age sorting but a subtle territoriality maintained by both unspoken understanding and overt, if minor, cross-age conflicts. Over and over, teenagers complained of the "bums" who spent all day at the plaza drinking. Young women were particularly annoyed by the unceasing verbal harassment they suffered in the presence of the men, especially in the spring and summer. The plaza, it was clear, was "owned" by this group, at least during the daytime and particularly from late spring through early fall. The young essentially stayed away—in their own "territories," such as O'Day Park. The use of the resource, that is to say, was highly conditional on the age of the resident, on the perceived group with primary use of it, which affected the extent to which it was really an available resource.

The group mechanisms in operation at JHCC were between locals and outsiders, while at the plaza they were between locals and other locals as the neighborhood stratified itself internally. Anderson (1978) found similar internal stratification processes in a very different setting, among patrons of a Chicago bar, where regulars and nonregulars occupied different positions in the internal status chain and claimed different levels of "ownership" of the local resource. In the context here, internal stratification processes mediate the relationship between residents and their use of local resources—and, by extension, between resource prevalence and internal and external social capital. Were it not for major events, such as the Festival Betances, the plaza's ability to strengthen local ties among residents might well be limited to that subsection of elderly, often more impoverished, regulars.

O'DAY PARK

The first time I saw it, O'Day Park looked like any park in any urban city. It was enclosed in a cyclone fence. At one end was a basketball court, its far wall painted over in graffiti; at the other end were four swings and a small spiral slide. In between were a water sprinkler for children, concrete benches, and a few small trees. Just as the plaza was, the park was designed to strengthen the local community, though in its own unique way. And as the plaza was, the park was also subject to internal stratification processes affecting who used it and when. However, O'Day Park was also what anthropologists would call a symbolically charged entity (Geertz 1972), an entity that elicited strong emotions for reasons independent of its obvious functions or observable characteristics. The park's history had been violent and scarring; it recalled memories of tragic, poignant events in the neighborhood's past. More than a mere park, O'Day was a symbol of violence in the neighborhood, a fact that contributed to many residents' reluctance to use it.

Much of park's history was told in its graffiti, if perhaps in random snapshots instead of a continuous narrative. At the far left, along the wall of the basketball court was a large letter *P* in white. Polito was a popular young person in the neighborhood, but one who had allegedly shared one too many heroin needles. He had died in the mid-1990s.

To the left of the *P* was spray painted the face of a young, dark-skinned man with a mustache wearing a wool Los Angeles Raiders cap. Next to his name, a twenty-five-foot long and eight-foot high spray-painted sign read "Domestik." Nearby on the wall was spray painted a eulogy from a sorrowful youngster:

> Why did you take my best friend.
> To make me suffer never hold again.
> The sun don't shine I need the light.

> To heaven he flies like a bird in flight.
> Days on the swings to be friends.
> He knocked on my heart and I let
> him in. Robbed from the things
> I loved most. Memories of Domestik.
> I see his ghost. I'm in so much
> pain! Iliana

Domestik was a beloved man in the neighborhood, a close and older friend of Laura's. On a Sunday in August of 1992, Laura and her friend were at the park, chatting and hanging out with other young teenagers of the neighborhood. There were people everywhere. As the sun set, Laura went home for dinner. She made it to the last step of her front stoop before she heard loud shots echo through the streets of the complex. The shots came from the park. She ran back toward the commotion, fearing, and witnessing, the worst. Packed into a car that sped through West Newton Street, a group of men in hoods had sprayed the park with bullets in retaliation over an earlier dispute with young men from Villa Victoria. Four people had been hit; Domestik, born Jorge Ramos, age twenty-one, was shot dead.

Another man, eighteen-year-old Rayton Walker, a brilliant athlete, was hit in the spine. Rayton lay screaming by a tree, the adrenaline rushing through his body as he tried to control the pain. In desperation, the other teenagers lifted him up and carried him home, urging his father to call an ambulance. "We tried to calm him down," recalled his father, "but he kept saying, 'I can't feel my legs'" (Manly 1992). The bullet had shifted. Rayton never walked again, trapped in a wheelchair for the rest of his life; he died shortly thereafter.

On the wall, next to "Domestik" was the word "A-Rock" in large blue block letters with soft edges that was spray painted over the image of an eight-foot-tall brown bottle. A-Rock might have been Angel Sánchez, a seventeen-year-old who loved drinking malt liquor. He was shot in the back and killed in May of 1994 as he stood outside his aunt's house in the South End (Comandini 1994). But "A-Rock" might also have been Al Martin, a sixteen-year-old from West Newton Street who was shot dead in September of 1993 in a lot off Worcester Street, a few hours after wishing his mother happy birthday. The alleged perpetrators were teenagers from another neighborhood who had a beef with young men from the Villa (Mashberg 1993).

Throughout the park, by the swings and spiral slides, were other memorials of various sorts, some old, others fresh: a rock with a plaque unofficially christening the area "Domestik/O'Day Park"; a few feet away, another plaque for a man killed while intervening in a stabbing; by the foot of a tree, a cross, some flowers, a few rocks, and a photograph. Some days, O'Day Park seemed less a recreation area than a cemetery, the memories of the dead not inscribed on tombstones but spray painted on the walls, carved into trees, and chiseled onto plaques.

Certain places in our social lives are more historically and symbolically charged than others—they have witnessed more contention, struggle, and lasting agony. O'Day Park is one such historically charged place. A knowledge of its history figures into understanding why there are frequently more teenagers than anyone else there, and why even they at times appear cautious and prematurely aged. Consider a sample of images of the park from my research there: a half dozen young men lined up against the cyclone fence, by the trees of the Villa, selling hard and soft drugs; teenage boys placing bets on dice under the shade of a tree; the strong scent of marijuana emanating from a group of girls babysitting for a dozen children; a tearful Laura recounting the death of her best friend; improbably young girls dancing to a reggae beat during the Betances Festival; young men doing the dozens; older women in shock at their vocabulary; a spent heroin needle on the sand. O'Day Park "belongs" to the young in the same sense the plaza does to the elderly; one remembers it as a park of young people. One can picture effortlessly what the park must have looked like during the horrid drive-bys of the past and imagine, just as effortlessly, what the current drug traffic and informal gang membership will later be associated with, for this is not just a reaction to the current structural poverty but a continuation of a history that preceded these particular boys and girls.

For the residents who use it, the park is a place at once comforting and distressing. Young men play basketball on a court, the wall of which is painted, top to bottom, with the fading but still stinging memories of the dead: friends, older brothers, and older brothers' friends. Children build tiny sand sculptures and play tag by the swings, while using Domestik's memorial rock for cover. The park was once the social center for young people in the neighborhood; now it is not quite that; it is still only the young who use it, but many of the neighborhood's youth would rather be elsewhere. The resource is not only group specific, as Plaza Betances is, but also historically charged with a very public set of symbols that colors, and often discourages, its use . Our understanding of the use of this resource, then, must confront the effects of history.

O'Day Park offers another cautionary tale with respect to social capital. Many sociologists believe that crime can be stopped in neighborhoods provided that informal social control mechanisms are in place, such as adults who are willing to supervise children, even from their windows, and to call the police when they see trouble (Shaw and McKay 1942, 1969; Sampson and Groves 1989). The quantitative evidence has shown, indeed, that informal social control is associated with at least some types of crime reduction (Sampson and Groves 1989; Sampson, Raudenbush, and Earls 1997).

However, it is not difficult to develop unrealistic assumptions about what the police can do to prevent violent acts. Robberies and car thefts can, indeed, be reduced by this mechanism; eyes on the street, as Jacobs (1961) has argued, discourage random robberies and make burglaries and car thefts more difficult. Yet several of the very violent crimes that took place in O'Day Park could not have been prevented by informal social control, no matter how willing the residents might be to call the police or to keep their eyes on the public spaces. Indeed, several of the drive-bys took place while the park was crawling with people.

Drive-bys, when compared to robberies or assault crimes, are relatively rare. Nonetheless—and this is the critical issue here—their effects on communities are lasting, much more powerful, disheartening, and debilitating than common robberies and burglaries. These are rare events that cause neighborhoods to deteriorate by virtue of the lingering memory— and, often, heavily recorded memory—associated with the neighborhood, its resources, or its public spaces. In a peculiar way, they affect quality of life not merely by making residents fearful of crime but also by attaching scarring memories to the local resources that sustain local ties among residents.

Resources and Social Capital

Two apparent paradoxes govern the relationship between resources and social capital in Villa Victoria: the neighborhood's high level of poverty increased the density of local resources, rather than the opposite, and this abundance of resources increased social isolation, rather than the reverse—which, from the residents' perspective, turned out to be quite convenient. These two relationships only appear paradoxical based on our most common assumptions about poor neighborhoods; a solid examination of this case suggests a quite natural relationship among these variables, underscoring the need to think more concretely about field cases.

Resource prevalence affects social capital—predictably with respect to critical resources but highly conditionally with respect to noncritical ones.

The first relationship is directly proportional: all other factors being equal, the greater the number of critical resources the fewer the opportunities to interact with residents of other neighborhoods and the middle class. If it is nearby, convenient, and of low enough cost and high enough quality, it will be used, much as a rational choice perspective would predict. But the use of noncritical resources does not conform to such expectations, since, not being necessities, they are more strongly affected by how the resource is run and managed, by which internal group has commanded "owner-ship" of the resource, and by what history accompanies residents' under-standing of the resource. As the JHCC, Plaza Betances, and O'Day Park make clear, intermediary conditions matter a great deal. At this juncture, it makes sense to turn again to such microlevel processes as residents' per-ceptions of their neighborhood—perceptions necessarily affected by the historical circumstances with which they associate it.

SEVEN

A Labyrinth of Loyalties

I never get out! — MELISSA

Villa Victoria is my community. Boston is my city. — OSCAR

I live here and I'm not isolated, and it's by choice. . . . Yet to some degree, I *am* isolated. — GLORIA

Residents as Individuals

The residents' diverse attitudes toward the park and the plaza allude to an important element of neighborhood effects: the same structural conditions are responded to differently by different individuals. Throughout the book, I have suggested that addressing this difference, rather than studying merely the average or most common response, is the key to understanding much of what we do not know about how neighborhoods work. In chapter 3 I examined why some residents were more likely than others to get involved, uncovering the importance of how and why different residents framed the neighborhood as they did. This chapter returns to the individual-level analysis in greater depth, addressing how and why they differ in their level of contact with the middle class.

The Villa bears evidence to the importance of studying both common responses and within-neighborhood differences to structural conditions, not merely the former. There is little question that the residents' ability to develop middle-class ties is affected by the Villa's particular type of neighborhood poverty, in which boundaries with the surrounding South End are fixed and in which most of the critical resources they need can be obtained "in-house." All residents are affected, in one way or another, by these factors. For most of them it is convenient to conduct their "third realm," day-to-day affairs nearby. And the overwhelming majority of them have few or no meaningful ties to white, middle-class South Enders. But residents vary widely in the number of ties they have to the middle class at large. For example, Ernesto, one of the elderly men who was involved in the ETC mobilization, has few middle-class friends, or even acquaintances, outside Villa Victoria, while Gloria, one of the highly involved young women of the neighborhood, maintains an active network of friends of all class backgrounds throughout the city, and, to some extent, the nation. Are these differences arbitrary, random? Are they patterned, but for reasons unrelated or unimportant to neighborhood poverty? Or, on the contrary, are they related to internal dynamics mediating in important ways the effects of neighborhood poverty?

Consider, in addition, the relationship between generating those external ties and local community participation. If policymakers on both the left and the right agree on any issue, it is their desire for both more community participation and less social isolation. The poor, they argue, should develop more social capital of both kinds: internal as well as external to the neighborhood (Wilson 1996; Sampson 1999; Putnam 2000). How feasible is this?[1]

What follows addresses this question in reference to the two types of social capital by presenting in-depth analyses of the lives of five residents who, at some time in their lives, have been highly involved in their neighborhood but who differ in the number of ties they have with the middle class. I consider here both why they differ and whether and how their local participation affects their ability to sustain those external ties, and discover the following. First, the most salient factor affecting differences among the cases is the residents' generational status. Second, the next most critical factor is whether and in what capacity they are employed (that "second realm" for network development ignored in the previous chapter). Third, local participation makes the development of external ties more difficult, not easier, for it leaves residents constantly struggling to balance competing loyalties and interests. Fourth, this struggle cannot be understood without taking into account the role of what I term "neighborhood affect" (on affect, see Scheler 1992). Finally, I assess the adequacy

---

1. One perspective might suggest it is not. Granovetter (1973) has famously demonstrated that our strongest ties are unlikely to be bridges, such that a tightly knit internal network is unlikely to have strong ties to another, external tightly knit network (also Wellman and Wortley 1990; Fernandez and Harris 1992; Tigges, Browne, and Green 1998). Nevertheless, this theorem, focused on strength, says nothing of the mere presence of both internal and external ties, the more pertinent issue with respect to neighborhood poverty. Researchers do not argue that residents of poor neighborhoods should be best friends with middle-class residents but, instead, simply that they know as many middle-class people as possible to gain information about jobs and other opportunities or to have potential role models. For persons to have large numbers of both internal and external ties is therefore not impossible. It must be asked, however, how likely it is.

of various possible approaches to understanding variation in a small number of cases (see also Ragin and Becker 1992).

Five Cases

ERNESTO

Ernesto carries himself with the serenity of someone who has seen and heard just about everything he expects to see and hear. Yet he remains incredulous at the unlikelihood of his own good fortune. He was born in the small town of Ponce, Puerto Rico, in the 1910s. Before migrating to Boston, he was a married man with several children, whom he supported by working as a laborer for construction and farming companies. When he moved to the South End in the early 1960s to help his brother run his business, he did so largely out of family loyalty not because of any hardship. Ernesto was not the type to worry about things he could not control; he was never weighed down by grudges or, in contrast, by heavy and idealistic virtues such as justice and responsibility. His brother needed help, so that matter was settled. Although poor, Ernesto had lived a comfortable enough life in Puerto Rico, had developed a tight network of friends, and was raising a family. A pensive, undisturbed man, he never thought of himself as particularly ambitious.

The Boston move proved to be an unexpected change of pace. When he first arrived, he brought along his eldest son; the rest of the family would arrive within a couple of years. His brother's business, a grocery store, went out of business despite his help, but Ernesto quickly found work at a local foundry. Ernesto's closest friends at the time were also Puerto Ricans who had moved to the South End at midcentury. He paid about $60 per month rent in the early 1960s for an old three-bedroom apartment in the South End, so, as long as he worked, he had expendable income. He partied a great deal and played cards incessantly.

Through his poker buddies, he developed a small network in one neighborhood outside the South End, for there was a great deal of gambling in Dudley Square, in Roxbury. Most of these men were as poor as he was. None of them could speak a word of English, and several of them could barely read or write, so they bonded, creating a community among themselves.

During the 1950s and 1960s, Ernesto worked odd jobs in the manufacturing sector, most of which caused him some physical injury or another. He never complained about it seriously, and were it not for his coworkers, he might never had thought to ask for any compensation from the com-

panies at all. Accidents, after all, happened; by definition they were nobody's fault. At his last job, he suffered an accident that cost him the use of
his left arm. He received $1,500 from the company for that, and he has col-
lected disability insurance ever since. The accident took place in the 1970s.
Since he had not graduated from high school back in Puerto Rico and
does not, in any case, speak English, Ernesto found it difficult to find a job
outside of the manufacturing sector. He has not worked for pay another
day since the accident.

Over the years, the number of relatives he had in the Villa grew dramatically; Ernesto's own children bore children, as did his wife's siblings.
The extended family congregated around Parcel 19 and, later, the Villa.
His involvement in the resistance efforts against relocation all but guaranteed him a place in the new Villa Victoria, and he would not have wanted
to live anywhere else. With overwhelming pride, Ernesto will tell anyone
he has never lived beyond the South End in the nearly half-century he has
lived in Boston.

On a typical day, Ernesto gets out of bed late—he needs rest as a result
of his failing health. He bathes, eats a small breakfast prepared by one of
his sons (who lives with him), and watches television. At noon, another
son brings him lunch and keeps him company; later, a few of his grandchildren stop by after school. They watch TV at the house and wait for
their mother or one of their aunts or uncles to pick them up. By dinner-
time, there are often—between sons, daughters, sons-in-law, daughters-
in-law, and grandchildren—about a dozen people at the house, fitting in
one way or another inside his modest two-bedroom apartment. By eight
o'clock, they are all gone, except for the son who lives with him as com-
panion and caretaker. The bulk of Ernesto's support network of friends,
relatives, and acquaintances lives right in the Villa. He no longer keeps in
touch with his old friends in Puerto Rico or with his old poker buddies.
Those ties are effectively dead.

EUGENIA

Eugenia, a woman at once optimistic and melancholic, was born in the
outskirts of San Juan, Puerto Rico, in the early 1940s. When her parents
brought her as a young girl to Boston, they did not enroll her in school.
Thus, although she speaks English well enough, she was never educated
formally beyond elementary school. Like Ernesto, Eugenia has lived
nowhere but the South End in her nearly forty years in Boston—in fact,
she has lived entirely within the few streets around Parcel 19, where she
bore a number of children and raised a large extended family.

Eugenia is a classic idealist and optimist, a twenty-year old in spirit. Her eyes sparkle when she speaks of the goods which could come to the Villa if only the second generation cared about neighborhood the way she did; if more of them ran for the board; if people just put in a few hours during the beautification campaign; if IBA distributed a video to new residents of the neighborhood's history; if this video were shown to potential donors—she is an ever-running fount of ideas for neighborhood improvement. She is deeply religious and incapable, for the most part, of uttering a word of disdain or contempt but is quick to criticize anyone who seeks his or her own betterment at the expense of the community. She is vocal, loquacious, fair, and highly intelligent.

Underlying her optimism, however, is a deep sense of grief. Eugenia does not work for pay, and she has not done so for much of her life, a fact that pains her. Part of her narrative of herself is that she has failed in life, as she will explain in so many words. Idealism, after all, is but a purer form of ambition, and the high expectations associated with both will often lead to despair. As a young girl, Eugenia wished to become "a social worker and a teacher," but without schooling this was impossible. She confided: "Until about three years ago I blamed my parents for my failure. They took me out of school and didn't put me back in the school year." There was no bitterness in her words. Through her activism during the sixties and later community involvement in the Villa, she has assuaged that grief, channeling her need for service toward community participation.

Most of Eugenia's friends are first-generation migrants, such as herself, who live in the Villa; she has a few friends who were former residents of Parcel 19 and now live in other Boston neighborhoods. With the notable exception of the acquaintances with professionals she made during the sixties, she has no close friends and almost no acquaintances who are middle class or higher. Of the surrounding South End, she says, "We are surrounded by condos, high-class people." She does not venture out into the South End, except when going to the supermarket. She does not patronize the restaurants or cafés in the area, for she "[doesn't] feel comfortable" there. With the exception of those former residents who lived in Parcel 19 and the people she knows from church, the bulk of her closest friends, family, and acquaintances are in Villa Victoria.

GLORIA

Gloria, an open-minded, active woman, was born in Boston in the 1960s; she has lived in the South End most of her life. Both of her parents were highly involved in the community during the late 1970s and early 1980s, whether running for IBA's board of directors, teaching ESL classes, or helping run the Festival Betances. Though both of Gloria's parents were born in Puerto Rico, they migrated at an early age. Thus, although Gloria understands and speaks Spanish, English is her native tongue. Curiously, as a young child she spoke only Spanish, not a word of English; one day, she explains, her mind "switched," and she is now much more comfortable in English. Her mother passed away a few years ago, and her father now lives in New York, but her brother owns a home in a working-class suburb of Boston, where he lives with his family. Gloria, along with the rest of her family, had moved out of the Villa years ago, but she returned with her son Victor, now eleven. She is not married. Both her father and mother have siblings throughout the city who serve as Gloria's main sources of support, especially while raising her son.

Gloria is a dancer. After graduating from high school, she toured the country with a prestigious Boston Puerto Rican folk dance troupe. Striking and immensely gifted, she considered (and was encouraged to pursue) a career in dance, but after having Victor, she realized she could not live a dancer's life. During those tumultuous years, she would leave Victor for weeks at a time with her parents. The performer's life was too taxing on Gloria's relationship with her son, so she quit. While dancing, however, she met scores of other dancers, musicians, artists, and students throughout Boston and the nation. Through them, she felt she broadened her horizons both personally and socially, meeting people of diverse class and racial backgrounds. Many of the people she met are now among her closest friends.

Mature beyond her years, Gloria is what many would call "a spiritual person." She is very attuned to her feelings (in the best sense of the phrase), and she is cautious, careful not to rush to judgment or to let her emotions get the best of her. Despite its trials, dance was an exceptional experience not just because of the people she met and places she visited but, above all, because she grew as a person. Gloria is a constant self-improver. She no longer smokes, she drinks less than she used to, and she is less confrontational, a better conflict manager.

To explain her relationship to people of different backgrounds, she has coined a term for herself: "I'm a weaver. I can go through all kinds of communities and be comfortable there. I can be in a black community. As a matter of fact, most of my friends are black. Because I felt comfortable." Although she knows a lot of people at the Villa, her closest friends live elsewhere in Boston. Gloria, in addition, is one of the relatively few persons under forty who, over the years, has run for the board of directors.

Gloria now works as a counselor-in-training. She hopes to return to school to pursue that career but probably won't do so until Victor is old enough to require less attention. On a typical day, Gloria waits for Victor's bus to take him to school, then drives to work on the opposite side of town. Victor participates in an after-school program that picks him up at school and brings him home around 5:00 p.m., by which time Gloria is already back from work. She then cooks, cleans the house, helps Victor with his schoolwork, and puts him to bed. When necessary, she picks up groceries at the bodegas in or around the Villa. During weekends, she deliberately tries to get out of the neighborhood. When Victor is with her, she takes him over to his cousins' house on the outskirts of Boston; on alternate weekends, when Victor is at his father's house, Gloria spends time with her friends outside the Villa at occasional parties throughout Boston or even some restaurants in the South End. Except for her childhood friends, many of whom live in the Villa, Gloria's family and close friends are spread throughout Boston, and she has acquaintances of all class backgrounds throughout the country.

MELISSA

Melissa is a sweet, complicated, and passionate young woman born in the 1970s in New Haven, Connecticut, to Puerto Rican parents. During her childhood, she lived with her father in New Haven during the school year and visited her mother in the Villa during the summer. At age eight, she moved in with her mother; when she turned ten, she was returned to Connecticut. By the time she was fourteen, she was "sick" of Connecticut. Furthermore, as she explains, "I felt I should spend more time with my mother," so she returned to Boston, to the Villa, where she has lived ever since.

The focal center of her most intimate network has shifted over her lifetime. Between the ages of eight and ten, during her first long-term residence in the Villa, she was bused, along with several of her neighbors, to the North End for elementary school. Most of her friends at the time were from the Villa. After returning to Boston from her second stay in Connecticut, she attended a high school in the city, along with many of the teenagers from the neighborhood. By now, she was not quite unpopular but still somewhat eccentric and reclusive; she still spoke with some of her childhood friends, but they were not close to her. Her two closest friends lived in other neighborhoods. After high school, Melissa found a clerical position with a local company, where she stayed for several years and met many people from different walks of life. She attended college for a few years, making many acquaintances but relatively few close friends.

Much of Melissa's family lives in the Villa, including siblings, step-siblings, aunts, and cousins. This family constitutes an important support network for her, and she is very close to all of them. She and her brother, who has a son, are particularly close.

Melissa, a musician, is an artist, true to form. She is passionate and lively, propelled by an incessant energy that makes her a quick, jittery speaker when she is excited about something. Her numerous creative outlets are outlets in the deepest sense—without them, she might explode from sheer excess of energy. Hardly ever bored and very attractive, she is at every minute busy with studies, socializing, random Villa activities, boyfriends, and work—lots of work. Stagnation would not bore her so much as drive her out of her mind. Her participation in local activities, from the Betances Festival to the beautification campaigns, is clearly in part an extension of her natural need to do something, anything, with her time.

Melissa was laid off some time after we first met when her firm downsized. Now she works with a temp agency, looking for something permanent. On a typical working day, Melissa gets up early and heads to work. She returns home exhausted, spends time with her brother and nephew, and busies herself with the house or one of her creative projects (music or writing) before returning to bed. On a nonworking day, she sleeps in and later runs errands. Her brother works full time, so Melissa often picks up her nephew at the Escuelita Boriken in the afternoon. She frequently complains about feeling "stuck" at the Villa. On weekends, she tries to spend time outside the neighborhood with people she has met over the years, at work or in college. The Villa's sense of being a small world unto itself is particularly troubling to her now that she is not permanently employed. "I never get out!" she explains, exasperated. "I don't see other places like I used to." Though many of her family members and many of her acquaintances are at the Villa, her closest friends live in other Boston neighborhoods, and she has both friends and acquaintances throughout the city.

OSCAR

Oscar, a talkative, sensitive young man, was also born in the 1970s, but he has lived in Villa Victoria his entire life. As a child, Oscar attended the Escuelita Boriken, and he was later enrolled in a public elementary school in Boston. His mother, a neighborhood activist, imparted to her son a rich knowledge of and appreciation for the history of the neighborhood, to which he felt intimately connected. Oscar was studious and not particularly popular as a young man. But he joined teen peer leader groups and attended church regularly. As he grew older, he started thinking about college, taking advantage of exchange programs, and generating a network of friends and acquaintances through summer camps, church, and events throughout Boston. He now commutes to a small college in western Massachusetts.

Over the years, Oscar's fondness for Villa Victoria has deepened. He is particularly pleased with the availability of resources in the neighborhood. We saw, in chapter 6, his appreciation for the local corner store, credit union, post office, community center, and other critical resources. Yet Oscar, something of an adventurer, also appreciates the central location of the neighborhood, the fact that he may leave at will: "If I need to go downtown, I'm two steps away from Tremont Street for the 43 [bus], two steps away from Washington for the 49. I'm ten minutes away from Back Bay Station. I'm fifteen minutes away from the Green Line. I mean, everything is around me. Like, where I'm at, I'm prime spot. I don't really need anything else." Though he has few close friends in the Villa, he cares for it deeply; though he appreciates its high resource base, he enjoys, just as much, his ability to leave the neighborhood at will. As his mother did, Oscar volunteers much of his time to "give back to the community," as he often explains. He serves as a mentor and an informal big brother to several of the younger residents in the neighborhood.

Many of Oscar's relatives live in Puerto Rico, where he goes often with his mother. His only sister, a married woman now in her thirties (and also a former, if occasional, neighborhood activist), lives in Dorchester with her husband. His mother, however, is his strongest source of support. He knows many of the Villa's residents, but he spends little time with them, since few are close friends.

Oscar is something of a loner, though hardly lonely. He admits to being unique among his peers, a fact that does not bother him. On the contrary, it seems to energize him. His closest friends—people he met in college and at random summer camps and other activities during his childhood—live throughout the state.

On typical days, Oscar wakes up early, at 5:30 a.m., to catch a train to go to college. He spends most of the day there, returning home late at night. On weekends, he heads out to one of the multiple organizations with which he seems to be affiliated throughout the city. With the exception of his mother, Oscar's family, close friends, and acquaintances live not in the Villa but elsewhere throughout the city, and they are of diverse class and ethnic backgrounds.

Five Types of Residents?

The experiences of Ernesto, Eugenia, Gloria, Melissa, and Oscar are as diverse as the individuals themselves, concretizing the fact that common structural conditions do not necessarily lead to identical or even similar levels of isolation from the middle class. They also suggest that local participation does not have a universal effect on one's likelihood of having middle-class ties (even if it may, however, have a common effect on the difficulty of sustaining such ties). How do we make sense of this variation?

The answer is by no means obvious. Among other things, we should be especially sensitive to the fact these are five case studies, not a statistical sample of five units (cf. Lieberson 1992). No five cases could be statistically representative of a neighborhood of several thousand. The cases should both lead to hypotheses about this variation and reveal the workings of those mechanisms that may only be studied from an in-depth, microlevel perspective.

Making sense of variation among a few cases is, fundamentally, a process of identifying patterns and associating those patterns with the phenomenon at hand. In this case, the task may be undertaken in one of two ways: by grouping the residents according to their end conditions (greater or lesser isolation) or by grouping them according to the potential causal factors. The former approach, common to this subfield, is probably inadequate to the tasks at hand. Below I discuss why and continue by exploring how the latter approach yields greater insight into the mechanisms by which individual factors mediate the effects of neighborhood poverty.

GROUPING RESIDENTS BY END CONDITION

The first approach would be to divide the residents into separate categories referring to different types of reactions to neighborhood poverty and to use the five cases above as exemplars of those categories. Following that approach, Ernesto and Eugenia would be categorized as "isolated"—people who behave as one would theoretically expect considering the neighborhood conditions described in the previous two chapters. Both Gloria and Oscar would be "not isolated," and Melissa would be "somewhat isolated." Categorizations such as this one (see also, e.g., Anderson 1999) have the clear benefits that they not only recognize the heterogeneity of the urban poor but also provide a straightforward device through which to interpret this variation.

This approach is common not only in the urban sociological tradition but also in sociology itself (Whyte 1955; Gans 1962; Hannerz 1969; Simmel 1971; Anderson 1999). In urban ethnographies, theorists have often resorted to typologies in an implicit attempt to break through societal perceptions or stereotypes about the urban lower or working class. Gans's (1962) distinction between "routine-seekers" and "action-seekers," for instance, suggests such an effort, as does Hannerz's (1969) distinction between "mainstream" and "ghetto-specific" forms of behavior among the urban poor. Reacting, in part, to the tendency of Americans during the 1950s and 1960s to homogenize the poor, these authors' works served to demonstrate the variety of responses to inner-city conditions among the poor.

Though all such typologies are concerned with the grouping of end conditions, there are at least three different kinds of them: those of people, states, and behavior. Among the first, Anderson's (1999) categorization between "street" and "decent" families is currently the best known. Those who Anderson calls street people engage in violent crime, are more sexually active, and are more likely to abuse drugs; decent people are law abiding, honest, and striving toward a middle-class existence. Anderson acknowledges the presence of decent people among street families and vice versa. But, contrary to the other typologies, individuals are of either one or the other type, not both. (Anderson does, however, suggest that decent adolescents can code-switch into street behavior when the circumstances warrant [1999, 98ff.].)[2]

One danger of this form of typology is that it can become a substitute for an explanation.[3] Anderson's work articulates in rich detail the differences between street and decent types. Yet, we do not know why street kids become street kids, other than knowing they are likely to have come from street families. In the case of Villa Victoria, we would want to understand

2. Also, Anderson writes, "One person may at different times exhibit both decent and street orientations, depending on the circumstances. Although these designations result from much social jockeying, there do exist concrete features that define each conceptual category, forming a social typology" (Anderson 1999, 35).

3. The approach is based on a symbolic interactionist framework by which social relations are thought to be governed by types of interactions among types of people (Goffman 1959, 1986; Simmel 1971). That tradition saw itself as articulating these forms of interaction, not necessarily as explaining why individuals would end up in one type and not the other. Simmel, e.g., is concerned with understanding how "the stranger" can be both "near and far at the same time" (Simmel 1971, 148), not with what factors (other than being a wanderer) affect one's likelihood of being a stranger.

why Eugenia is more isolated than Melissa is and why Melissa is more so than Oscar.

A second limitation is the approach's implicit assumption that people's conditions do not change over time, much as the category of criminal (or murderer or rapist) in popular parlance is a sort of unshakable condition from which people are assumed never to change. In our context, assuming one were to explain why some people are isolated and others not, the approach might still assume that one's isolation level is fixed. However, as I show below, the five aforementioned cases cannot be fit into fixed categories. Ernesto's case already provides hints as to why: although he is relatively isolated now, during his years resisting dislocation from Parcel 19, he had a few friends and many middle-class acquaintances throughout the city of Boston. His current isolation is, in part, a manifestation of the dwindling and eventual disappearance of these ties. In short, poor people's exposure to middle-class networks shifts over their lifetimes.

The second approach—categorizing end states—helps solve this problem because, by fundamentally conceiving of the end phenomenon as a state, it allows the researcher to ask why residents enter and leave a state of social isolation. Nevertheless, this approach is ultimately inadequate to our purposes. The term "socially isolated" is not a state the way "liquid" or "gaseous" are for water; there is no universally agreed on definition of social isolation that would allow us to identify such a state, nor should we seek for one. Any such attempt would be entirely artificial. Individuals do not enter or leave states of social isolation; they simply have fewer or greater active ties to members of the middle class. Their volume of external networks, in other words, is a continuum.

Among typologies of behavior—the third approach—probably the most influential has been Hannerz's (1969) distinction between mainstream and ghetto-specific modes of behavior (see also Wilson 1987, 1996). Any given individual in Hannerz's urban community could exercise either type of behavior, though some had greater facility than others in employing mainstream cultural repertoires. However, the approach is of little use to us since social isolation is not a form of behavior, such as using drugs or engaging in violent crime, but a condition, namely, the number of ties the resident has outside the neighborhood.

GROUPING RESIDENTS BY CAUSAL FACTOR

Thus, sorting residents by end condition is inappropriate for our question. The approach I followed here was partly deductive, partly inductive, a continuous dialectical movement between middle-range theories and microlevel observed behavior. I identified supraindividual factors that, based on either past research or observations on other topics in the Villa, I hypothesized would affect why some individuals knew more middle-class people than did others and examined whether such factors were at play in the cases. If they were, I explored how; if not, I explored other factors. Such an examination, furthermore, assumed that the number of external ties would not necessarily be fixed over a resident's lifetime and sought to uncover why. Finally, recognizing that residents have choices when it comes to generating networks, I sought to understand the motivations behind why they made some choices over others. Following this approach, I uncovered the roles of generational status, employment status, and neighborhood affect.

Generational Status

A critical factor associated with the residents' extent of isolation is their generational status. In this context, generational status refers to two separate issues: the residents' current position in the life course and their generation of migration (see Portes and Rumbaut 2001). The cases of Ernesto and Gloria elucidate this relationship.

Part of what affects Ernesto's propensity to spend most of his time at the Villa is his current position in the life course. He is an elderly man. That the elderly are often socially isolated—not just with respect to people outside their neighborhoods but in general—is well known, and part of Ernesto's current status is simply an extension of his old age. As a young man, Ernesto routinely went to Dudley Square in Roxbury to play cards, meeting a number of persons, Puerto Rican and otherwise, from the other neighborhood. But, now, he says, when people out at Dudley ask, "'And [Ernesto]? Did he go to Puerto Rico?' [His friends reply,] 'What? He hasn't gone anywhere! Go to the *placita* and you'll see him.'" Indeed, when the weather allows it, just about all of his leisure time is spent at the plaza, "telling jokes and playing dominoes and whatnot." He is not so frail that he cannot go elsewhere, but extensive traveling on public transportation is much harder than it used to be. The plaza serves as a central gathering place for long-term residents, reinforcing local ties and providing the opportunity for social intercourse Ernesto would otherwise be compelled to search for elsewhere. But even then, he probably would not; he would merely be lonelier. In this respect, Ernesto resembled many of the Villa residents of his age cohort.

But Ernesto's situation is not just tied to his age; it is also determined, in part, by his status as a first-generation immigrant with little education. Ernesto speaks no English, which probably has had the most significant effect on his opportunities to develop networks outside the neighborhood. When he was active in ETC during the late sixties and early seventies, Ernesto met many of the activists and professionals who helped the council in its cause. Yet as a result of the language barrier, these contacts never attained a level of intimacy beyond the issues associated with the movement, and he did not keep in touch with any of those people after that period. Over time, he became well known as "a pioneer." However, as he confides—matter-of-factly, not boasting: "Everyone knows me, but I hardly know anyone at all." Since he no longer plays cards, his old poker friends are no longer part of his circle, and since he is not an activist, he is no longer engaged with activists and professionals. His interactions with both groups revolved around specific activities; once the activities ceased, the contacts withered and disappeared. As a first-generation migrant speaking a different language, those interactions with middle-class, English-speaking individuals—facilitated by the rare sequence of events surrounding the tenants' movement—could not sustain themselves or develop into lasting ties. Thus, as a consequence of the factors associated with his immigrant status, the potential positive relationship between participation and greater external ties did not materialize.

Unlike Ernesto, Gloria, a young adult, was born in Boston and raised at the Villa. As a second- or third-generation migrant, she was in a much better position than Ernesto was to take advantage of opportunities to develop contacts outside the neighborhood. Though she speaks Spanish, English is her native language. When she toured the country with the folkloric dance troupe, she made a number of acquaintances. The initial contact took place under the framework of her dance performances, just as Ernesto's initial contact with the middle class took place under the framework of the tenants' movement. Yet Ernesto's interactions with middle-class activists took place with the aid of translators or else were limited to gestures and simple communications. Thus, while Ernesto's language barrier precluded the strengthening and sustenance of those ties, Gloria's facility with language cemented many of hers, which she has kept alive over her lifetime.

The fact that Gloria grew up not in rural Puerto Rico but in urban Boston also affected her possibilities for interaction with persons from other neighborhoods, even if those others were not always middle class. Though Gloria identifies herself as Latina, she grew up embedded in the

symbolism of urban hip-hop culture. Many of her own friends, and some
people she has dated, have been African-American, and she feels a particular affinity with the black community. She evinces, in part, what Portes
and others have called segmented assimilation (Portes and Zhou 1993).[4] In
fact, as she says of older Villa residents' opinions of her later-generation
status, "they view me as being Americanized. . . . They don't see me as not
Puerto Rican, but they don't think I encompass it. I don't know how else
to describe it. I am third generation here. And I don't speak a lot of Spanish." As a result, making friends across ethnic barriers comes more easily
than it does to Ernesto. How she and others of her generation came to
identify in these terms is related, in part, to the fact that they attended
school in Boston, an issue described in the section below. In addition, I
later address how her local involvement affected her ability to sustain these
external networks.

The generational differences among residents affect the body of linguistic and cultural capital with which they can negotiate interactions
with non-Latinos and the nonpoor (see Portes and Zhou 1993; Portes and
Rumbaut 2001). How these differences affect the relationship between local participation and external networks is evident, in part, from Ernesto's
case, where his linguistic limitations precluded sustained contact with the
new networks that community participation had made available. But I
will return to an examination of that relationship later in the chapter. For
now, I examine the second factor affecting the variation in social isolation:
whether and where the residents worked or went to school.

Employment and Schooling

In the previous chapter I elaborated on the location of those resources at
which residents conducted all business except for work since most residents who work do not do so in the Villa. It is well known that work is a
critical avenue for network development, and, like generational status, it
will fundamentally affect residents' opportunities for developing middle-
class ties. Work affects associational opportunities (Huckfeldt 1983) because employed individuals spend most of the day at work, as schooling
does among the young for the same reason.

As discussed earlier, the unemployment rate in the Villa is 26 percent,

---

4. Her assimilation, however, has not been associated with the development of an "oppositional" or "adversarial" culture (Waters 1999; Ogbu 1978; Fordham and Ogbu 1986).

which is high, but which still leaves 74 percent of those adults in the labor force with jobs, and it is unlikely that the bulk of those people work at the Villa.[5] Thus, one would expect that a large number of the neighborhood's adults find at least the opportunity to generate lasting ties outside the neighborhood. However, that figure is misleading. Though the unemployment rate is about 26 percent, the figure of real interest with respect to external ties is the jobless rate, which also includes those people who are not actively seeking employment. If we include those people over age sixteen who either cannot or do not wish to find work, the rate is a high 60 percent, which means, of course, that more than half of all adults are not working and, thus, lack the most salient avenue through which people develop ties outside their neighborhood (see Wilson 1996). This certainly contributes to the high prevalence of persons on the streets of Villa Victoria.

Still, for those who are employed, we do not know whether and how the relationships they make at work sustain themselves over time. What effect does work have and what are the factors contributing to that effect? The cases of Ernesto, Eugenia, and Melissa are instructive on this point.

Ernesto's status as a first-generation migrant interacts with the circumstances of his employment. When he was employed, Ernesto worked mostly in manufacturing jobs in which there was little opportunity or need to learn English and which did not result in greater contact with the middle class; as a laborer, he was simply exposed to other poor laborers. After his accident, manual work was out of the question, and since he had neither the education nor the linguistic abilities, he was unable to find work in other sectors. Thus, just at the time both his poker playing and his activism during the seventies subsided, Ernesto lost another key opportunity to generate outside networks—his work. Living in the Villa, with an array of services available within easy reach, as well as a community of Spanish-speaking Puerto Ricans congregating daily in a public space created explicitly for that purpose, Ernesto's disconnection from external ties and his attachment—perhaps even dependence—on networks local to the Villa was all but inevitable.

Eugenia is a generation younger than Ernesto and able to speak English. But she has not worked for pay for most of her life. Thus, like that of Ernesto, her network of acquaintances outside the neighborhood is small. Ernesto spends time at the plaza or with his family; Eugenia cares for her

5. These, as before, are 1990 Census figures. The figures for the 2000 Census were not available at the time of this writing.

ailing father and raises her family. Ernesto and Eugenia have experiences, personalities, and approaches to life as different as those of any two persons, yet none of these factors overwhelms the fundamental significance of work. Without it, associational opportunities with the middle class simply decrease drastically.

Melissa's case differs markedly from those of Ernesto and Eugenia. One of the main reasons is schooling, which, in this setting, serves the same function as employment, an avenue for the generation of networks in other neighborhoods. Through school, Melissa did, indeed, expand her networks. In Boston, the school system provides greater opportunities for interaction across neighborhoods than the systems of other cities. The district operates under a controlled choice program, whereby parents submit their first, second, and third choice of public school for their children, and students are allocated to different schools throughout the city. Thus, children from the South End do not necessarily attend school in the South End. In cities where children attend schools in their same neighborhoods, the effect of neighborhood isolation is probably more pronounced.

Melissa attended a high school not too far from the South End, a school she bitterly remembers as "one of the *worst* schools in the area" because of its third-rate teaching and ubiquitous violence. However, the school, which required students to work at a job in order to graduate, did provide her the opportunity to broaden her horizons. She explains: "At ——— you go to school from seven to eleven, that's how it is. It's kind of like a vocational school. After [attending classes] you get a job —at McDonald's, the shoe store—anything, basically. But if you didn't work you couldn't get credit." She continues: "When I was in high school I worked a lot. Class ended at 11:00. I worked from 11:30 to 6:00, and then at another job from 6:00 to 10:00. I just wanted to work, you know. Make some money. I got a paycheck. I was doing better."

Melissa found work at a department store, where she met a number of people, most of whom were older and in college. She spoke with and learned a great deal from her new friends. Most of them were nothing but acquaintances, constituting "weak" ties (Granovetter 1973). But they became significant weak ties, for they began to change her outlook. She explains: "At the [store] I worked with a lot of college kids. And they were like [*mocking the accent of a college-educated white person*] 'Have you read *Catcher in the Rye?* Have you read this and that?'" In most cases, she had not. "So, I would go out and do it. I didn't want anyone to look at me and say 'poor thing.' So I went to the guidance counselor and I said I needed college help."

Her basic narrative of herself changed as a result of her exposure to the college students at work. She began to see herself as a person with the potential to discuss books such as *Catcher in the Rye* with others, something she had not done before. As she developed this perception of herself, she began to act in light of it, pursuing an opportunity that, through her school, had been there all along: guidance in the college application process. Schooling had provided an opportunity for Melissa that Eugenia—whose parents never enrolled her in school in Boston—never had. Eventually, she set her mind on going to college and did so. Melissa's is a case of not just exposure—the type of exposure people such as Eugenia did not experience—but also of the self-feeding effects of such exposure. Melissa's interactions with college students at work contributed to her considering college; attending college expanded her middle-class network even further (see also Newman 1999).

However, college was difficult for her since her high school preparation was inadequate. Melissa dropped out after her first year. She found a short-term job with a temporary placement agency in the South End, very near the Villa. She is now considering whether to move to Florida with her boyfriend or stay at her low-paying job in the South End. Interestingly, having been exposed to a wider network of persons and situations, it is now distressing for her to work so close to the Villa, since she spends most of her time there and nearby elsewhere in the South End. ("I never get out!") Her inability to "meet other people" as she used to has been difficult for her.

It is important to keep in mind that neither school nor employment guarantee the development of external ties. They simply provide the associational opportunities for doing so. Agency matters. Consider the case of Melissa many years earlier, when she was in elementary school. Between the ages of eight and ten, when she lived in Boston, Melissa attended an elementary school in the North End; she was bused there along with several other children from the Villa. Yet this hardly resulted in the type of interaction with children from other neighborhoods one might expect; on the contrary, while in the North End she kept her ties to children from the Villa. She recalls: "The people on the bus were the people from Villa Victoria or Mass Ave. Yeah, I spent my time with kids on the bus, waiting for the bus, getting over to school. I guess most of the kids I hung out with in school were from the Villa. We were just always together. We lived in the same neighborhood. Went to the same park . . . the park right here in the Villa [O'Day Park]." Though they attended school in a different neighborhood, and, in part, because of it, the children from the Villa stuck together.

No factor increasing associational opportunities is a guarantee that external ties will develop. Such a relationship is conditional on a host of intermediary factors, such as, in the case above, the ability to remain within one's familiar network. In addition, the resident's agency—deciding not to be thought of as a "poor thing," going to guidance counselors, attending college—is critical.

Neighborhood Affect and Local Participation

The mechanisms by which employment and generational status affect middle-class ties are similar in some ways and different in others. Both affect social capital by generating or limiting opportunities to develop external and potentially middle-class ties. Yet all factors associated with generational status are those over which residents have no control, while those regarding employment may or may not be beyond the control of the resident. Local community participation, by and large, works differently.

Whether to become involved in their community is entirely the resident's choice (though one affected, to be sure, by their narratives of the neighborhood). Thus, whatever effect participation has on the development of external ties, it does so less under the influence of a limited opportunity structure than under the influence of deliberate actions and chosen trajectories of living. Understanding those choices forces us to enter deeper into the realm of human motivation, especially when residents' actions do not conform to the easy assumptions of rationality. The narrative approach (Taylor 1989; Somers 1992; Somers and Gibson 1994), if employed cautiously, is helpful in this regard.

In the following, I suggest that the relationship between community participation and social isolation or lack thereof—between internal and external social capital—is best understood as part of larger type of effect that may be labeled affect toward the neighborhood. Below, I first explore how neighborhood affect, in general, alters the likelihood that residents will have ties to the middle class. I then turn to the specific way that community participation is tied to this relationship.

In his classic study of the North End, Whyte (1955) argues that there is a relationship between people's attachment to their local community and their chances for upward mobility. He proposes a distinction between the "college boy" and the "corner boy" and explains why the college boy is more likely to move upward into middle-class society. Whyte writes, "Both the college boy and the corner boy want to get ahead. The difference between them is that the college boy either does not tie himself to a group of close friends [in the neighborhood] or else is willing to sacrifice his friendship with those who do not advance as fast as he does. The corner boy is tied to his group by a network of reciprocal obligations from which he is either unwilling or unable to break away" (1955, 107) The college boys in Whyte's work were dissociated from, if not downright unpopular with, local friends. Their local ties were weak. Corner boys, by contrast, were so strongly tied to their local networks that their chances for mobility were limited, since strong local ties implied a series of reciprocal obligations—including lending money or paying for others' expenses if others could not pay—that made mobility difficult (see also Coleman 1988; Portes 1998).

Whyte's work can serve as a point of departure to understand one critical factor affecting the residents' abilities to develop external ties: their sentiment about diverse elements of the local community. Whether residents are strongly tied to or dissociated from local networks is one component of whether they are strongly attached to or dissociated from the collective of individuals, groups, and institutions that make up the neighborhood. When understood this way, it becomes clear that attachment or dissociation are "meaningful" states partly motivated by nonmaterial interests, by sentiments such as loyalty, fear, or responsibility. To this extent, it becomes imperative to understand these sentiments, which I subsume under the term "neighborhood affect" (on affect, see Scheler 1992).

"Neighborhood affect" can be defined as the sentiment tied to individuals, groups, or institutions in the neighborhood that motivates individuals to wish attachment to the neighborhood or wish dissociation, regardless of whether such attachment or dissociation does, in fact, materialize. Sentiments producing a desire for greater attachment may be loyalty, appreciation, pride, guilt, or responsibility; those producing a wish for dissociation may be alienation, ridicule, shame, or fear. The individuals, groups, or institutions to which these sentiments are attached may be a family, a gang, a youth group, a spouse, a child, a church—in short, the collective of people and institutions that makes up a neighborhood—provided that such individual, group, or institution is perceived to be of the neighborhood. Indeed, in some cases, the symbolic idea itself of a neighborhood may incite a particular affect.

Researchers rarely examine the role of affect on mediating the effects of poor neighborhoods (but see Kasarda and Janowitz 1974; Austin and Baba 1990; Lee, Campbell, and Miller 1991). I suggest that the relationship between neighborhood affect and external capital depends on the type of affect—whether it incites attachment or dissociation. One way to understand how neighborhood affect (a sentiment) causally affects social capital is to contrast it to two common explanations: rationality and cultural valuation. Rationality assumes that individuals generate external networks or fail to do so because one action or the other maximizes their rational or economic interests; cultural valuation assumes individuals generate such networks or fail to do so because of their value systems. Neighborhood affect assumes that individuals generate such networks or fail to do so because they feel loyalty, guilt, pride, ridicule, fear, or other sentiments about their neighborhood or the individuals, groups, and institutions that compose it.

Among the five individuals in Villa Victoria discussed in detail above, these sentiments affected external social capital more strongly than either rationality or cultural valuation. Neighborhoods, and the institutions and individuals that compose them, incite sentiments in people. Those sentiments affect their motivation to develop external networks or sustain local ones.

One can think of positive or attachment-related affect as a mechanism behind Granovetter's (1973) strength-of-ties effect. Granovetter argued that strong ties were likely to be linked to other strong ties and that among a network of particularly strong ties it was unlikely there would be a link to a different, external network except via a weak tie. In the case of the Villa, Granovetter would suggest that residents embedded in a strong and dense local network would be unlikely to know many people outside Villa Victoria. His argument would be one of reduced likelihood, one of probability rather than causality. The cases at the Villa, however, suggest that strong local ties generate sentiments of loyalty, responsibility, or even guilt, which make it difficult for residents to break away from the neighborhood, much as they did in Whyte's case. That is, strong local ties may impede the generation of many strong external ones if the local ties are embedded in active sentiments.

Dissociation-related affect motivates individuals to reject association with the neighborhood. Here, the contrast with the Granovetter model is instructive. It is not merely that people with weak local ties will find it easier to develop external ties (provided they find the opportunity, in school, work, or other settings, to do so). It is that the sentiments they associate with local individuals, groups, and institutions may compel them to develop and sustain external ties.

The relationship between positive neighborhood affect and social isolation is clear in the cases of Eugenia and Ernesto. Despite their differences in age, personal history, and ability to speak English, Eugenia and Ernesto exemplify the effects of loyalty, pride, and comfort, all of which are inextricably tied to the neighborhood. Both have lived in the neighborhood for more than four decades; neither could imagine living anywhere else. Ernesto, as noted earlier, was proud to live in the Villa; Eugenia felt blessed, even as she felt the neighborhood could improve. Ernesto believed that he had made it in life, and Villa Victoria was an important component of that belief. Eugenia was less convinced that she had made it, but she had no doubts that making it would take place in the neighborhood, among locals, not anywhere else. While Ernesto will hardly involve himself in improving his lot at his advanced age, Eugenia will—though by no means will that involve leaving for another neighborhood. Her sentiments toward the neighborhood motivate her to focus her energies toward the neighborhood, to sustain friends locally rather than searching for them elsewhere, and to seek fulfillment in participation here rather than participation elsewhere, all of which ultimately limits her external networks. Yet in her case, at her age, she would not be bothered by this isolation. Indeed, Eugenia very much wants what turns out to be, in the sociological mind, social isolation.

Positive neighborhood affect among poor neighborhoods may be noticeably salient in the case of Villa Victoria, but it is not particularly rare. Suttles (1968) documents the territorial sense of ownership that developed among young men not in an entire neighborhood but in a collectively understood subsection of the Addams area. Indeed, much of the research on gangs has been about precisely this issue (Sánchez-Jankowski 1991).

A Labyrinth of Loyalties

The effect of neighborhood affect, nonetheless, is not always so straightforward. Sentiments, after all, are complicated and often contradictory, and sentiments about neighborhoods are no different. Residents alternately hate and love their Villa: they feel ashamed about the prevalence of drug dealing but feel possessiveness toward Villa Victoria when others berate it. Indeed, much of what took place among residents was neither persistently positive nor persistently negative neighborhood affect but a waxing and waning of one or another version of both.

Such sentiments are often meek, with hardly the push or pull necessary to affect social relations with others. At times, residents felt loyal to the Villa but not loyal enough to do much about it. Other times they complained about the violence but not because they had any intentions of moving elsewhere.

But among those residents who had actively devoted themselves in one or another form to local participation, neighborhood affect was an intense sentiment. For them, such sentiments led their social isolation to wax and wane dramatically over time. These residents were often of the second generation, for whom the benefits of moving, and severing their ties to the neighborhood, were much clearer than they had been to their ancestors. A generation much more exposed to American society, with greater access to its mainstream symbols and culture and its accompanying aspirations, they found generating external ties was not impossible but increasingly difficult owing to their participation in the Villa's activities.

Gloria, Oscar, and Melissa were all caught in what we can think of as a labyrinth of competing loyalties, in which neighborhood affect competes with their ambitions for mobility, most of which involve sustaining and developing external social capital. For the elders, Eugenia and Ernesto, becoming locally engaged was a way to sustain their ambitions and to improve their status; for Gloria, Oscar, and Melissa, becoming locally engaged was at least as much a hindrance to their ambitions as it was personally rewarding. For none of the three has local participation been a forgone conclusion. All of them have questioned their local engagement, and all of them have, after a history of participation, stopped for good, and then reinitiated their involvement. Theirs is a true labyrinth of loyalties and competing interests.

GLORIA: LOVE OF NEIGHBORHOOD, DISAPPOINTMENT WITH PEERS, PERSONAL AMBITION

Gloria's situation suggests that, though she is not particularly isolated, she would be even less so were it not for the effect of what can only be described as her loyalty (a sentiment) to the neighborhood. Gloria's parents were both highly involved in the community; they taught her the history of the neighborhood, how she might not be living there were it not for the efforts of pioneers in the late sixties. Through them, she developed an appreciation for, and even love of, the Villa.

Her fondness was deepened by her own experiences. Gloria was raised in the Villa during its golden years, between the late seventies and early eighties. She remembers that life there during her youth generated a sense of a supportive local community. "There was love," she says openly. "There was always lots of love between my friends and their family members, and even with us. It was always like family." As a child and a young teenager, much of her social life centered, as Ernesto's does now, around peers from the Villa and, in fact, Plaza Betances.

"It was beautiful, beautiful," she recalls. "We used to always hang out. People were always around. All the time. You wanted to socialize? Go to the plaza!" "More so than now?" I ask. "Way more than now." She elaborates:

> I wish there was still some of that stuff that I experienced as a kid, and being able to go out and have fun. Like "C'mon let's go roller-skating: let's go to *Spin Offs* [a rink]!" And we'd just have a ball, and our parents kind of felt like we were safe because we [all the children of the neighborhood] would all hang in like big groups. It wasn't like anybody could just come and do something to us. . . . We would go roller-skating together, go to movies together, go do all these fun things. And our parents trusted us. We had this trust thing going on and we were good kids.

Her descriptions hint at many of the elements sociologists argue as critical to a sense of community: local trust, intergenerational closure (Coleman 1988), the increased safety generated by informal social control, and the presence of many eyes on the street. These memories—of youth, her local friends, and the times they had at the Villa—are vivid to Gloria now in her thirties.

But things got complicated as she aged. "When I was younger [as a young teen] I used to be involved in this community. All my friends were Puerto Rican. But I couldn't handle it. The competition was too much, the boyfriends, et cetera. I experienced a lot of them not being loyal as friends." After her mother passed away, her father moved out, and her brother got married and went to live with his wife elsewhere, Gloria's family was no longer at the Villa. She moved out, too, for several years.

This was accompanied by a major shift in her narrative of herself. Prior to that time, she saw herself primarily as a Villa resident, one whose social life circled largely around the neighborhood, its people, its streets, and its plaza. But at the time she left, she started touring the country with her folkloric dance troupe. As a result, she met new people of diverse ethnic and class backgrounds. Some were people in the dance troupe, others were artists, dancers, and musicians that she had met from touring throughout the nation. She also began to generate networks among the many African-Americans in the new neighborhood in which she lived, just at the time she was turning into an adult. Slowly, she began to see herself differently, not as the member of a single community, the Villa, but as a "weaver." Now, she says of herself, "I can go through all kinds of communities and be comfortable there."

Eventually, however, she settled down. She abandoned the hectic life of the performer and dedicated herself to raising her son. When deciding what to do for a living after giving up dancing, she returned to Villa Victoria.

Gloria now has strong aspirations toward upward mobility, and she has considered buying a small house in the outskirts of Boston, where houses are still affordable to low-wage workers. However, she cannot fathom the thought of leaving the Villa, which she finds tantamount to abandoning her community. Her own involvement in local activities only serves to sustain these local ties and reinforces that sense of duty, complicating her desire to leave.

Particularly salient is that Gloria is attached not just to individuals who grew up with her but also to the community itself, to the highly symbolic sense of "Villa Victoria" as a representation of the outcome of an earlier generation's struggles. It is here where neither Granovetter's nor Whyte's frameworks are sufficient. Local attachment may limit residents' opportunities for generating outside networks not just by tying individuals to other individuals but also by tying them to communities in the broader sense, and even to the symbolic ideal of a community. Although Gloria's conception of herself had become that of a weaver, someone comfortable in different locations and willing to live just about anywhere, the Villa Victoria community has become so tied to her narrative of who she is, and to her sense of belonging and responsibility, that actually leaving the neighborhood permanently has become difficult. It is a constant struggle. In her words, "I live here and I'm not isolated, and it's by choice. . . . Yet to some degree I *am* isolated." The sentiments of love and loyalty on one hand and both the sentiment of disappointment (at betrayal by old friends) and her ambition of mobility on the other pull her in opposite directions.

MELISSA: PEER ALIENATION, LOVE OF FAMILY

Most of Melissa's friends and acquaintances live in other neighborhoods. During those years of her childhood when she lived at the Villa, Melissa went to school with other children from the Villa and developed friendships with them. But Melissa's stay at the Villa was sporadic, punctuated by prolonged periods of residence in Connecticut. Indeed, she considers herself to have been "raised" in Connecticut. Her attachments to individuals at the Villa, interrupted by long periods of disconnection, were ultimately weak.

In Connecticut, she lived in a working- and middle-class African-

American neighborhood that had a good public school system. At her school, there was a particularly strong art program, where Melissa discovered she had a talent for music. She took as many music courses as she could, spent much of her time around artists, young and old, and began seeing herself as a potential musician in training.

By the time Melissa moved back to the Villa as a teenager, she had already developed her own, eccentric style of dress, hair, and makeup, closer to the retro funk-rock style of the music bands she admired than to the break dance and early hip-hop style of the rest of the teenagers of the Villa. Her peers at the Villa did not take this well, and when she returned to the Boston area from Connecticut she was not very popular. She explains: "I was very expressive, I dressed very eccentrically. I'll be honest with you, I didn't have too many friends in high school. Because I listened to house music and beats, I was called a house-head. I didn't dress in Gap [clothing], and that type of thing. I wore platform shoes, big hair, things like that. . . . Like Lenny Kravitz. I liked him. [I dressed like this] at fourteen. I was going to clubs." Within a year or two, her peers' rejection, though not necessarily malicious or complete, was firm. Hence, she remembers, "when I'd walk through the Villa, they'd say 'There's [Melissa] and her weirdos.' . . . I wasn't in that loop anymore. My girlfriends and I were spreading apart. I didn't have many friends in high school." For her part, she believed she now had little in common with the children with whom she had gone to grade school. "I thought they were—let me be blunt— kind of 'ghetto.' [They were] very street smart [but]. . . . [*her voice trails off*] Maybe because I grew up in [Connecticut]. . . ." As she was forging her identity as an adolescent, her interests, already different in part because of her upbringing in Connecticut, became more and more detached from those of her peers; she was, therefore, an outcast, forced to search elsewhere for a close friendship network. Narrative theorists suggest that changes in one's narrative of oneself will result in changes in one's actions. In this case, the changes in Melissa's self narrative, coupled with the rejection of her peers, resulted in her search for networks in locales where her new narrative of herself would be supported.

She found these at work, in clubs, and through music. "When I was sixteen I met my boyfriend. He was six years older. The people I was working with were older. [So] I hung out with older people. People from Emerson [College]," a local college of communications, music, and media. Now, as a young adult, her friends are no longer in the neighborhood. The detachment, initiated by her place of birth and exacerbated by her upbringing in a different neighborhood and divergence of musical and stylistic tastes, became solidified. "[The kids in the neighborhood] know me. But we don't say hi anymore. We've drifted apart. It's weird because I've distanced myself but I'm still here." Though her feelings about her neighborhood and her relationship to it are mixed, ultimately, Melissa cannot wait to move out of the Villa.

Yet her family is still here, and they constitute her most critical support network. Indeed, her mother, who lives at the Villa, was the reason she left Connecticut at fourteen. Just as the alienation from her local peers drives her dissociation, her loyalty to and need for her family pulls her back in; both types of affect are working on her, driving her in different directions.

She also feels a sense of profound responsibility toward the neighborhood, one probably inherited from her mother, one of the pioneers of the neighborhood. Thus, although she has been highly involved in the past, and still feels a responsible to "do something," she also wants to leave. Her struggle is palpable, magnified by her own impassioned personality. At times, she had decided unequivocally she needed to depart; at others, that she could easily make a rewarding life for herself in the neighborhood. She resembled Gloria in this sense, experiencing periods in which living in the Villa seemed out of the question and others in which living there seemed the best and most rewarding option. Yet whereas Gloria went back and forth between these extremes over the course of years, Melissa went back and forth over the course of a month. No one would doubt the honesty of either of their commitments.

OSCAR: LOVE OF COMMUNITY, PERSONAL AMBITION

Oscar shares Melissa and Gloria's combined sense of attachment and dissociation, though in his own idiosyncratic way. In one sense, Oscar is intimately attached to Villa Victoria. When speaking of what paths his career may take him, he says, colorfully:

> I'll always, always remember where I come from, and I'll always give back to my community, I will always be there to lend a hand, lend a leg, lend an arm, lend a mind, lend a mouth, lend an eye. And if possible be there financially. If it ever gets to that point. Because that's how much my community means to me. It means so much to me. It would be disheartening to see that my community does not exist any more. Because this is my life. It's all I've known for———years. It's the only place that I've called home [in my entire life]. I've called little bits and places like, you know, my dorm room at

school, and, you know, when I go away, these are my little homes, but this is my *home* home. This is where my mom lives. This is where [I and my sister] were raised.

For Oscar, Villa Victoria constitutes an important element of his narrative of himself. In this sense he resembles Gloria. However, he lacks the strong attachments to childhood friends that constituted such a central part of Gloria's memories of the neighborhood. His strongest local ties are to his family.

Furthermore, Oscar, like Melissa, is somewhat eccentric. He is bookish, bespectacled, conservatively dressed. He is not quite rejected by his peers the way Melissa was as an adolescent. He is considered different but is hardly ostracized. In his case, then, the dissociation effect is modest. He experiences distance more than outright rejection. His response to that distance is instructive:

> A lot of people [from the Villa] look at me and say, "you're different." But how am I different? My thing is, like I said, it all goes back to being open-minded. As a child I went to these places. We used to go to the Prudential sprinkler system, you know. I still hung out with my friends [from the neighborhood] and stuff like that but I didn't want to sell myself short. I didn't want to just keep myself in an environment. I've always been a person who always wanted to do more and get out, learn more. . . . So, I feel like when people go, well, "you're different," but how am I different? Just because I think a certain way or do things different, [or because] I don't have quote-unquote "the lifestyle" or the way some people act in this community? Because I don't act the same way you guys do, I'm different? I don't see myself as different. I just see myself as a person who has not limited myself. I've always kept myself open . . . to be able to . . . do things, you know, to go to ———— Academy for the summer, which is a great accomplishment. To go . . . overseas [in a high school exchange program], and in high school [to] study four years . . . [a different language,] and not just take Spanish just to pass. I've always wanted to challenge myself.

While the community is an important component of his narrative of himself, it is by no means the only one. He understands himself as someone who has been nurtured by Villa Victoria but who must also transcend it. The soft dissociation from his local ties and his willful search for external ties and opportunities feed on each other in a continuous cycle. Oscar's struggle is the least emotionally challenging among himself, Gloria, and Melissa, probably in part because of his unusually positive outlook on life. Yet the struggle is just as penetrating; it is just as difficult for him to say, with any certainty, whether he wishes to remain in the Villa for much of his life.

That much, at least, Oscar shares with Gloria and Melissa, while Eugenia and Ernesto, in contrast, have no interest in ever living anywhere else. The conflicting desires of the three about whether to stay or leave also set them apart from most uninvolved residents of their generation, who would probably leave the neighborhood if they could. They want to move up the social ladder, yet they also want to remain involved. They are all committed to the Villa but all are aware of the socioeconomic possibilities elsewhere; they have all experienced dissociation in some way, yet all feel profound attachment because of loyalty, fondness, or love of family. All of them have been loners without being isolated: "I was always a loner. And it didn't bother me. I never hung out with any particular group. I always jumped around." These comments were Gloria's, but they could have been Melissa's or Oscar's just as well. They are all "weavers" in Gloria's term, or "chameleons," in the words of another second-generation resident who shares this predicament. Theirs is a continuous search for the way out of this labyrinth.

Generating Networks

Are Ernesto, Eugenia, Gloria, Melissa and Oscar socially isolated? The question now seems hopelessly simplistic (though not, I hope, hopelessly complex). What researchers have called social isolation has varied over these people's lifetimes, even if not to the same extent and not always for the same reasons. As a young man, Ernesto was less isolated than he is now. When she attended college and before she started working in the South End, Melissa was also less isolated than she is now. Gloria, in contrast, broke through her local ties when she began touring with her dance troupe, going from a degree of moderate isolation to very little if any.

We learn less about these differences by developing an overarching typology than by conceiving of the relationship between neighborhood poverty and social isolation as dynamic, a process that changes over residents' lifetimes and depends on intermediary conditions, such as generational status (including age, language ability, and immigration status) and being employed or in school. These conditions present opportunities of which the residents, in turn, may or may not take advantage. At the neighborhood level, we saw in the previous two chapters that the impact of the neighborhood's poverty on residents social ties was affected by a set of ecological conditions that provided, among other things, a resource-rich, Spanish-friendly environment with plazas and public spaces within short walks of their apartments. At the individual level, we now see that the residents' personal circumstances at any given time, such as whether they are employed, affect the impact of these neighborhood-level attributes. For the jobless Ernesto, the effects are much greater than for the busy Gloria.

These relationships become more complicated when we introduce community participation. The latter does not prevent external networking so much as complicates it, as neighborhood affect becomes salient. Sociologists in this field have steered clear of studying the effects of affect—loyalty, local pride, ridicule, alienation—but in the Villa this neglect would miss an important element of whether and how residents are able to generate external networks. Recent scholars of social movements have rediscovered these factors (Goodwin, Jasper, and Polletta 2001); urban social scientists may gain much from doing so as well.

EIGHT

Social Capital in Poor Neighborhoods

Are ghettos and housing projects socially isolated? Are they devoid of social capital? Are they deprived of resources? Are they politically apathetic? For the past fifteen years, we have, more often than not, answered these questions affirmatively and turned to ethnographic work (or waited for ethnographic work) to explain how or why this happens. We have often expected ghettos to look more or less the same in cities across the country. Indeed, that is the general conclusion of the conception of the ghetto as an institution. At the very least, we have assumed that whatever differences exist among actual poor neighborhoods- -however much variance there is in any particular characteristic of such neighborhoods—their main effects are common, such that the mechanisms by which neighborhood poverty affects individuals must also be common to most poor neighborhoods. These assumptions are rarely articulated, but they are implicit in the standard hypotheses about what these mechanisms are, hypotheses that happen to correspond neatly with lay assumptions: that poor neighborhoods reduce trust and increase fear and that they provide few role models and numerous bad peers for the young. Thus, whatever the most important mechanisms are, they must operate independently of the particular context in which they occur in any given neighborhood. In this specific sense, we have assumed, the mechanisms must be decontextualized.

Villa Victoria suggests that if we remain exclusively tied to this approach we are unlikely to understand many of the critical mechanisms by which neighborhood poverty affects individuals. The standard approach assumes what should be tested: that these mechanisms manifest themselves universally, that differences between poor neighborhoods are either minimal or unimportant to opening the black box. The Villa suggests, on the contrary, that differences between poor neighborhoods are critical to opening the box.

The approach followed in this book is to use heterogeneity in responses to neighborhood poverty as the starting point rather than to ignore that element. At issue is the reason why poor neighborhoods and the people who live in them are often *not* deprived of social capital—not politically apathetic, not socially isolated. I have assumed here that their positive response to this negative condition is no mere artifact of chance, which in turn assumes that the relationship between neighborhood poverty and social capital is neither automatic nor spurious but conditional on factors that must be identified.

The case of the Villa has brought to light several of these conditional factors. Some of these were neighborhood-level factors, such as the availability of resources in the neighborhood, the quality of boundaries (fixed or loose) between the poor households and surrounding nonpoor ones, the ethnic and class composition of the neighborhood and its adjacent neighborhoods, and the characteristics of cohorts of residents. Others were individual-level factors, such as age, immigration status, employment status, affect toward the neighborhood, and the narrative frames through which a resident perceives her or his neighborhood. Poor neighborhoods are not homogeneous on the first set of factors, and poor individuals are not homogeneous on the second. But the relationship between these two sets of factors and neighborhood poverty is not arbitrary, as we have seen in the Villa. Thus, the Villa suggests that understanding this heterogeneity should be the priority if we wish to uncover internal neighborhood mechanisms. For example, poor neighborhoods with a paucity of institutional resources affect individuals differently from poor neighborhoods with a preponderance of such resources. And, under the right conditions, neighborhood poverty can be predictably associated with *either* a paucity *or* a preponderance of resources. Many important mechanisms are related to intermediary conditions in this fashion.

This approach is explored in greater detail in the pages that follow; it is compared to similar approaches in other subfields of sociology and contrasted with the standard approach to how neighborhood poverty affects life chances. This is not a method, per se, but a perspective from which to consider these questions, a perspective that, in addition, is consistent with both quantitative and qualitative research. The discussion will place the specific analyses throughout the book within a broader perspective about poor neighborhoods.

That discussion is largely conceptual. However, there are substantive lessons that the case of Villa Victoria offers to the questions of community participation and personal networks among the poor. Thus, we temporarily bracket the discussion of this approach and elaborate on the contributions of this case to our understanding of local community participation and networks in poor neighborhoods.

Notes on Community Participation

Most of the substantively important issues about community participation in the Villa, such as the interaction between structural and cultural factors and the role of neighborhood framing processes, were discussed in chapters 3, 4, and 7. Here we elaborate on what the Villa suggests about community participation more generally.

Villa Victoria crystallizes an important characteristic of community participation. The relationship we uncovered between community participation and neighborhood interpretive frames was a peculiar macro-micro phenomenon: A neighborhood's participation level is technically a macro-level variable; its residents' narrative framing of the neighborhood is a microlevel phenomenon (or at least a phenomenon observed at the microlevel). Yet microlevel phenomena were instructive about macrolevel change because so few of the residents were involved that understanding something about that small group told us much about the neighborhood as a whole. Since the vast majority of people in any neighborhood are not involved in voluntary, neighborhood-related activities, a small number of people—even less than 1 percent of a total population—can make a large difference in a neighborhood's overall level of participation.

Neighborhood participation is an instance of what economists and business strategists have called the 80/20 phenomenon, or the principle of the "vital few" and "trivial many" (see Juran 1954; Gladwell 2000). By this principle, 80 percent of the change in a given phenomenon will likely be perpetrated by 20 percent of the population. In the words of an early proponent: "In any series of elements to be controlled, a selected small fraction, in terms of numbers of elements, always accounts for a large fraction, in terms of effect" (Juran 1954, 749). This was certainly the case at Villa. In fact, the Villa suggests community participation might be a 90/10 or even a 98/2 phenomenon, since the involvement of a couple of dozen residents made the neighborhood a place more organized than many other poor neighborhoods.

This principle helps explain the ease with which participation could theoretically change. The Villa contains roughly 3,000 persons and eight hundred households. Suppose a time in which there is no local involvement. A change in the participation rate from 0 to 1 percent of the population would constitute an increase from none to thirty engaged individuals. In percentage points the change is minuscule, but the dedicated participation of thirty individuals can have a robust impact on the number of visible activities available in the neighborhood. For example, if every three of them dedicated themselves to a separate activity, there would be ten activities or programs of some sort, more than exist in many neighborhoods of this size. The reality, of course, is more diffuse, as individuals become less or more involved over time, increasing or decreasing the apparent number of involved persons at any given time. But understanding something about those thirty persons would reveal a great deal about the conceptual macrolevel question of neighborhood change.

Another important aspect of community participation is its relative rarity—or, to be more precise, its rarity as a sustained phenomenon over an extended time period. In the Villa, extended community participation in the 1970s and 1980s began as a result of the residents' positive experience with political mobilization in the late 1960s. Yet threats of the particular magnitude experienced by the residents of Parcel 19 in the 1960s occur infrequently in any given neighborhood and only within a small portion of neighborhoods at any given time. Furthermore, only a small portion of these threats result in a successful mobilization effort. Since it was this success that convinced residents of the newly constructed Villa that community participation was important, what can we derive from the historical case of the Villa about community participation in other neighborhoods?

One cannot determine, a priori, the historical circumstances that will drive a particular group of residents to perceive their neighborhood through symbolic channels that make participation seem important. Yet one can hypothesize what types of conditions are necessary for this to happen. Using the Villa, I suggest two different types of conditions: sustaining mechanisms and inciting mechanisms.

Cultural frames, I have suggested, are dynamic not static or unchanging entities (Benford 1997; Steinberg 1998, 1999). As such, in order for any set of categories to sustain themselves, reinforcement mechanisms are required, for they are bound to change as the lives of individuals and groups change. In the case of residents of poor neighborhoods such mechanisms are bound to be tied to the relationship between their neighborhood and their life chances, insofar as poverty is a state that one—in theory—wishes to escape or whose effects one wishes to alleviate. The situation of the Villa suggests that the sustenance of the types of neighborhood narratives conducive to participation is more likely to occur among individuals (or cohorts) for whom their best opportunities are perceived to be tied to the neighborhood. For Ernesto, Eugenia, Roberta, and others of that first generation, returning to the Villa after construction was an instance of upward mobility and about as much upward mobility as they expected in their lifetime. In this instance, their existing perception of the Villa as symbolically important was likely to sustain itself.

But for Tommy, Don, and others of the second cohort, the Villa was a ghetto one ought to transcend. Even if they heard—as everyone in the Villa eventually did—the tales of the political struggles of the 1960s, they were unlikely to sustain a perception of the Villa as beautiful or important in light of the possibility of mobility they saw and wanted for themselves, a possibility that could only come to fruition if they left Villa Victoria. As we saw, while this cohort evinced less social capital of a particular type—community participation—it had much more social capital of another type: sustained networks with residents of other neighborhoods. Part of the effect of this latter social capital was the broadening of their aspirations. When a resident's aspirations involve or require leaving the neighborhood, a narrative of the type of the first generation is difficult to sustain. Thus, one can formulate as a necessary mechanism for the sustenance of such narratives the belief that one's life chances would not realistically be much improved by living elsewhere. This belief does not imply despair. Rather, it implies they have not concluded they can do better by going elsewhere; in those instances when that conclusion is reached, it becomes extremely difficult to sustain such narratives.[1]

Equally important are those mechanisms that help incite, rather than sustain, a perception or narrative frame of the neighborhood conducive to participation. Here, I generate some hypotheses extrapolating from the Villa. The question can be posed thus: What will drive a group of residents who were previously not involved locally to develop a perception of their neighborhood that is conducive to community participation? Few poor

---

1. Observing who the members of the second cohort are that are nonetheless highly involved is instructive. All of them shared much of their older relatives' conception of the neighborhood, but their perception, tempered by their experience of a more deteriorated landscape, was second hand, more impressionistic, and often less articulate. As we saw in chap. 7, several of these young leaders struggled with their felt responsibility to contribute somehow to community life in the Villa versus their ambition for upward mobility. Their perception of the neighborhood, despite its similarities to the first cohort's, was more ambiguous, for it relied on a more precarious sustaining mechanism. Indeed, one suspects it will not last as long as it did for their parents.

neighborhoods have experienced the spectacular and volatile birth that Villa Victoria did. But the basic mechanism is easily replicable on a smaller scale: a sudden, exogenous threat (in Parcel 19, of displacement) produces a momentary spurt of engagement (in this case, to resist displacement), whose outcome contributes to a reconfiguration of the running narrative of the neighborhood. Momentary crises, large or small, incite short-term reactions, which distort the established social order and have the potential of transforming cultural perceptions as communities attempt to reestablish normalcy.

This pattern parallels Swidler's (1986) argument that "unsettled times" bring symbolic categories to the fore, creating the possibility for their contestation, reimagination, and transformation. Sewell (1996, 867) found something similar at a much larger scale, when he argued that political dislocations of the social structure (in his case, in France in the spring of 1789) produce a transformation of the symbolic channels through which society is interpreted. But events may be much smaller in scale—such as a particularly atrocious crime perpetrated in the neighborhood or the imminent threat of a new runway at a nearby airport—leading to short-term action that creates "unsettlement," allowing for the reconfiguration of cultural perceptions of the neighborhood and the possibility (on a smaller scale) of the conception of community participation as important. It is under such times that cultural perceptions are likely to change radically, as crises heighten cultural activity.[2]

An inciting mechanism of this nature, coupled with the sustaining mechanisms described above, has the potential to transform an unengaged community into one in which participation for its own sake is supported for more than just the very short term. To be clear, this process relates to local community participation, as the term has been employed throughout this book, and not necessarily to sustained political mobiliza-

---

2. Here, it is important to distinguish a shock from mere neighborhood change. To be sure, "settled" and "unsettled" are relative terms, and neighborhoods, especially urban neighborhoods, are constantly in flux (see Schwirian 1983; Taub, Taylor, and Dunham 1984). However, not all changes should be considered crises; that is, although urban neighborhoods may be constantly in flux, they are not constantly experiencing shocks. The distinguishing characteristics of a shock probably lie at the juncture of intensity and suddenness. In the case of Parcel 19, the crisis was high in magnitude; in neighborhoods were the crisis is lower in magnitude, it probably must be higher in intensity (e.g., with a higher number of interested and contentious parties) or in suddenness or unexpectedness (e.g., as in the case of a horrid crime) to generate an "unsettled time" likely to produce cultural reassessment. Furthermore, larger crises are probably more likely to lead to cultural reassessment and revaluations. One possibility for generating formal predictions in this respect lies in adapting the models of neighborhood change in Taub, Taylor, and Dunham (1984), which take into account ecology, corporate decisions, and individual decisions.

tion around specific issues (e.g., voter registration), though the latter may well be affected by similar dual mechanisms. Nor does this argument preclude that other factors, such as local institutions or favorable political environments, serve important sustaining functions as well. The issue here is the role of how residents perceive their neighborhoods.[3]

Notes on Social Isolation

The question of social isolation in ghettos or poor neighborhoods is, at heart, an issue of how people develop networks. Why should a person's address affect who her friends are? This was the challenge to proponents of social isolation theory, for whom neighborhood poverty, independent of individual poverty, limited a person's social networks. The challenge was complicated by the fact that recent advances in technology and communications have made geographic boundaries less restrictive than they used to be. Network sociologists have argued that networks are not concentrated in a single location but "ramified" across space, rendering neighborhoods increasingly irrelevant to network formation (Wellman 1979, 1999; Fischer 1982). If these researchers are correct, then living in a poor neighborhood should bear little or no relevance to one's social circle.

The case of the Villa has suggested that poor neighborhoods may have an impact on residents' social capital under certain conditions. The most salient condition in this instance was the prevalence of resources. Having access to not only basic goods and services—such as health care, day care, groceries, grooming, and mail—but also those specific services targeted at Spanish-speaking and Latino groups—such as Spanish-speaking health care workers, Spanish religious services, and ethnic foods—meant the residents had significantly fewer incentives to leave their neighborhood than others might in equally poor but resource-deprived neighborhoods. In a very concrete sense, their address affected their likely social circles.

What this book referred to as the ecology of resources in poor neigh-

---

3. Anyone wishing to understand this process as it unfolds over time in a given neighborhood may well be forced to confront the transformations in collective memory experienced by its residents. The memory of the Villa's creation was maintained through both physical symbols—such as the murals on Plaza Betances and the Jorge Hernández Cultural Center—and oral histories. Indeed, the very name of the neighborhood is an incitement to not forget. But histories such as these are constantly reinterpreted in light of new cohorts, new interests, and new economic circumstances, as thinkers as varied as Nietzsche ([1887] 1967) and Schudson (1992) have made clear. Significant events are not merely remembered as they were but are reinterpreted. In neighborhoods without the benefit of the relative residential stability Villa Victoria enjoyed, remembering will be an increasingly difficult task.

borhoods is a version of what Breton (1964) calls "institutional completeness" among ethnic groups. The extent to which a neighborhood or group can provide necessary services is inversely related to the level of interaction that residents or members will have with people from other neighborhoods or ethnic groups. The abundance of local institutions and businesses attenuates the effects of poverty but accentuates social isolation.

In a sense, the impact of resource prevalence on social isolation is a softer version of the institutional effect documented by Gamm (1999) in his *Urban Exodus: Why the Jews Left Boston and the Catholics Stayed.* Gamm also finds that institutions attach people to their neighborhoods, though the institutions he identifies are religious. He uncovers that the rules governing the relationship between people and either churches or synagogues in a neighborhood strongly affect whether the community remains territorially bound to the neighborhood, that is, whether it is willing to move out of its geographic community. Nevertheless, that attachment to religious institutions differs from the Villa residents' attachment to the neighborhood's local resources. Among Catholics in Dorchester, institutional attachment was driven by complex ecclesiastical rules about the roles of the church in a community; among the Puerto Ricans of the Villa, it was driven by convenience.

Having said this, it was not merely convenience that limited many residents' networks to the local scene. The Villa's eventful past highlights an issue that is noted in some ethnographic studies (Gregory 1998, Venkatesh 2000) but that is largely neglected in large-sample tests: people develop emotional reactions to their neighborhoods. These reactions may range from disgust through apathy to loyalty, but they may well affect the types of social investments residents make on their neighbors, as they did among Melissa, Gloria, and Eugenia. It is a truism that humans are emotional creatures. On the question of poverty, emotion about one's neighborhood is likely to play a critical role.

A Conditional Approach

THE BASIC PERSPECTIVE

In this book, I have attempted to show the benefits of employing a conditional approach to understand how poor neighborhoods affect social capital and, indeed, to think about poor neighborhoods or ghettos. This approach may be contrasted to the universalistic perspective that predominates the research and the particularistic critique that may be its principal alternative. The three general approaches have strengths and limitations. But the conditional approach is especially well suited to address much of what we do not know about how neighborhood poverty affects life outcomes.

The crux of the universalistic approach is its search for mechanisms that work across poor neighborhoods, regardless of the neighborhoods' other particular traits. Some researchers assume that poor neighborhoods—say, those with a poverty rate greater than 40 percent (Jargowsky and Bane 1991)—share a bundle of characteristics that affect social outcomes more or less universally across these neighborhoods. Indeed, this is the foundation behind the idea of the inner-city ghetto as an institution (Wilson 1987; Wacquant 1997). Others assume, more simply, that regardless of the differences across poor neighborhoods, they differ little in those key factors that affect social outcomes. This is the assumption behind the recent Moving to Opportunity experiments, where participants in the treatment group were offered vouchers that could only be used in a neighborhood, any neighborhood, with a poverty rate under 10 percent (Katz, Kling, and Liebman 2001). The idea is that even though, by design, participants in the treatment group are moving to neighborhoods that differ in a host of traits, they are still considered to be subject to the same single "treatment" (a neighborhood less than 10 percent poor). When searching for mechanisms, followers of this approach expect to find a common set of factors, such as the absence of educated role models (Cutler and Glaeser 1997), across most poor neighborhoods affecting a particular outcome.

The crux of the particularistic approach is its search for the mechanisms working to produce an outcome in a particular case. The assumption is that poor neighborhoods differ so radically from one another that generalizations about all of them, though statistically valid (if phrased in probabilistic terms), are necessarily removed from their local contexts and, thus, likely to relate to issues of little importance or salience in actual neighborhoods. The particularist perspective is less prevalent in the urban poverty field than in others such as historical sociology, but it has informed some important critiques of Wilson's work. The case studies in Moore and Pinderhughes's (1993) *In the Barrios: Latinos and the Underclass Debate* showed that social isolation theories about the ghetto failed miserably among some Latino communities, where poverty as severe as that described by Wilson was not accompanied by the "social pathologies" he hypothesized.

In common with the universalistic perspective, a conditional approach searches for regularities across neighborhoods; however, it does not assume that those mechanisms common to most poor neighborhoods will be necessarily the most important. In fact, *it assumes that the notion of a "typical" poor neighborhood is unhelpful to unpacking the black box.* It treats observed mechanisms as conditions, not universal traits of poor neighborhoods. As a result, it would conceive of the absence of critical resources that Wilson famously described to be not attributes necessary for poor neighborhoods but attributes of a set of black inner-city neighborhoods in Chicago. Universalists develop theories about mechanisms in place in all (or most) poor neighborhoods; conditionalists develop theories about mechanisms in place only in those poor neighborhoods meeting specified conditions.

In common with the particularistic perspective, a conditional approach focuses on context and intermediary factors; however, it does not aim to explain all the factors leading to a particular outcome in a given case. Rather, it tends to focus on those conditions at least theoretically capable of manifesting themselves in different neighborhood settings. In this sense, its analyses of a particular neighborhood tend to be less holistic and idiographic and more targeted and aimed at comparison. Thus, rather than seeing cases as historically arbitrary, it seeks to place them within the context of testable theories about conditional relationships—for example, that high poverty will contribute to high isolation from surrounding neighbors, provided the boundaries between poor and nonpoor areas are fixed, or that the prevalence of critical resources in the neighborhood will contribute to high isolation, provided such resources cannot be had in better quality or at lower costs elsewhere.

An instructive exercise is comparing how the three approaches would undertake ethnographic research. A universalist searches for a "typical" (i.e., roughly representative) poor neighborhood, with the assumption that these mechanisms could later be tested among the universe of poor neighborhoods. The neighborhood would represent, in statistical language, a sample with an n of 1, and the more representative its characteristics the better. This general approach is undoubtedly useful when studying populations about which little is known. The social relations expertly depicted in Pattillo-McCoy's (1999) *Black Picket Fences* study of the pseudonymous Groveland neighborhood in Chicago contrasted life among this group of middle-class blacks to what most of us assume is life in white middle-class neighborhoods. The author's observations were meant to apply (potentially) to the black middle class as a whole, not exclusively to the particular black middle-class residents in these few blocks in Chicago.[4] The idea would be later to test whether these patterns are in place across the universe of black middle-class neighborhoods. Though useful when intended to bring attention to previously unknown (or understudied) groups, this approach would perform less adequately, I suggest, in identifying many of the mechanisms behind neighborhood poverty in the ways we are interested. Since it deliberately ignores mechanisms dependent on the particular context of the neighborhood, it will miss all factors that depend on a specific manifestation of neighborhood poverty (e.g., resource prevalence) likely to be found in many but not present in all poor neighborhoods.

A particularist searches for a neighborhood without regard for representativeness but with an interest in accounting for all major influences producing a specific outcome in that neighborhood. Here, a particular neighborhood is not a sample with an n of 1; it is, in statistical language, the universe, because the explanatory interest is in what happened in that particular case, not what happened or might happen anywhere else. This general approach is especially useful under two circumstances. The first is where the universe does, in fact, constitute only one or two cases. Cold War studies of the United States as a superpower were, in a sense, highly sophisticated studies with a sample of one (the United States) from a population of two (the United States and the USSR). They were not concerned with what happened in other countries. The second is when the population is relatively unknown but, unlike the universalist case, also very small, as in the early anthropological ethnographies. Thus, even though one might test whether the community patterns in Pattillo-McCoy's Groveland were in place among black middle-class neighborhoods in, say, Baltimore, one would not test whether the cockfights Geertz (1972) found in Bali were in place among the Tarahumara in Mexico. Here, cases are important in their own right. The difficulty with this approach is that it provides little information as to how to tie the case to other settings.

A conditionalist also searches for a neighborhood without regard to representativeness. However, here the neighborhood is neither a sample

4. Indeed, the use of a pseudonym for the neighborhood is a nod to the idea that the particular historical circumstances in which the neighborhood is found are unimportant to the general story. A different instance of this is Venkatesh's (2000) *American Project,* a social history of the Robert Taylor Homes. Though a case of a single neighborhood, the work (which is not titled, e.g., *One American Project* or *The Robert Taylor Homes*) is meant to provide a window into "the fabric of 'project living'" in general (2000, 10).

nor the universe but a case with a specific configuration of conditions.[5] Although the configuration is unique to the neighborhood, each of the conditions may manifest itself in other neighborhoods. Like the particularist, the conditionalist tends to focus on the context at hand but, unlike the particularist, pays special attention to those conditions at least theoretically capable of manifesting themselves elsewhere, such as the presence of external threats or fixed neighborhood boundaries. In this sense, conditionalist studies are by definition incomplete accounts of the particular neighborhood. For example, as in the case of this book, these studies do not account for every historical factor that may have affected a neighborhood's decline in participation or its residents' tendencies to remain within its boundaries. They do not seek to be comprehensive accounts of the particular community; they seek, rather, to be comprehensive accounts of the particular condition (e.g., the fixed boundary). Herein lies the conditionalist's tradeoff between generality and context.[6] Generalizable hypotheses, that is, are critical, but they should be thought of differently.

Contrasting the different approaches to ethnographic research is appropriate because uncovering the black box will require more historical ethnographic and comparative ethnographic work. Indeed, several (though not all) of the processes discussed in this book can only be addressed with any seriousness through ethnographic field research. Nevertheless, the conditional perspective is not an approach exclusive to ethnographic fieldwork. It is a way of thinking applicable to multiple methods, including large-scale quantitative studies. The issue is the approach to the data, not the data themselves.

OTHER PERSPECTIVES

The standard approach first tests that neighborhood poverty has an effect on social capital net of other factors and then searches for mechanisms at play in the typical (statistically average) poor neighborhood. The conditional approach assumes that the effect of neighborhood poverty on social

---

5. To be sure, particularists often call their studies "cases" as well. For lack of a better word, it is used here to contrast how particularist and conditionalist approaches would address the issue of generalizability.

6. Universalist, particularist, and conditionalist approaches to ethnographic research are ideal types. Probably no ethnographic studies, including this book, fall strictly within any of these categories. The contrast in the approach to fieldwork is instructive because understanding many of the mechanisms underlying how neighborhood poverty affects life requires fieldwork.

capital is not automatic but also not spurious; it assumes that the effect is conditional on intermediary factors and sees its task as identifying those conditions. Under identifiable conditions, it assumes, neighborhood poverty will not affect social capital.[7] This conditionalist perspective is by no means new to sociology. In many ways, it follows a type of thinking similar to (though distinct from) that in at least two other strands of sociological thought: the early Chicago school and Qualitative Comparative Analysis (Ragin 1987).

The early ethnographies of the Chicago school, concerned as they were with space and time, also prioritized context, though not within the explicit framework about mechanisms described above and certainly not within the context of recent theoretical advances in neighborhood poverty research. Discussing the early Chicago school work, Abbott (1997) calls this a "contextualist paradigm," in which understanding context is the key objective of the research. This paradigm is contrasted to what he calls the "variable paradigm" currently dominant in sociology. Abbott presented a formidable critique of the variable paradigm's tendency to search for variables having an effect after all other factors are held constant. In social reality, all other factors are not constant, and practitioners, according to Abbot, have come to reify variables at the expense of society and to substitute association for explanation.

Abbotts's critique, as well as those of others (Lieberson 1985; Ragin 1987), have been refreshing and promising. However, the standard statistical models still have, at least in theory, much to offer to the question of neighborhood mechanisms. Some of the propositions advanced in this book could be tested using large samples of neighborhoods and estimating models with interaction terms between neighborhood poverty and the intermediary conditions. But this would require first positing what these conditions are and then collecting new large-scale data on these conditions. The variables found in traditional datasets such as the decennial census only provide a minuscule portion of the potential conditions to examine. They do not have measures, for example, on whether the boundaries between poor and nonpoor areas are fixed or on the number of businesses and nonprofit institutions in a neighborhood. Creative new data collection methods would be required. An example is systematic so-

7. One might argue that asking whether a relationship exists logically precedes asking under what conditions it exists, but that is not the case. The difference between the questions is not in the sequence they should be asked but in the type of answers they demand. If we assume a conditional approach and then find no such conditions, then that in itself would be a finding. Yet it is clear from both this study and the existing evidence that at least certain such conditions exist.

cial observation, where observational data are collected from a representative cross-sectional sample of neighborhoods using video cameras and trained observers (Sampson and Raudenbush 1999). In addition, employing the standard statistical models would require abandoning the tendency to think of variables, including these interactions, as something to "control away," rather than using them as tools toward theorizing social processes (Lieberson 1985).[8]

Besides its parallels to the early Chicago school, the conditional approach implies what Ragin (1987) has called "conjunctural causation," the notion that a certain outcome results not from a single variable but from a combination of causal factors. Rather than searching for which variables produce an outcome "net of other factors" one searches for the combination of variables that produce an outcome. The issue is the intention of the research. For example, such research would not aim to uncover that neighborhood poverty produces social isolation after controlling for selection bias; it would aim to uncover that social isolation results from, say, the combination of neighborhood poverty, resource prevalence, and ethnic homogeneity (at the neighborhood level), and the inability to speak English and positive neighborhood affect (at the individual level). Ragin's Qualitative Comparative Analysis (QCA) method, used often, though not exclusively, in studies in which the universe of cases is small (e.g., all east European countries) employs Boolean algorithms to simplify complex interactions of variables by reducing the number of possible relationships among them that leads to the outcome of interest. The approach assumes that a specific combination of variables (or two or more combinations of variables) will always produce the outcome of interest.

The idea of conjunctural causation is consistent with the conditional perspective, since both focus on the operation of combinations of factors to produce an observed outcome. Whether probabilistic or deterministic approaches are best, however, is a matter to be addressed in other work, though a nonprobabilistic perspective might seem difficult to embrace in the study of neighborhood-level processes. The appeal of QCA is that it forces the shift in perspective that, I have suggested, we require in order to open the so-called black box of neighborhood effects, a shift toward conditional causation.

Poor neighborhoods are not always isolated or uninvolved. And not all

8. For example, whether the main neighborhood poverty variable remained statistically significant after the interactions were included would be immaterial because the interest is in understanding the interactions.

people in a given poor neighborhood are isolated or uninvolved. I suggest that understanding the conditions affecting the reasons why should be the central, not peripheral, focus of our analysis if we are to understand how neighborhood poverty affects isolation and lack of involvement. Our conditional perspective shares with both the early Chicago school and QCA the belief that such conditions are central.

After reading sociological depictions of poor neighborhoods in inner cities, the writer Ralph Ellison famously complained that "I simply don't recognize Harlem in them" (Ellison 1967, 76). Indeed, it is difficult to recognize actual poor neighborhoods in many of our large-sample studies. They resonate strongly with a few depictions of ghettos but weakly with many existing poor neighborhoods in Boston, Cincinnati, Tucson, Minneapolis, Eugene, or St. Louis. Perhaps a greater focus on intermediary conditions, and the patterns in their heterogeneity across such neighborhoods, might bring our research closer to reality, sharpening our theories by forcing them to deal more concretely with the diversity of the field.

Six months after leaving Boston I returned to Villa Victoria. The neighborhood had changed dramatically in that short time. Many of the houses were experiencing rehabilitation, as were much of the landscaping and other areas surrounding the plaza. The houses were being outfitted with new doors, new front stoops, new kitchen cabinets, new tiles, new floors, and new bathrooms; they were being wired for the Internet. Their exteriors were being painted, each house in one of four gorgeous pastels. Midway through construction, the neighborhood already looked drastically better. I could suddenly imagine what the elders of the neighborhood had experienced when the Villa was constructed in the midseventies. The word "beautiful" did not seem so incongruous. The neighborhood's landscape, in quality and upkeep, if not in architecture, suddenly approximated that of the surrounding South End. Indeed, it was clear that, within a year or two, my descriptions in chapter 5 of the physical differences between the Villa and its surrounding neighborhood would no longer be of the current Villa but of a former one, one part of the neighborhood's rich collective memory.

There had been other changes, many made possible by a new manager, who had started his tenure at about the time, two and a half years earlier, I had begun my study. The Escuelita day-care center had finally been moved completely to a new, much larger, more accessible location in the basement of the Jorge Hernández Cultural Center; the day-care center's former locale had been turned into a youth center with a large television set, lounge chairs, tables, and some video games. The Batey Technology Center no longer existed; it had been replaced by the highly professional Villa Tech Center, equipped with state-of-the-art computers with giant flat panel screens and Windows 2000, staffed by paid full- and part-time experts offering a full schedule of courses. (Funds had been provided by a large technology corporation.) The South End Community Health Center had finally relocated to a larger, more modern location a few blocks south. Inquilinos Boricuas en Acción now had a fully functioning Web site, with full text access to *The New Villa,* its new, professional-looking and bilingual newsletter. Thanks to a series of outside grants, the resident of every house being refurbished was offered a free computer with the newly available Internet access. The requirement for eligibility: to complete a course in introductory computing at Villa Tech.

Not all of the changes I was made aware of were positive. Beginning in the late spring of that year, for example, a series of young men either from or at the Villa had been stabbed or shot. In response, security cameras had been mounted high up at locations throughout the neighborhood, including O'Day Park. This combination of events had a chilling effect on the community. I ran into Tommy, who was sitting in his car across from the park, directly below one of the cameras. We started chatting and were later joined by three or four other men. We quickly went our separate ways—I, as the others, uncomfortable at the thought of being watched. The original vision of large windows facing the parks and public areas designed to ensure informal social control had turned into a much uglier vision of twenty-four-hour observation and extremely formal social control. The effects on crime were questionable: a few weeks after the cameras were installed, a young man, his head covered under a hood, shot a nonresident with whom he had a conflict who was visiting the neighborhood. The camera caught the act but could not discern the actor. The young men who used to hang around O'Day Park now spend their time on Tremont Street, much to the chagrin of a few South End neighborhood associations.

The changes I witnessed in Villa Victoria underscored the importance of conceiving ethnographies as situated studies, of treating observational and interview data as historically constituted, not random samples of the average poor neighborhood. Villa Victoria, when I last visited, was a different neighborhood from the one of the early nineties, and a different one then from that of the early eighties. That the sociologist must keep up with such changes and incorporate them into the analysis is not a burden but a blessing, an opportunity for generating theories that assume the dynamic nature of our inner cities.

The various aspects of social capital in the neighborhood are likely to continue changing over time. Through IBA, the Villa seems to be establishing a rather strong institutional foundation, reinforcing much of what had been done in the past. This foundation, and the programs that ensue, are likely to keep alive the collective history of the neighborhood, which benefits the strengthening of local social bonds. Yet establishing institutional foundations is partly affected by economic cycles, the generosity of those supplying funds, and the viability of state and local governments. And the current and future cohorts' concerns for upward mobility might produce dynamics increasingly different from those of the past, rendering strong local attachments more difficult to maintain. One might be justified in concluding, then, on a note of cautious optimism about the future of community participation and the development of beneficial social ties in Villa Victoria.

In what follows, I discuss the book's methodology, the core of which is ethnographic (Hammersley and Atkinson 1983; Fetterman 1998). I describe the perspective from which I approached most of the subject matter and attempt to systematize what by necessity is a largely unsystematic process. I conclude by covering the logistics of data collection itself and how I complemented my ethnographic observations with other validating sources.

Historically Informed Observation

As discussed in chapters 1 and 8, the general approach I took in this book was neither univeralist nor particularist but conditionalist; it sought to use the case of Villa Victoria to understand (some of) the conditions under which neighborhood poverty decreased social capital. This implied a deliberate search for these conditions, rather than a traditional community study. Unlike, for example, Gans's ([1967] 1982) *The Levittowners*, this study did not intend to depict all aspects of social life among residents of the neighborhood. Conditionalism can be thought of as a general approach to a case, but it does not prescribe much about the mechanics of actual data collection in the field. A few observations on this issue are worthwhile.[1]

---

1. There are many approaches to collecting data once in the field. Burawoy (1991) has identified four. One approach, grounded theory, is to collect data on everything of interest without prior explicit assumptions about the what will affect what and to inductively generate theories based on these observations (Glaser and Srauss 1967). Another, the interpretive method, is to gather information on cultural symbols one expects to interpret rather than processes one wishes to explain (Geertz 1972). A third, ethnomethodology, is to chart the patterns in very microlevel, one-on-one social interactions. A fourth, the extended case approach, relies on a macrolevel theory of domination and resistance and, based on that theory, searches for power dynamics in a particular case (Burawoy 1991). There are many others. For recent discussions, see Jessor, Colby, and Shweder (1996) and Atkinson et al. (2001).

My main approach to data collection itself can be thought of as "historically informed." Most ethnographies on urban poverty are concerned with the present, providing only a limited discussion of the history of a neighborhood and rarely connecting that history to the present in systematic fashion (but see Gregory 1998; Venkatesh 2000). My approach was not to develop a history of the neighborhood but to interpret the observed present conditions in light of continuously invoked elements of the past, at both the individual and collective levels. This did not constitute a new ethnographic method; it was simply a perspective from which to investigate the phenomena I observed. In the field, the ethnographer has to make choices about which phenomena to investigate or pursue and how to investigate such phenomena. In many cases in this book, my choices involved uncovering more about the past of the individuals involved or the about neighborhood itself.

I came to this historical approach for largely (though not exclusively) pragmatic reasons. I began this project, as most ethnographers do, hoping to attain what Max Weber meant by *verstehen:* an empathetic understanding of social relations and situations in Villa Victoria as the residents themselves experienced it. It soon became clear that to attain this understanding I would have to ascertain the history of Villa Victoria as they knew it because this history colored how they saw the world. The elderly saw the Villa as important because of the history they experienced; without knowledge of that history, I would have been unable to understand how they saw the Villa, why they saw beauty where outsiders saw poverty and destitution. The neighborhood's youth saw O'Day Park as an emotionally charged space, one both painful and comforting, an initially tender wound that had healed—and scarred—over time. Without knowing the park's violent history, it would have been impossible for me to understand its emotional valence. *Verstehen*—the understanding of meaning from the perspective of the residents—therefore, had to be undertaken by means of a historical method; an "ahistorical *verstehen*" was simply impracticable.

I was also motivated by my belief in a basic but often neglected sociological fact—that cross-sectional and historical analyses of the same phenomenon may yield apparently contradictory but equally correct explanations. Quillian (1999) had shown that Wilson's out-migration and Massey's segregation theses were not necessarily contradictory, as was typically assumed. Out-migration was a stronger account of the causes behind change over time; segregation was a stronger predictor of neighborhood poverty across space. In the Villa, structural changes explained very little about changes in participation over time; but structural conditions were critical for understanding participation in the present. Thus, my ethnographic research had to examine both the present conditions and their historical transformation.

My third and final motivation was straightforward: the Villa had an interesting past, and I was curious to learn about it. Its history of participation was especially intriguing.

Over the course of the study, as my thoughts about the Villa crystallized, I came to understand Wilhelm Dilthey and Friedrich Schleiermacher's notions of the hermeneutic circle more concretely than I ever had. The more I understood the Villa's history, the better I understood its present conditions; the more I knew about the present, the keener eye I could bring to my understanding of its history. As a sociologist, however, my ultimate interest was always in the present. The resulting product became "historical" in very different senses: it was concerned with the residents' knowledge of the Villa's history, with the subjective significance they gave to that history, with the objective historical conditions they had or had not faced as individuals, with their personal histories, and with the transformations over time in the Villa's structural and ecological conditions.

After conducting most of the research, I came to several conclusions about how to report my findings. First, I had to identify the neighborhood. Because of confidentiality concerns, many ethnographers have concealed the location of their sites. And, indeed, with the fear of lawsuits driving human subjects committees at today's universities, there is often no choice in the matter (Shea 2000). Yet without identifying the neighborhood, it is impossible to present research in which historical evidence is introduced, rendering a historical perspective impossible. In addition, only when neighborhoods are identified can they be thought of as concrete cases depicting conditions in a meaningful location, which is key to the accumulation of evidence and to the comparison of conditions in one case to another; only under these conditions is replicability possible. A recent example of this is Duneier's (1999) *Sidewalk.*

Second, I had to make use of existing ethnographies as substantive, not just theoretical, cases. If I was going to treat my findings as those about a specific place in specific times, I had to do the same with respect to existing ethnographies, especially if I expected to use them to draw contrasts or parallels. That Gans (1962) identified Boston's West End in the *Urban Villagers* made possible placing Parcel 19's crisis within the context of changes taking place in Boston for the decade prior to the late 1960s and comparing Parcel 19 to how other neighborhoods responded to similar conditions.

Third, I had to examine changes across different dimensions. The most critical dimensions in the Villa were structural, generational, and ecological. This forced me to think critically about which changes made a difference with respect to a specific question and which did not. Indeed, the most fundamental danger behind adopting a historical perspective to a case study is to assume that all conditions in the neighborhood's past are causally related to all conditions in the present. In the Villa, it was clear that changes in structural conditions, generational differences across cohorts, and the ecological evolution of the neighborhood vis-à-vis the surrounding South End affected certain aspects of contemporary social capital but not others, so it was important to study each change in its own light.

The major weakness with this approach concerned the treatment of individual data. Since the neighborhood was identified, and it is, in addition, quite small, I was forced to go to extra lengths to protect the confidentiality of my respondents. My basic belief was that I should alter the data as little as possible. As a result, I was forced to limit the amount of material I presented about individual cases. For example, if I provided extensive detail of all the activities an individual had engaged in with regard to the community, it would be possible to identify her or him. Chapter-length biographies, used effectively by Pattillo-McCoy (1999) in *Black Picket Fences* and by Anderson (1999) in *Code of the Street,* were out of the question.

Data Collection

The study relied on multiple sources. The sources included ethnographic observation over two years, interviews with key informants, the U.S. Census, archival records, and newspaper articles. I describe these below.

ETHNOGRAPHIC OBSERVATION

In an early phase of the research, I investigated the Villa with an emphasis on the institutions and organizations of the Villa and the South End that dealt with issues relevant to poor women with children. I interviewed service providers and spent a lot of time observing social interactions in the neighborhood, around the plaza, the parks, and streets and sidewalks. I am a native Spanish speaker of Latin American origin, so getting to know the neighborhood's residents was unhampered by linguistic or cultural barriers. Within a short time, I came to know a large number of people in the community, and most new residents I met were in some way related to others I had met previously. About a dozen large, extended families account for a sizable portion of the residents of the Villa. Over time, I made some very close friends in the neighborhood and developed several key informants who were the most important source for correcting, elaborating on, and validating what I was observing.

My research was by no means limited to detached observation. Over the two years I studied the neighborhood, I volunteered in the yearly membership drives for IBA corporate members, in the Betances Festival, and in beautification efforts; served on career panels and "career shadowing" days with neighborhood youth; taught bilingual courses in computing for adults; and attended countless meetings, public events, and celebrations. I routinely ate at the local restaurants, visited with friends, old and young, at their homes, attended the dances and performances at the JHCC, hung around the offices of IBA, and, generally, spent a great deal of leisure time in the central plaza, the local park, and public spaces throughout the neighborhood. These experiences gave me a solid sense of life in the Villa and in the South End.

In addition to my observations, the comments of key informants and oral histories of several elders helped me both understand the present conditions of the Villa and reconstruct its past. I interviewed service providers, present and past activists, professionals, residents, and clergy. In the vast majority of these conversations, I took notes by hand, either during or after the encounters took place. This method, however, makes it difficult to produce extended quotes with any accuracy. Thus, to supplement these conversations, I taped several interviews; all extended quotes in the article were taken from these taped interviews. It was not always practical, or advisable, to carry a tape recorder around, so most of the data are derived from handwritten notes. In addition to the statements of key informants and my oral histories, I relied on the personal accounts and testimony documented in Green (1975), Lukas (1985), Hardy-Fanta (1993), Meza and Buxbaum (1995), and Toro (1998). These sources help produce first-hand accounts by residents of both the Villa and the South End at different points in its history.

ARCHIVAL RECORDS

The research was also supplemented with records and written documentation, for which my two sources were the census and archival records. Census data were used to obtain information on poverty and income rates, educational status, and residential stability in the Villa. The census does not provide tract data for Villa Victoria. However, it is possible to obtain Villa data because of a fortunate peculiarity of census tract 0705 in Boston.

The tract is a rectangular plane with its two long sides running neatly along Tremont and Washington Streets and the short sides running along East Berkeley and Rutland Streets. Within that rectangular plane, the only place in which there are Latinos is, with a tiny number of exceptions, Villa Victoria. Furthermore, Villa Victoria is overwhelmingly Latino. Thus, I used the statistics for Latinos in tract 0705 as a proxy for the statistics of Villa residents. This is by no means a perfect measure, not just because it includes the very few Latinos in that tract who do not live in the Villa but also because there is a severe undercount problem of Latinos. Nevertheless, it is by far the best measure available. Instead of census data, for example, I might have used the narrower block group data. However, there are two problems with block data. Three of the four block groups that make up tract 0705 cover parts of the Villa, but they cover more than just the Villa, so they only do slightly better in terms of geographic accuracy than the census tract does. And fewer statistics are available at the block group than at the tract level. Furthermore, in 1970 the block groups in tract 0705 were drawn differently, and there were only two, not four of them, so comparisons over time are impossible with block group data. Another potential source of these data for Villa Victoria would have been ETC, the management company, which at one time collected statistics on some measures of interest. However, as the administration of ETC has changed hands over the years, hundreds of records have been destroyed and it now manages part, not all, of the local properties in Villa Victoria. Thus, ETC has no historical data and only incomplete current data.

In addition to census data, I relied on newspaper articles in the *Boston Globe, La Semana,* the *South End News,* and to a lesser extent the *New York Times.* Finally, I made use of flyers, pamphlets, meeting minutes, newspaper clippings, and other archival data that were generously made available to me by the staff of IBA. These sources served to reconstruct life in the Villa in the 1970s, 1980s, and early 1990s, and to substantiate and document the oral histories I had obtained from lifelong residents. The archives, originally accumulated not for an academic to read through but as remnants of past mobilization and institutionalization efforts, were imperfect and incomplete but nonetheless extremely useful. These files are cited as "IBA Archives," for there is no other consistent organization. Since the time of my study, many of these papers, in about 135 boxes, have been donated to a collection at the Northeastern University Special Collections Department. I have accessed those archives and matched where possible my earlier records to the files at Northeastern. These files are cited as "NU IBA Z02-20," and identified by box number. The full citation is Northeastern University, Archives and Special Collections Department, Inquilinos Boricuas en Acción (Z02-20). The current boxes were simply numbered as they arrived from IBA, so that documents on a single topic are scattered throughout them. The staff at the university is applying for grants to reorganize the files in a more intuitive fashion; if and when they do so, a correspondence index (between the old and new box numbers) should be available.

Abbot, Andrew. 1997. "Of Time and Space: The Contemporary Relevance of the Chicago School." *Social Forces* 75 (4): 1149–82.

Aber, J. Lawrence, Martha Gephart, Jeanne Brooks-Gunn, and James Connell. 1997. "Development in Context: Implications for Studying Neighborhood Effects." In Brooks-Gunn, Duncan, and Aber 1997a, 44–62.

Abu-Lughod, Janet. 1997. "The Specificity of the Chicago Ghetto: Comment on Wacquant's 'Three Pernicious Premises.'" *International Journal of Urban and Regional Research* 21 (2): 357–62.

Ainsworth-Darnell, James, and Douglas Downey. 1998. "Assessing the Oppositional Culture Explanation for Racial/Ethnic Differences in School Performance." *American Sociological Review* 63:536–53.

Anderson, Elijah. 1978. *A Place on the Corner.* Chicago: University of Chicago Press.

———. 1990. *Streetwise: Race, Class, and Change in an Urban Community.* Chicago: University of Chicago Press.

———. 1994. "The Code of the Streets." *Atlantic Monthly.* 273 (5): 80–91.

———. 1999. *Code of the Street.* New York: Norton.

Atkinson, Paul, Amanda Coffey, Sara Delamont, John Lofland, and Lyn Lofland, eds. 2001. *Handbook of Ethnography.* London: Sage.

Austin, D. Mark, and Yoko Baba. 1990. "Social Determinants of Neighborhood Attachment." *Sociological Spectrum* 10:56–78.

Banfield, Edward. 1968. *The Unheavenly City.* Boston: Little, Brown, & Co.

Barth, Fredrik. 1969. *Ethnic Groups and Boundaries: The Social Organization of Culture Difference.* Boston: Little, Brown, & Co.

Benford, Robert D. 1997. "An Insider's Critique of the Social Movement Framing Perspective." *Sociological Inquiry* 67 (4): 409–30.

Bluestone, Barry, and Mary Huff Stevenson. 2000. *The Boston Renaissance: Race, Space, and Economic Change in an American Metropolis.* New York: Russell Sage Foundation.

Bond, Evagene. 1982. *La Comunidad: Design, Development, and Self-determination in Hispanic Communities.* Washington, D.C.: Partners for Livable Places.

Boston Landmarks Commission. 1983. *The South End.* Boston: Boston Landmarks Commission.

Boston Redevelopment Authority (BRA). 1958. *Final Relocation Report: New York Streets Project_UR Mass.2–1.* Boston: Boston Redevelopment Authority.

———. 1964. *Castle Square Residential Relocation Program: Summary.* Boston: Boston Redevelopment Authority.

————. 1965. *South End Urban Renewal Plan*. Boston: Boston Redevelopment Authority.

————. 1977. *South End: District Profile and Proposed 1978–1980 Neighborhood Improvement Program*. Boston: Boston Redevelopment Authority.

————. 1978. *Subsidized Housing in the South End*. Boston: Boston Redevelopment Authority.

————. 1997. *A New Washington Street: Boston's Main Street for the New Century*. Boston: Boston Redevelopment Authority.

Bott, Elizabeth. 1971. *Family and Social Network: Roles, Norms, and External Relationships in Ordinary Urban Families*. New York: Free Press.

Bourdieu, Pierre. 1977. *Outline of a Theory of Practice*. Cambridge: Cambridge University Press.

————. 1984. *Distinction: A Social Critique of the Judgment of Taste*. Translated by Richard Nice. Cambridge, Mass.: Harvard University Press.

————. 1985. "The Forms of Capital." In *Handbook of Theory and Research in the Sociology of Education*, edited by J. G. Richardson, 241–58. New York: Greenwood.

Bourdieu, Pierre, and Loïc Wacquant. 1992. *An Invitation to Reflexive Sociology*. Chicago: University of Chicago Press.

Bourgois, Phillipe. 1995. *In Search of Respect: Selling Crack in El Barrio*. Cambridge: Cambridge University Press.

Brand, Janice. 1987. "The South End." *Boston Magazine* (April).

Breton, Raymond. 1964. "Institutional Completeness of Ethnic Communities and the Personal Relations of Immigrants." *American Journal of Sociology* 70 (2): 193–205.

Brooks, David. 2000. *Bobos in Paradise: The New Upper Class and How They Got There*. New York: Simon & Schuster.

Brooks-Gunn, Jeanne, Jill Denner, and Pam Keblanov. 1995. "Families and Neighborhoods as Contexts for Education." In *Changing Populations, Changing Schools: Ninety-fourth Yearbook of the National Society for the Study of Education*, edited by Erwin Flaxman and Harry Passow, 233–52. Chicago: University of Chicago Press.

Brooks-Gunn, Jeanne, Greg Duncan and J. Lawrence Aber, eds. 1997a. *Neighborhood Poverty*. Vol. 1, *Context and Consequences for Children*. New York: Russell Sage Foundation.

————, eds. 1997b. *Neighborhood Poverty*. Vol. 2, *Policy Implications in Studying Neighborhoods*. New York: Russell Sage Foundation.

Bryk, Anthony, and Stephen Raudenbush. 1992. *Hierarchical Linear Models: Applications and Data Analysis Methods*. Newbury Park, Calif.: Sage.

Burawoy, Michael, et al. 1991. *Ethnography Unbound: Power and Resistance in the Modern Metropolis*. Berkeley: University of California Press.

Burgess, Ernest. 1925. "The Growth of the City." In Park, Burgess, and McKenzie 1925.

Burton, Linda, T. Price-Spratlen, and M. B. Spencer. 1997. "On Ways of Thinking about Measuring Neighborhoods: Implications for Studying Context and Developmental Outcomes for Children." In Brooks-Gunn, Duncan, and Aber 1997b, 132–44.

Chacon, Richard. 1997. "Mismanagement, Fiscal Woes Push Villa Victoria into Crisis." *Boston Globe*, May 8.

Chaskin, Robert 1997. "Perspectives on Neighborhood and Community: A Review of the Literature." *Social Service Review*, 71 (4): 521–47.

Clifford, James, and George E. Marcus. 1986. *Writing Culture: The Poetics and Politics of Ethnography.* Berkeley: University of California Press.

Cohen, Cathy, and Michael C. Dawson. 1993. "Neighborhood Poverty and African American Politics." *American Political Science Review* 87 (2): 286–302.

Coleman, James. 1988. "Social Capital in the Creation of Human Capital." *American Journal of Sociology,* suppl. to vol. 94:S95—S120.

Comandini, Michele 1994. "South End Rivals March to Fight Gang Violence; Organizers Say Event Is a First Step in Restoring Peace to Neighborhood." *Boston Globe,* August 28.

Cook, Phillip, and Jens Ludwig. 1998. "The Burden of 'Acting White': Do Black Adolescents Disparage Academic Achievement?" In *The Black White Test Score Gap,* edited by Christopher Jencks and Meredith Phillips, 375–401. Washington, D.C.: Brookings Institution.

Cook, Thomas D., Shobha C. Shagle, and Serdar M. Değirmencioğlu. 1997. "Capturing Social Process for Testing Mediational Models of Neighborhood Effects." In Brooks-Gunn, Duncan, and Aber 1997b, 94–119.

Crane, Johnathan. 1991. "Effects of Neighborhoods on Dropping Out of School and Teenage Childbearing." In Jencks and Peterson 1991, 299–320.

Cutler, David and Edward Glaeser. 1997. "Are Ghettos Good or Bad?" *Quarterly Journal of Economics* 112:827–62.

Duncan, Greg, and J. Lawrence Aber. 1997. "Neighborhood Models and Measures." In Brooks-Gunn, Duncan, and Aber (1997a, 62–78.

Duncan, Greg, James Connell, and Pam Keblanov. 1997. "Conceptual and Methodological Issues in Estimating Causal Effects of Neighborhoods and Family Conditions on Individual Development. In Brooks-Gunn, Duncan, andAber (1997a, 219–50.

Duneier, Mitchell. 1992. *Slim's Table: Race, Respectability, and Masculinity.* Chicago: University of Chicago Press.

———. 1999. Sidewalk. New York: Farrar, Straus & Giroux.

Edin, Kathryn, and Laura Lein. 1997. *Making Ends Meet: How Single Mothers Survive Welfare and Low-wage Work.* New York: Russell Sage Foundation.

Elliott, Dilbert, William J. Wilson, David Huizinga, Robert Sampson, Amanda Elliott, and Bruce Rankin. 1996. "The Effects of Neighborhood Disadvantage on Adolescent Development." *Journal of Research in Crime and Delinquency* 33 (4): 389–426.

Elliott, James. 1999. "Social Isolation and Labor Market Insulation: Network and Neighborhood Effects on Less-Educated Urban Workers." *Sociological Quarterly* 40 (2): 199–216.

Ellison, Ralph. 1967. "A Very Stern Discipline: An Interview with Ralph Ellison." By James Thompson, Lennox Rafael, and Steve Cannon. *Harper's Magazine* 234 (March): 76–95.

Emirbayer, Mustafa, and Jeff Goodwin. 1994. "Network Analysis, Culture, and the Problem of Agency." *American Journal of Sociology* 99 (6): 1411–54.

Emirbayer, Mustafa, and Anne Mische. 1998. "What Is Agency?" *American Journal of Sociology* 103 (4): 962–1023.

Famuliner, Charles C. 1999. "Opinion and Comment." *Journal of Housing and Community Development* 56 (6): 8–9.

Ferguson, Ronald, and William Dickens, eds. 1999. *Urban Problems and Community Development.* Washington, D.C.: Brookings Institution.

Fernandez, Roberto, and David Harris. 1992. "Social Isolation and the Underclass." In *Drugs, Crime, and Social Isolation: Barriers to Urban Opportunity,* edited by Adele Harrell and George Peterson, 257–93. Washington, D.C.: Urban Institute Press.

Fetterman, David. 1998. *Ethnography: Step by Step.* Thousand Oaks, Calif.: Sage.

Fischer, Claude. 1976. *The Urban Experience.* New York: Harcourt, Brace, Jovanovich.

———. 1982. *To Dwell among Friends: Personal Networks in Town and City.* Chicago: University of Chicago Press.

Fordham, Signithia, and John Ogbu. 1986. "Black Students' School Success: Coping with the Burden of 'Acting White.'" *Urban Review* 18 (3): 176–206.

Freeman, Donald. 1970. *Boston Architecture.* Boston: Boston Society of Architects.

Furstenberg, Frank, Thomas Cook, Jacquelyne Eccles, Glen Elder, and Arnold Sameroff. 1998. *Managing to Make It: Urban Families and Adolescent Success.* Chicago: University of Chicago Press.

Furstenberg, Frank, and Mary Elizabeth Hughes. 1997. "The Influence of Neighborhoods on Children's Development: A Theoretical Perspective and a Research Agenda." Brooks-Gunn, Duncan, and Aber 1997b, 23–47.

Gamm, Gerald. 1999. *Urban Exodus: Why the Jews Left Boston and the Catholics Stayed.* Cambridge, Mass.: Harvard University Press.

Gamson, William. 1992. "The Social Psychology of Collective Action." In *Frontiers in Social Movement Theory,* edited by Aldon Morris and Carol Mueller, 53–76. New Haven, Conn.: Yale University Press.

Gans, Herbert. 1962. *The Urban Villagers: Group and Class in the Life of Italian-Americans.* New York: Free Press.

———. [1967] 1982. *The Levittowners: Ways of Life and Politics in a New Suburban Community.* New York: Columbia University Press.

Garelick, James. 1986. "Jazzing Up the South End." *Boston TAB,* October 14, sec. 2.

Gaziano, Emmanuel. 1996. "Ecological Metaphors as Scientific Boundary Work: Innovation and Authority in Interwar Sociology and Biology." *American Journal of Sociology* 101 (4): 874–907.

Geertz, Clifford. 1972. *The Interpretation of Cultures.* New York: Basic Books.

Gephart, Martha. 1997. "Neighborhoods and Communities as Contexts for Development." In Brooks-Gunn, Duncan, and Aber 1997a, 44–61.

Gephart, Martha, and Jeanne Brooks-Gunn. 1997. Introduction to Brooks-Gunn, Duncan, and Aber 1997b, xiii–xxii.

Gieryn, Thomas. 1995. "Boundaries of Science." In *Handbook of Science and Technology Studies,* edited by Sheila Jasanoff, Gerald Markle, James Petersen, and Trevor Pinch, 393–443. Thousand Oaks, Calif.: Sage Publications.

Gladwell, Malcolm. 2000. *The Tipping Point: How Little Things Can Make a Big Difference.* Boston: Little, Brown, & Co.

Glaser, Barney, and Anselm Strauss. 1967. *The Discovery of Grounded Theory: Strategies for Qualitative Research.* New York: Aldine De Gruyter.

Goffman, Ervin. 1959. *The Presentation of Self in Everyday Life.* New York: Anchor.

———. 1986. *Frame Analysis: An Essay on the Organization of Experience.* Boston: Northeastern University Press.

Goodman, Phebe S. 1994a. *Boston's South End Squares: Inventory, Analysis, and Recommendations.* Boston: Phebe Goodman.

———. 1994b. *The Residential Square Transplanted: London to Boston.* Boston: Phebe Goodman.

Goodwin, Jeffrey, James Jasper, and Frances Polletta. 2001. *Passionate Politics: Emotions and Social Movements.* Chicago: University of Chicago Press.

Granovetter, Mark. 1973. "The Strength of Weak Ties." *American Journal of Sociology* 78:1360–80.

Green, James. 1975. *The South End.* Boston: Boston 200 Neighborhood History Series.

Gregory, Stephen. 1998. *Black Corona: Race and the Politics of Place in an Urban Community.* Princeton, N.J.: Princeton University Press.

Hammersley, Martyn, and Paul Atkinson. 1983. *Ethnography: Principles in Practice.* 2d ed. London: Routledge.

Hannerz, Ulf. 1969. *Soulside: Inquiries into Ghetto Culture and Community.* New York: Columbia University Press.

Hardy-Fanta, Carol. 1993. *Latina Politics, Latino Politics: Gender, Culture, and Political Participation in Boston.* Philadelphia: Temple University Press.

Harrison, Lawrence E., and Samuel P. Huntington. 2000. *Culture Matters: How Values Shape Human Progress.* New York: Basic Books.

Hart, Janet. 1992. "Cracking the Code: Narrative and Political Mobilization in the Greek Resistance." *Social Science History* 16 (4): 631–68.

Hoyt , Margaret, and Tomas Rivera. n.d. *Villa Victoria: Boston's South End Victory Village.* Boston: Urban Schools Collaborative at Northeastern University.

Huber, Joan, ed. 1991. *Macro-Micro Linkages in Sociology.* Newbury Park, Calif.: Sage.

Huckfeldt, Robert. 1983. "Social Contexts, Social Networks, and Urban Neighborhoods: Environmental Constraints on Friendship Choice." *American Journal of Sociology* 89 (3): 651–69.

Hynes, John B., and Greater Boston Chamber of Commerce. 1957. *Urban Renewal in Boston: An Outline Prepared for the Boston Redevelopment Tour.* Boston: Greater Boston Chamber of Commerce.

Inquilinos Boricuas En Acción (IBA). 2000a. *Festival Betances 2000: Unidos Siempre.* Boston: IBA.

———. 2000b. *Inquilions Boricuas En Acción: Annual Meeting June 7, 2000.* Boston: IBA.

Jacobs, Jane. 1961. *The Death and Life of Great American Cities.* New York: Vintage Books.

Jargowsky, Paul. 1997. *Poverty and Place: Ghettos, Barrios, and the American City.* New York: Russell Sage Foundation.

Jargowsky, Paul, and Mary-Jo Bane. 1991. "Ghetto Poverty in the United States, 1970–1980." In Jencks and Peterson 1991, 235–73.

Jencks, Christopher, and Kathryn Edin. 1990. "The Real Welfare Problem." *American Prospect* 1 (Spring): 31–50.

Jencks, Christopher, and Susan Mayer. 1990. "The Social Consequences of Growing up in a Poor Neighborhood." In *Inner-City Poverty in the United States,* edited by Lawrence Lynn and Michael Mcgreary, 111–86. Washington, D.C.: National Academy Press.

Jencks, Christopher, and Paul Peterson. 1991. *The Urban Underclass.* Washington, D.C.: Brookings Institution.

Jessor, Richard, Anne Colby, and Richard A. Shweder, eds. 1996. *Ethnography and Human Development*. Chicago: University of Chicago Press.

Johnston, Hank, and Bert Klandermans. 1995. *Social Movements and Culture*. Minneapolis: University of Minnesota Press.

Jonas, Michael. 2000. "Puzzlement over Cellucci's Cut of Summer-Job Funding." *Boston Globe,* June 25.

Juran, Joseph M. 1954. "Universals in Management Planning and Control." *Management Review* 43 (11): 748–61.

Kain, John. 1992. "The Spatial Mismatch Hypothesis: Three Decades Later." *Housing Policy Debate* 3 (2): 371–460.

Kanter, Rosabeth Moss. 1972. *Commitment and Community: Communes and Utopias in Sociological Perspective*. Cambridge, Mass.: Harvard University Press.

Kasarda, John, and Morris Janowitz. 1974. "Community Attachment in Mass Society." *American Sociological Review* 39:328–39.

Kasinitz, Philip. 2000. "Red Hook: The Paradoxes of Poverty and Place in Brooklyn." *Research in Urban Sociology* 5:253–74.

Kasinitz, Philip, and Jan Rosenberg. 1996. "Missing the Connection: Social Isolation and Employment on the Brooklyn Waterfront." *Social Problems* 43 (2): 180–96.

Katz, Lawrence, Jeffrey Kling, and Jeffrey Liebman. 2001. "Moving to Opportunity in Boston: Early Results of a Randomized Mobility Experiment." *Quarterly Journal of Economics* 116 (2): 607–54.

Katz, Michael. 1997. "Comment on Loïc J. D. Wacquant, 'Three Pernicious Premises in the Study of the American Ghetto.'" *International Journal of Urban and Regional Research* 21 (2): 354–56.

Kennedy, Lawrence W. 1992. *Planning the City upon a Hill: Boston since 1630*. Amherst, Mass.: University of Massachusetts Press.

Keyes, Carleton Langley. 1969. *The Rehabilitation Planning Game: A Study in the Diversity of a Neighborhood*. Cambridge, Mass.: MIT Press.

Kling, Jeffrey. 2000. "Index: Moving to Opportunity Research." (http://www.mtoresearch .org/index.html).

Kornhauser, Ruth R. 1978. *Social Sources of Delinquency: An Appraisal of Analytic Models*. Chicago: University of Chicago Press.

Labov, William, and Wendell Harris. 1986. "De Facto Segregation of Black and White Vernaculars." In *Diversity and Diachrony,* edited by David Sankoff, 1–24. Current Issues in Linguistic Theory, vol. 53. Amsterdam: John Benjamins Publishing.

Lamont, Michele. 1992. *Money, Morals, and Manners*. Chicago: University of Chicago Press.

———. 1999. *The Cultural Territories of Race: Black and White Boundaries*. Chicago: University of Chicago Press.

Lamont, Michele, and Michael Fournier. 1992. *Cultivating Differences: Symbolic Boundaries and the Making of Inequality*. Chicago: University of Chicago Press.

Lamont, Michele, and Annette Lareau. 1988. "Cultural Capital: Allusions, Gaps, and Glissandos in Recent Theoretical Developments." *Sociological Theory* 6 (2): 153–68.

Lee, Barrett A., and Karen E. Campbell. 1999. "Neighbor Networks of Black and White Americans." In *Networks in the Global Village: Life in Contemporary Communities,* edited by Barry Wellman, 119–46. Boulder, Colo.: Westview Press.

Lee, Barrett A., Karen E. Campbell, and Oscar Miller. 1991. "Racial Differences in Urban Neighboring." *Sociological Forum* 6 (3): 525–50.

Lee, Barrett A., R.S. Oropesa, Barbara J. Metch, and Avery M. Guest. 1984. "Testing the Decline-of-Community Thesis: Neighborhood Organizations in Seattle, 1929 and 1979." *American Journal of Sociology* 89 (5): 1161–88.

Lewis, Oscar . 1965. *La Vida: A Puerto Rican Family in the Culture of Poverty—San Juan and New York.* Random House: New York.

———. 1968. "The Culture of Poverty." In *On Understanding Poverty: Perspectives from the Social Sciences,* edited by Daniel Patrick Moynihan, 187–220. New York: Basic Books.

Lieberson, Stanley. 1985. *Making It Count: The Improvement of Social Research and Theory.* Berkeley: University of California Press.

———. 1992. "Small *N*'s and Big Conclusions: An Examination of the Reasoning in Comparative Studies Based on a Small Number of Cases." In Ragin and Becker 1992, 105–18.

Liebow, Elliot. 1967. *Tally's Corner: A Study of Negro Streetcorner Men.* Boston: Little Brown & Co.

Lin, Nan. 1999. "Social Networks and Status Attainment." *Annual Review of Sociology* 25:467–87.

Logan, John R., and Harvey L. Molotch. 1987. *Urban Fortunes: The Political Economy of Place.* Berkeley: University of California Press.

Lukas, J. Anthony. 1985. *Common Ground.* New York: Vintage Books.

Macleod, Jay. 1995. *Ain't No Makin' It: Aspirations and Attainment in a Low-Income Neighborhood.* Boulder, Colo.: Westview Press.

Manly, Howard. 1992. "A South End Neighborhood Digs into Task of Healing: Villa Victoria's Residents Aim to Reclaim Turf." *Boston Globe,* September 14.

Mannheim, Karl. [1928] 1952. *Essays on the Sociology of Knowledge.* London: Routledge & Kegal Paul.

Maranrz, Steve. 2000. "Mayor Finds $1.7m for Teen Job Program." *Boston Globe,* August 9.

Mashberg, Tom. 1993. "Youth, 16, Slain in South End Lot; Some Say He May Have Been Innocent Victim of Dispute between Two Gangs." *Boston Globe,* September 12.

Massey, Douglas. 1998. "Back to the Future: The Rediscovery of Neighborhood Context." *Contemporary Sociology* 27 (6): 570–72.

Massey, Douglas, and Nancy Denton. 1993. *American Apartheid: Segregation and the Making of an Underclass.* Cambridge, Mass.: Harvard University Press.

Matos Rodríguez, Felipe. 2000. "'Saving the Parcela': A Short History of Boston's Puerto Rican Community." Photocopy, Hunter College, New York.

McCarthy, John D., and Mark Wolfson. 1996. "Resource Mobilization by Local Social Movement Organizations: Agency, Strategy, and Organization in the Movement against Drinking and Driving." *American Sociological Review* 61:1070–88.

McCarthy, John D., and Mayer N. Zald. 1977. "Resource Mobilization and Social Movements: A Partial Theory." *American Journal of Sociology* 82 (6): 1212–41.

McPherson, Miller, Lynn Smith-Lovin, and James Cook. 2001. "Birds of a Feather: Homophily in Social Networks." *Annual Review of Sociology* 27:415–44.

Mead, George Hebert. 1934. *Mind, Self, and Society.* Chicago: University of Chicago Press.

Mead, Lawrence. 1992. *The New Politics of Poverty: The Nonworking Poor in America*. New York: Basic Books.

Melucci, Alberto 1989. *Nomads of the Present: Social Movements and Individual Needs in Contemporary Society*. Philadelphia: Temple University Press.

Merton, Robert. 1967 *On Theoretical Sociology: Five Essays, Old and New*. New York: Free Press.

Meza, Tito, and Laura Buxbaum. 1995. "Headaches, Tears, and Healing: Organizing for Ownership and the Role of a Community Development Corporation." The 1995 Richard Schramm Paper on Community Development. Tufts University, Lincoln Filene Center, Boston.

Moore, Joan, and Raquel Pinderhughes eds. 1993. *In the Barrios: Latinos and the Underclass Debate*. New York: Russell Sage Foundation.

Moritz Bergmeyer Associates, Inc. 1979. *Preservation Feasibility Study: The Allen House, 16882 Washington Street, South End, Boston*. Boston: Massachusetts Historical Commission.

Morris, Aldon, and Carol Mueller. 1992. *Frontiers in Social Movement Theory*. New Haven, Conn.: Yale University Press.

Moynihan, Daniel P. 1965. *The Negro Family: A Case for National Action*. Washington, D.C.: Office of Policy Planning and Research, U.S. Department of Labor.

Murray, Charles. 1984. *Losing Ground: American Social Policy, 1950–1980*. New York: Basic Books.

Newman, Katherine. 1992. "Culture and Structure in *The Truly Disadvantaged*." *City and Society* 6:3–25.

———. 1999. *No Shame in My Game: The Working Poor in the Inner City*. New York: Knopf.

Nietzsche, Friedrich. [1887] 1967. "On the Genealogy of Morals," translated by Walter Kaufmann and R. J. Hollingdale. In *On the Genealogy of Morals and Ecce Homo*, edited by Walter Kaufmann, 16–200. New York: Vintage Books.

Nightingale, Carl. 1993. *On the Edge: A History of Poor Black Children and Their American Dreams*. New York: Basic Books.

Ogbu, John. 1978. *Minority Education and Caste: The American System in Cross-Cultural Perspective*. New York: Academic Press.

Olson, Mancur. 1965. *The Logic of Collective Action: Public Goods and the Theory of Goods*. Cambridge, Mass: Harvard University Press.

Padilla, Felix. 1992. *The Gang as an American Enterprise*. New Brunswick, N.J.: Rutgers University Press.

Park, Robert. 1952. *Human Communities: The City and Human Ecology*. Glencoe, Ill.: Free Press.

Park, Robert, Ernest Burgess, and Robert McKenzie. 1925. *The City*. Chicago: University of Chicago Press.

Parsons, Talcott, ed. 1937. *The Structure of Social Action: A Study in Social Theory with Special Reference to a Group of Recent European Writers*. New York: McGraw-Hill.

———. 1947. *Max Weber: The Theory of Social and Economic Organization*. New York: Free Press of Glencoe.

Patterson, James T. 1996. *Grand Expectations: The United States, 1945–1974*. New York: Oxford University Press.

Patterson, Orlando. 1997. *The Ordeal of Integration: Progress and Resentment in America's "Racial" Crisis.* Washington, D.C.: Civitas.

———. 2000. "Taking Culture Seriously: A Framework and an Afro-American Illustration." In Harrison and Huntington 2000, 202–18.

Pattillo-McCoy, Mary. 1999. *Black Picket Fences: Privilege and Peril among the Black Middle Class.* Chicago: University of Chicago Press.

Piven, Frances Fox, and Richard Cloward. 1977. *Poor People's Movements: Why They Succeed, How They Fail.* New York: Vintage.

Pollard, Gayle. 1980. "South End Solar Greenhouse: A Community Self-Help Report." *Boston Globe,* April 22.

Portes, Alejandro. 1997. "Immigration Theory for a New Century: Some Problems and Opportunities." *International Migration Review* 31 (4): 799–825.

———. 1998. "Social Capital: Its Origins and Applications in Modern Sociology." *Annual Review of Sociology* 24:1–24.

Portes, Alejandro, and Rubén Rumbaut. 2001. Legacies: The Story of the Immigrant Second Generation. Berkeley and New York: University of California Press and Russell Sage Foundation.

Portes, Alejandro, and Min Zhou. 1993. "The New Second Generation: Segmented Assimilation and Its Variants (Interminority Affairs in the U.S.: Pluralism at the Crossraods)." *Annals of the American Academy of Political and Social Science* 530:74–97.

Putnam, Robert D. 2000. *Bowling Alone: The Collapse and Revival of American Community.* New York: Simon & Schuster.

Quillian, Lincoln. 1999. "Migration Patterns and the Growth of High-Poverty Neighborhoods, 1970–1990." *American Journal of Sociology* 105 (1): 1–37.

Ragin, Charles C. 1987. *The Comparative Method: Moving beyond Quantitative and Qualitative Strategies.* Berkeley and Los Angeles: University of California Press.

Ragin, Charles C., and Howard Becker. 1992. *What Is a Case? Exploring the Foundations of Social Inquiry.* Cambridge: Cambridge University Press.

Rainwater, Lee. 1970. *Behind Ghetto Walls.* Chicago: Aldine Publishing Co.

Rankin, Bruce, and James Quane. 2000. "Neighborhood Poverty and the Social Isolation of Inner-City African-American Families." *Social Forces* 79 (1): 139–64.

Rivas, Maggie. 1981. "New Life for a South End Group." *Boston Globe,* January 19.

———. 1982. "Villa Victoria: Where Families Stay." *Boston Globe,* April 26.

Rodriguez, Richard. 1981. *Hunger of Memory: The Education of Richard Rodriguez.* Boston: David R. Godine.

Rosenbaum, James, and Susan Popkin. 1991. "Employment and Earnings of Low-Income Blacks Who Move to Middle-Class Suburbs." In Jencks and Peterson 1991, 342–56.

Rumbaut, Rubén, and Alejandro Portes, eds. 2001. *Ethnicities: Children of Immigrants in America.* Berkeley: University of California Press.

Ryan, William. 1976. *Blaming the Victim.* Rev., updated ed. New York: Vintage Books.

Ryder, Norman B. 1965. "The Cohort as a Concept in the Study of Social Change." *American Sociological Review* 30 (6): 843–61.

Sampson, Robert. 1988. "Local Friendship Ties and Community Attachment in Mass Society: A Multilevel Systemic Model." *American Sociological Review* 53:766–79.

———. 1991. "Linking the Micro- and Macrolevel Dimensions of Community Social Organization." *Social Forces* 70 (1): 43–64.

———. 1999. "What Community Supplies." In Ferguson and Dickens 1999, 241–92.

Sampson, Robert, and W. Byron Groves. 1989. "Community Structures and Crime: Testing Social Disorganization Theory." *American Journal of Sociology* 94.774–802.

Sampson, Robert, and Jeffrey D. Morenoff. 1997 "Ecological Perspectives on the Neighborhood Context of Urban Poverty: Past and Present." In Brooks-Gunn, Duncan, and Aber 1997b, 1–22.

Sampson, Robert, Jeffrey Morenoff, and Felton Earls. 1999. "Beyond Social Capital: Spatial Dynamics of Collective Efficacy for Children." *American Sociological Review* 64 (5): 633–60.

Sampson, Robert, Jeffrey Morenoff, and Thomas Gannon-Rowley. 2002. "Assessing 'Neighborhood Effects': Social Processes and New Directions in Research." *Annual Review of Sociology* 28:443–78.

Sampson, Robert, and Stephen Raudenbush. 1999. "Systematic Social Observation of Public Spaces: A New Look at Disorder in Urban Neighborhoods." *American Journal of Sociology* 94:774–802.

Sampson, Robert, Stephen Raudenbush, and Felton Earls. 1997. "Neighborhoods and Violent Crime: A Multilevel Study of Collective Efficacy." *Science* 227:918–24.

Sampson, Robert, and William J. Wilson. 1995. "Toward a Theory of Race, Crime, and Urban Inequality." In *Crime and Inequality,* edited by John Hagan and Ruth Peterson, 37–55. Stanford, Calif.: Stanford University Press.

Sánchez-Jankowski, Martín. 1991. *Islands in the Street: Gangs and American Urban Society.* Berkeley and Los Angeles: University of California Press.

Scheler, Max. 1992. *On Feeling, Knowing, and Valuing: Selected Writings.* Chicago: University of Chicago Press.

Schelling, Thomas. 1978. *Micromotives and Macrobehavior.* New York: Norton.

Schudson, Michael. 1992. *Watergate in American Memory: How We Remember, Forget, and Reconstruct the Past.* New York: Basic Books.

Schuman, Howard, and Jacqueline Scott. 1989. "Generations and Collective Memories." *American Sociological Review* 54:359–81.

Schuman, Howard, Charlotte Steeh, and Lawrence Bobo. 1985. *Racial Attitudes in America.* Cambridge, Mass.: Harvard University Press.

Schwirian, Kent. 1983. "Model of Neighborhood Change." *Annual Review of Sociology* 9:83–102.

Sewell, William H. 1996. "Historical Events as Transformations of Structures: Inventing the Revolution at the Bastille." *Theory and Society* 25 (6): 841–81.

Shaw, Clifford, and Henry McKay. 1942. *Juvenile Delinquency and Urban Areas.* Chicago: University of Chicago Press.

———. 1969. *Juvenile Delinquency and Urban Areas.* Rev. ed. Chicago: University of Chicago Press.

Shea, Christopher. 2000. "Don't Talk to the Humans. The Crackdown on Social Science Research." *Lingua Franca* 10, no. 6: 27–34.

Simmel, Georg. 1971. *On Individuality and Social Forms.* Chicago: University of Chicago Press.

Small, Mario L. 1999. "Departmental Conditions and the Emergence of New Disciplines: Two Cases in the Legitimation of African-American Studies." *Theory and Society* 28:659–707.

Small, Mario L., and Katherine Newman. 2001. "Urban Poverty after *The Truly*

Disadvantaged: The Rediscovery of the Family, the Neighborhood, and Culture."
    Annual Review of Sociology 27:23–45.
Smith, Steven, and Michael Lipsky. 1993. *Nonprofits for Hire: The Welfare State in the Age
    of Contracting.* Cambridge, Mass.: Harvard University Press.
Snow, David, and Robert Benford. 1992. "Master Frames and Cycles of Protest." In
    Frontiers in Social Movement Theory, edited by Aldon Morris and Carol Mueller, 133–
    55. New Haven, Conn.: Yale University Press.
Somers, Margaret. 1992. "Narrative, Narrative Identity, and Social Action: Rethinking
    English Working-Class Formation." *Social Science History* 16 (4): 591–630.
Somers, Margaret, and Gloria Gibson. 1994. "Reclaiming the Epistemological 'Other':
    Narrative and the Social Constitution of Identity." In *Social Theory and the Politics of
    Identity,* edited by Craig Calhoun, 37–99. Oxford: Blackwell.
South, Scott, and Kyle Crowder. 1999. "Neighborhood Effects on Family Formation:
    Concentrated Poverty and Beyond." *American Sociological Review* 64 (1): 113–32.
Stack, Carol. 1974. *All Our Kin.* New York: Basic Books.
Stainton, John. 1972. *Urban Renewal and Planning in Boston: A Review of the Past and a
    Look at the Future.* Boston: Citizen's Housing and Planning Assoc.
Stein, Maurice R. 1960. *The Eclipse of Community: An Interpretation of American Studies.*
    New York: Harper & Row.
Steinberg, Marc W. 1998. "Tilting the Frame: Considerations on Collective Action
    Framing from a Discursive Turn." *Theory and Society* 27:845–72.
———. 1999. "The Talk and Back Talk of Collective Action: A Dialogic Analysis of
    Repertoires of Discourse among Nineteenth-Century English Cotton Spinners."
    American Journal of Sociology 105 (3): 736–80.
Stinchcombe, Arthur L. 1968. *Constructing Social Theories.* Chicago: University of
    Chicago Press.
Stockman, Farah. 2000. "A Community's Stand Is Honored." *Boston Globe,* August 23.
Sucoff, Clea, and Dawn Upchurch. 1998. "Neighborhood Context and the Risk of
    Childbearing among Metropolitan-Area Black Adolescents." *American Sociological
    Review* 63 (4): 571–85.
Susser, Ida. 1982. *Norman Street.* New York and Oxford: Oxford University Press.
Suttles, Gerald. 1968. *The Social Order of the Slum: Ethnicity and Territory in the Inner
    City.* Chicago: University of Chicago Press.
———. 1972. *The Social Construction of Communities.* Chicago: University of Chicago
    Press.
Swidler, Anne. 1986. "Culture in Action: Symbols and Strategies." *American Sociological
    Review* 51:273–86.
Taub, Richard, D. Garth Taylor, and Jan Dunham. 1984. *Paths of Neighborhood Change:
    Race and Crime in Urban America.* Chicago: University of Chicago Press.
Taylor, Charles. 1989. *Sources of the Self.* Cambridge, Mass.: Harvard University Press.
Teltsch, Kathleen. 1982. "Boston Project Is a Showcase for Group That Helps Rebuild
    Neighborhoods." *New York Times,* November 12.
Thomas, W. I. 1936. "The Comparative Study of Cultures." *American Journal of Sociology*
    42 (2): 177–85.
Tienda, Marta. 1991. "Poor People and Poor Places: Deciphering Neighborhood Effects
    on Poverty Outcomes." In Huber 1991, 244–62.
Tigges, Leann, Irene Browne, and Gary Green. 1998. "Social Isolation of the Urban Poor:

Race, Class, and Neighborhood Effects on Social Resources." *Sociological Quarterly* 39 (1): 53–77.

Tolnay, Stewart, and Kyle Crowder. 1999. "Regional Origin and Family Stability in Northern Cities: The Role of Context." *American Sociological Review* 64 (1). 97–112.

Toro, Angel A. 1998. "An Oral History of the Puerto Rican Socialist Party in Boston, 1972–1978." In The Puerto Rican Movement: Voices from the Diaspora, edited by Andrés Torres and José Velázquez, 246–58. Philadelphia: Temple University Press.

Urban Field Service. 1968. *Report on South End Urban Renewal Plan for Boston City Council Hearing, March 25, 1968.* Boston: Urban Field Service.

Uriarte-Gastón, Mirén. 1988. "Organizing for Survival: The Emergence of a Puerto Rican Community." Ph.D. diss. Boston University.

U.S. Census Bureau. 1970. *Census of Population and Housing.* Washington, D.C.: Government Printing Office.

———. 1980. *Census of Population and Housing.* Washington, D.C.: Government Printing Office.

———. 1990. *Census of Population and Housing.* Washington, D.C.: Government Printing Office.

Valentine, Charles. 1968. *Culture and Poverty: Critique and Counter-Proposals.* Chicago: University of Chicago Press.

Venkatesh, Sudhir. 2000. *American Project: The Rise and Fall of a Modern Ghetto.* Cambridge, Mass.: Harvard University Press.

Wacquant, Loïc. 1997. "Three Pernicious Premises in the Study of the American Ghetto." *International Journal of Urban and Regional Research* 21 (2): 341–55.

Wacquant, Loïc, and William J. Wilson. 1990. "The Cost of Racial and Class Exclusion in the Inner City." *Annals of the American Academy of Political and Social Science* 501 (January): 8–25.

Waters, Mary. 1999. *Black Identities: West Indian Dreams and American Realities.* New York: Russell Sage Foundation; Cambridge, Mass.: Harvard University Press.

Weiss, Robert S. 1994. *Learning from Strangers: The Art and Method of Qualitative Interview Studies.* New York: Free Press.

Wellman, Barry. 1979. "The Community Question: The Intimate Networks of East Yorkers." *American Journal of Sociology* 84 (5): 1201–31.

Wellman, Barry. 1988. "The Community Question Re-evaluated." *Comparative Urban and Community Research* 1:81–107.

Wellman, Barry. 1999. "The Network Community: An Introduction." In *Networks in the Global Village: Life in Contemporary Communities,* edited by Barry Wellman, 1–48. Boulder, Colo.: Westview Press.

Wellman, Barry, and Barry Leighton. 1979. "Networks, Neighborhoods, and Communities: Approaches to the Study of the Community Question." *Urban Affairs Quarterly* 14 (3): 363–90.

Wellman, Barry, and Scot Wortley. 1990. "Different Strokes from Different Folks: Community Ties and Social Support." *American Journal of Sociology* 96:558–88.

Whitehill, Walter M. 1968. *Boston: A Topographical History.* Cambridge, Mass.: Belknap Press.

Whyte, William Foote. 1943. *Streetcorner Society.* Chicago: University of Chicago Press.

———. 1955. *Streetcorner Society.* 2d ed. Chicago: University of Chicago Press.

Willis, Paul. 1977. *Learning to Labor.* New York: Columbia University Press.

Wilson, William Julius. 1987. *The Truly Disadvantaged: The Inner City, the Underclass, and Public Policy.* Chicago: University of Chicago Press.

———. 1996. *When Work Disappears: The World of the New Urban Poor.* New York: Knopf.

With, Tatiana. 1996a. "Onetime Model Faces the Future." *Boston Globe,* April 21.

———. 1996b. "Latino Community Looks to the Future; Merced Departure Sparks Concern." *Boston Globe,* November 13.

Wirth, Louis. 1938. "Urbanism as a Way of Life." *American Journal of Sociology* 44 (1): 1–24.

Woods, Robert. 1898. *The City Wilderness: A Settlement Study, by Residents and Associates of the South End House.* Boston: Houghton Mifflin. Cited in Green 1975.

Yin, Robert. 1994. *Case Study Research: Design and Methods.* Thousand Oaks, Calif.: Sage.

Youngerman, Elizabeth. 1969. A Profile of Boston's Spanish Speaking Community: Characteristics and Attitudes. Boston: Action for Boston Community Development.

Wilson, W. J., xii, 133, 196
and isolation of poor and middle class, 100
particularistic critiques of, 183
and poor neighborhoods as resource-deprived, 125, 184
and research on neighborhood poverty, 2
and social isolation theory, 7, 26, 99

Women, Infants, and Children (WIC) Program, 93
women as head of households in Latino community of 1968 and 1970, 26
work. *See* employment
worldview and culture, 9

Youngerman, Elizabeth, 36